The Joseph Narrative in Genesis

The Joseph Narrative in Genesis

AN INTERPRETATION
by
ERIC I. LOWENTHAL

KTAV PUBLISHING HOUSE, INC.
NEW YORK, N.Y.
1973

Library of Congress Cataloging in Publication Data

Lowenthal, Eric I   1901-
   The Joseph narrative in Genesis.

   "Book interprets ... Genesis 37-50, omitting chapters
38 and 49: 1-27"
   Bibliography: p.
   1. Bible, O. T. Genesis XXXVII-L--Commentaries.
2. Joseph, the patriarch. I. Title.
BS1235.3.L69   222'.11   73-12044
ISBN 0-87068-216-4

MANUFACTURED IN THE UNITED STATES OF AMERICA

Contents

* *Sidrah* is the Hebrew word for the larger *Torah* subdivisions, already mentioned in BT *Megillah* 29b. The first *sidrah* is read in the synagogue at the beginning of the Jewish calendar year; the last at its end. The Joseph Narrative comprises the last four of the twelve Genesis subdivisions. The Hebrew Bible verse-divisions are masoretic. But the "chapters" were added to the MT from the Vulgate Christian translation. That is why a *sidrah* does not necessarily conclude with the end of a chapter.

TO MY WIFE, SUZANNE; OUR CHILDREN,
ABRAHAM AND JUDITH
AND TO THE MEMORY OF
MY PARENTS, RABBI ABRAHAM AND JENNY;
MY SON, PETER; AND MY BROTHER, LUDWIG
זכרונם לברכה

Acknowledgments

The many people who encouraged and stimulated me to write this book are too numerous to mention individually. Yet I want to acknowledge my gratitude to my congregation of 23 years, Agudath Achim, Leominster, Mass. for making my creative retirement possible.

I am also grateful to the following scholars and colleagues who by their interest in my work fortified me to hold on and overcome periods of low spirits: Professor Simon Greenberg who helped me with his constructive criticism at the initial stage following my retirement. Professor Nahum N. Glatzer for taking out time to read my manuscript and giving me valuable advice and suggestions. Most of all Professor Nahum M. Sarna for the benefit of his knowledge and scholarship at all times to guide me.

I am greatly obliged to Doctor John B. Wight for his stylistic assistance, Batya Bauman for her painstaking editing and to Judith Neufeld who applied her remarkable scrutiny to the editing of my notes and bibliography.

I am deeply grateful to my daughter Chaninah Maschler, who responded in scores of most stimulating letters to my first drafts, and brought her great gifts for textual analysis as well as her insights to bear upon her reading of the text. Some of her finding are listed in my exposition, but many of my own interpretations are the result of her critique and her challenging participation. To her I also owe the acquaintance with her friend, Professor Priscilla W. Shaw whose annotations to my interpretations of Genesis 37 helped me to free myself from my Germanisms in style and method.

Most of all I want to thank my wife, Suzanne, who as always has been my severest critic, but without whose wise counsel, help and understanding my persistence in writing and completing this book would not have been possible.

Preface

This book interprets the Biblical Story of *Joseph,* henceforth called "the Narrative." It comprises Genesis 37-50, omitting chapters 38 and 49: 1-27. Goethe ends his remarkable paper "The Patriarchal Family"[1] with the Narrative, which he cherished immensely. But he complains, "It seems too short; and one is tempted to carry it out in all its details." Thomas Mann heeded this challenge in his novel-tetralogy. Though, as this will show, Mann contributes a few original and valuable expositions of the Narrative-text, his work paints in the detail by fictionalizing it in 2000 pages:[2] Another method, attempted in this book, is to scrutinize the immensely condensed diction of the text so that *its* details will yield the intent.

A.   The Narrative in Its Context

By scriptural standards, the Narrative is, of course, not short at all; it is the longest Biblical literary unit—391 verses. We should, therefore, ask why it covers as much as the last fourth of Genesis. The immediate answer is certainly that Joseph is the link between Canaan and Egypt, "responsible" in some manner for the "descent" (see expos. on 37:28).[3] But only when we reflect upon the fact that Genesis ends with the death of Joseph, and that Exodus opens with the reminder that it was the small Jacob clan, "seventy souls" in all, "that entered Egypt . . . Joseph being already in Egypt" ((cf. Exodus 1:1,5) do we begin to see Joseph as the bridge between the Patriarchs and Moses. As the Narrative unfolds, we come to recognize that Joseph's destiny was to cause *Bene Ya-'aqov,* "Jacob's offspring," the consanguine clan, to become the spiritual unit *Bene Yisrael,* "The Children of Israel." This destiny begins to take shape at the outset of the Narrative, when "Joseph was seventeen years old," when *toledoth Ya-'aqov*—the History of Jacob —(see expos. on 37:2) begins.

So the Narrative only seems to be a "novel." In reality it is *Torah,* 'teaching' how Jacob's clan became, through Joseph, the germ cell of the Sinaitic-Covenant-People. This is the essence of the Narrative which, accordingly, neglects to elaborate as we would have expected had a novel of "Joseph and his Brothers" been intended. This is why we never once hear Benjamin speak and why, of all the brothers, only the words of Reuben and Judah appear. The Narrative also consummates the motif of brotherly strife that recurs in Genesis again and again. Of the first pair of brothers the *Torah* teaches that the one who slew the other asked, "Am I my brother's keeper?" Of the twelve who became *Bene Yisrael,* we learn the answer by the one who was hated, but who sought his brothers.

B. The Narrative and Documentary Analysis

Modern Bible scholarship views the Pentateuch as a compilation of different sources by a redactor. But, as von Rad[4a] observes,

> . . . one of the glaring failures of . . . expositions to date is that, with their separate interpretations of the . . . sources, they have consistently held back from contemplating the reciprocal relations among the sources.

A little later, p. 32, von Rad writes:

> Franz Rosenzweig once remarked wittily that the sign 'R' (for the redactor of the Hexateuch documents, so much slighted in Protestant research) should be taken to mean Rabbenu, "our master," since ultimately we depend on him and only on him, on his great work of compilation and on his theology and since, in any case, it is from his hands that we receive the Hexateuch. (M. Buber und Fr. Rosenzweig, *Die Schrift und ihre Verdeutschung,* 322). From the standpoint of Judaism, this is cogent (translations the author's).

The passage from Rosenzweig, here paraphrased by von Rad, was originally part of a letter Rosenzweig wrote on April 21, 1927 to Jacob Rosenheim, a leader of Orthodox Judaism in Frankfurt am Main, with whom he had discussed in the forenoon the new Bible translation of Martin Buber and himself.[5] The letter begins with Rosenzweig's attempt to explain the essential reason for the profound difference between their views and Rosenheim's.

> Where we differ from orthodoxy is in our reluctance to draw from our belief in the holiness or uniqueness of the Torah, and its character of revelation, any conclusions as to its literary genesis and the philological value of the text as it has come down to us. If all of Wellhausen's theories were correct . . . our faith would not be shaken in the least. This is the profound difference between you and us— a difference which, it seems to me, may be bridged by mutual esteem but not by understanding.[6]

The passage paraphrased by von Rad runs as follows:

> We also treat the Torah as the one book. To us too it is the work of one spirit. We do not know who it was; that it was Moses we cannot believe![7] Among ourselves we refer to him by the sigil under which scholarship denotes him as the finalizing redactor. But to us "R" denotes *"Rabbenu,"* 'our master-teacher.' For whoever he was and whatever materials may have been available to him, he is our teacher and his theology is our teaching [5](translation the author's).

What von Rad did not paraphrase is the following sequence:

> One example: Even if Criticism were right, even if chapters 1 and 2 of Genesis are indeed from different authors (which I don't dare to aver after a man like B. Jacob tells me that he doubts it), even then I hold that what it behooves us to know about Creation cannot be learned from just one of the two chapters but only from their actual *Zusammenstehen und Zusammenklingen,* 'standing side-by-side and being hearkened to simultaneously'[5] (translation the author's).

Yet just a little before citing Rosenzweig, von Rad had made the same point at the hand of the same example:

> Must we not add that the two stories of creation are in some respects *gegeneinander hin offen?,* 'open to each other'?

What von Rad means by this and Rosenzweig by his *"Zusammenstehen und Zusammenklingen"* should perhaps be called "stereoscopic understanding."

According to Milton Himmelfarb, "Most of the non-Orthodox [American rabbis] (and perhaps a few Orthodox [ones] too, privately) would say what Rosenzweig said . . . ."[8] It is, therefore, worth noting that almost thirteen years before Rosenzweig wrote his letter (and many years before he became known in this country), Mordecai M. Kaplan anticipated much of Rosenzweig's view:[9]

> The method of interpretation . . . will have to view the Torah *sub specie unitatis*. It must assume that, however diverse the age, authorship and circumstances of the different fragments that constitute the Torah—if the theory of the critics as to its documentary character be the correct one—they become tributary to some dominating ideal in the mind of Israel the moment they were woven into the context of the Torah. . . . From that time on the Jewish interpretative imagination began to weld the Torah into a consistent unity .

In a recent publication by Nahum Sarna[10] the following two passages on the history of "Higher Criticism" occur:

> Many of the 'scientific' methods it claimed to have employed have not been validated by subsequent research, and the hypercritical process of source fragmentation into which it degenerated became self-defeating. Nevertheless, in its general outlines, the non-unitary origin of the Pentateuch has survived as one of the finalities of biblical scholarship. . . .
> In its enthusiasm for documentary analysis the critical school failed to take account of the fact that things in combination possess properties and produce qualities neither carried by, nor inherent in, any of the components in isolation. For this reason, the disentanglement of literary strands does not constitute the apotheosis of scholarship. This is not to decry the importance of source-criticism. On the contrary. . . . But the inspired genius at work behind the interweaving of the originally disparate elements is ultimately of greater significance. This is a fact that often escapes recognition by both fundamentalists and 'scientists' and constitutes a serious deficiency in their understanding of the Bible.

C. Hermeneutics

The preceding remarks go beyond a mere vindication of my constant practice of cross-reference. They are intended to caution the reader against the still prevalent but gratuitous self-assuredness of modern source criticism[11] on the one hand and of exegetics on the other hand. Again I start with a citation from von Rad's *Genesis,* this time from his "Foreword to the First Edition, 1944":[4b]

> . . . the author is prepared . . . for objections on a point where he feels especially sure of himself, namely, the reproof that he has "overinterpreted" the texts and "gone beyond" their content. . . .

I too am prepared to be criticized for having "overinterpreted" the Narrative and having gone "beyond" its content precisely where *I* feel "especially sure" of myself. An unbiased study of my work will, I hope, vindicate as exegesis what conventional modern scholarship may consider "eisegesis," that is, fanciful reading into the text. An important contributing factor to the bias we must overcome is, I believe, the strangely "modern" air of the Narrative; it appears to be cast in the secular mold of historical and psychological accounts with which we are familiar. This makes it harder for us to become aware of the differences between modern and ancient standards of consistency in narration. In particular, it has led those by whom the "redactor" is "so much slighted" to naively consider certain passages incompetent duplications, dislocations, redundancies, and discrepancies when actually they are meant to be charts to pilot the ardent student toward the deeper meaning. The text has to be approached not only with the seriousness and respect which our seminars instill in the student of ancient Greek classics, but with the expectation of finding "Torah,"[12] i.e., direction and teaching, "speaking with authority." What appears at first to be an incongruity will turn out to be, as long ago recognized by some of the early Jewish exegetes, a technique of the Torah to evoke deeper pondering. Such postulation of the Torah's masterly stylistic competence does not require a "revelational" attitude on the student's part.

A key feature of my exegesis is "speculation." E. A. Speiser[13] touches on this point: "Good writers are not given to spelling things out; the reader, too, has his part to play." I would go much further: Not only the reader, but also the *exegete* has his part to play in spelling things out. Speculation should be recognized as a legitimate tool of textual hermeneutics just as "historical imagination" has become accepted in "historical thinking."[14] Restrained use of speculation in exegetics, inquiring "what really happened?" must not be rejected because of its occasional abuse by homilists. The Torah solicits speculation. It requires the engagement of imagination not only of the reader, but of the scholar as well. Part of its exegesis is to ponder imaginatively what the text deliberately does not "spell out." If the exegete protests that this would degrade his "science," making it "subjective," he should realize that in the last analysis, hermeneutics is not a science but an art and, thus, inextricably subjective. Exegetics as science, i.e. circumspect text-phenomenology, is merely the prerequisite. However, hermeneutics, i.e. ascertaining a message, depends on the spirit of the interpreter; and the spirit is subjective.

D. Commentaries Used

That I have profited from modern Bible scholars is evidenced throughout. But my exposition abounds in reference to classic and later Jewish exegetes.[15] Their frequently cryptic condensed Hebrew is worth studying because they often show surprisingly keen insight into the subtleties of Biblical idiom and style. I have learned much, too, from the Jewish Aramaic Torah translations, TO (Targum Onkelos) and TJ (Targum Jonathan). They embody long-established rabbinic traditions and contain much valuable philological lore. I have also used the B(abylonian) Talmud and the *midrash*, dealing with items in the Narrative. I have often found valuable suggestions in the *haggadic*—morally instructive—legends collected by Louis Ginzberg.[16] Yet I have learned most from Benno Jacob whose monumental work on Genesis has had a decisive influence on me.[17] But for three reasons it did not have its deserved general impact: 1) Shortly after its publication, most copies were destroyed by the Nazis. 2) The study of this great, but cumbersome work (it has no index) strains the patience and energy of even the dedicated scholar who would master the condensed German diction. 3) The most important reason, however, (explaining why it has, so far, not found any publisher to undertake its translation) is Jacob's militant polemic against the methods and results of "Higher Criticism," the dissection of Genesis into "sources," which takes up the last 100 pages (48 lines each) of his Appendix. Thus, Jacob is not even mentioned in Speiser's *Genesis*. Yet, though the scope of my work allows but a selection from Jacob's exegesis, his name appears on almost every page.

E. Miscellaneous

1) The interpretation of the Joseph Narrative begins with 37:1. Wherever such numbers appear, lacking the name of the scriptural book, they refer to Genesis. The translated text-verse is preceded by its number. The interpretation is preceded by *The Background of the Narrative*.
2) For abbreviations cf. *Abbreviations* at the end of the book, preceding *Bibliography*.
3) If only the exegete's name is referred to, not his work, the reference is to his commentary on the relevant Narrative passage. If his name is preceded by "see," it means that my exposition has been arrived at thanks to his (different) one.
4) My translation and interpretation hardly ever take up more than one verse at a time. Occasionally, to facilitate the exposition, a verse is even subdivided.
5) Whenever my translation differs essentially from all others, my exposition gives the reason.
6) At times my translation includes in brackets obvious ellipses in the text.
7) Occasionally transliterated Hebrew words appear in my translation to explain the reason for so translating.
8) The *Appendix* deduces and ponders chronological data from the Narrative.
9) My interpretation abstains from characterizing the "art" behind the Narrative.
10) The *Bibliography* omits listing many sources cited in works to which reference is made.

11) My interpretation constantly refers to certain exegetes, traditionally called by the following acronyms:

MaLBYM	R. Meier Loeb ben Yehiel Michael Berlin, 1809-1879, Russia.
NaTsYB	R. Naphtali Tsevi Yehudah, 1817-1893, Russia.
RaDaQ	R. David Qimchi, 1160-1235, France.
RaLBaG	R. Levi ben Gerson, 1288-1344, France.
RaMBaN	R. Moshe ben Nachman, 1194-1260, Spain, Palestine.
RaShBaM	R. Rabbenu Shmuel ben Meir, 1085-1174, France.
RaShI	Rabbenu Shlomo Itschaki, 1040-1105, France.
ShaDaL	R. Shmuel David Luzzatto, 1800-1865, Italy.

The Background of the Narrative

This chapter sums up passages from Genesis that precede Chapter 37, but are relevant to the Narrative.

1) JOSEPH'S FIRST SIX YEARS IN HARAN

Joseph's parents were Jacob and Rachel. She was the younger daughter of Laban, Leah the older. Laban was the brother of Rebekah, Jacob's mother. He lived at Haran, north of Canaan. To him Jacob fled from his brother Esau, and was to him in servitude for fourteen years. Leah became his wife at the lapse of the first septennial, Rachel, eight days later. Joseph was born at the lapse of the second septennial, during which Jacob sired nine other sons (see *Appendix* 2 and 3), five of Leah and two each by Bilhah and Zilpah who became his concubines after they had been handmaids of his wives. During Jacob's last six years in Haran, he was Laban's partner and acquired considerable wealth in livestock. Precocious as little Joseph must have been, he was quite aware of the tensions between his father and his maternal grandfather as well as those between his mother and Leah. He must surely have sensed also the friction between Leah's children and the concubines' sons and the contrast between his father's and Laban's way of life.

2. JACOB'S FLIGHT FROM HARAN

His family's flight from Laban (cf. 31:17), particularly the feud with Laban at Mitspah (cf. 31:25-32:1), must have made a deep impression on Joseph. He may not have understood what the quarrel was all about, but when his father's wives and children at last received Laban's kisses and farewell blessing, he knew that peace had been restored and that reconciliation was possible.

3. THE ENCOUNTER WITH ESAU

Then came the great moment when the family crossed the border and entered Canaan, the father's homeland, which, twenty years before, he had left in flight from his brother Esau. Joseph watched the elaborate preparations for the encounter with the fierce man, approaching with four hundred men. The father instructed his four wives to prostrate themselves before Esau one by one, each to be followed by her children. Yet, when at last it came to be his mother's turn, "Joseph and Rachel came forward and bowed low" (cf. 33:7b). Thus, already at the age of six, he manifested boldness and initiative. *Genesis Rabbah* 78:1 suggests, "He wanted to conceal his mother from Esau's eyes." How relieved must Joseph have been when Esau "ran to meet, to embrace and kiss" his father and when "they wept" (33:4).

4) JACOB BUILDS "A HOUSE" IN SUCCOTH

After Esau's departure, the family settled close to the Jabbok river (cf. 32:23), east of the Jordan, obviously to stay there for good, for Jacob built there "a house"[1] and *succoth* booths, shelters—for his livestock. Such *succoth* seem to have been something novel, for they gave the place its name (cf. 33:17; Josh. 13:27; Judg. 8:15). The Torah, informing us (cf. 31:18) that Jacob intended to return to his father, does not explain why he did not do so. He may have heard that his mother was no longer alive. Nor do we learn why Jacob left Succoth after having built that house and the shelters.

5) *EL-ELOHE-YISRAEL*

The family crossed the Jordan river and reached Shechem (now called Nablus, some thirty miles north of Jerusalem). Jacob "encamped within the sight of the town and bought a plot of ground where he pitched his tent. . . ." (33:18f.). Presumably, he did not tell his family the purpose of this purchase (see expos. on 48.22), but Joseph—then about eight years old— must have watched with keen interest how the father hallowed the field by erecting on it an altar-monument. It was in that vicinity, the father may have told him, that God revealed Himself for the first time to Abraham, who built an altar there (cf. 12:7). Considering the family's veneration for its elders and these elders' passion for transmitting their tradition—a sacred obligation (cf. 18:19)—the young Joseph must have known about his clan's past, *sancta* and destiny. In fact, he may have learned more about it than what the Torah transmits.

Before long, he must have learned about "YHWH, the Creator" (cf. 14:22), "God of heaven and earth" (cf. 24.3), "the Judge of all the world" (18:25), and have known that Abraham had reached the highest rung where "it becomes visible" (22: 14; B. Jacob), having been God's partner in Council and Judgment (cf. 18:17ff.) and "prophet" (20:7).[2] As an explanation for his father's naming the altar-monument *"El-elohe-Yisrael,"*—El is the God of Israel or El, the God of Israel— Joseph must have learned about the father's nocturnal contest with the mysterious "man" who predicted, "Not [only] Jacob . . . but [also] Yisrael will your name be called, for *sarita*—you have striven—[whence Yisra] with *El,* and you prevailed" (32: 29). His father surely told him also that when the "man" wrenched his "hip-socket," it actually was in answer to his prayer (cf. 32:10-13), for that very pain which contorted him seemed to have transformed Esau's thirst for revenge to pity and love (B. Jacob). During the "many years" (Ibn Ezra on 33:20) of the family's stay near Shechem, Joseph also learned about God's promise to and covenant with Abraham and his offspring.[3]

6) THE MASSACRE AT SHECHEM

Chapter 34 reports how Dinah, Jacob's last child born in Haran, was dishonored. She seems to have been born two years after Joseph (cf. *Appendix* 3). She was not older than fourteen when violated, at a time when Simeon and Levi were not older than twenty-one and twenty, and when almost ten years had passed since Jacob had returned to Canaan (cf. *Appendix* 7). "Having heard the news [of their sister's defilement], the men [her brothers] were distressed and very angry, because he [Hamor's son] had committed an outrage in Israel by lying with Jacob's daughter—a thing not to be brooked!" (34:7). They met Hamor's proposition of appeasement through fraternization of the two clans "with guile" (v. 13), pretending their consent if Shechem's males would undergo circumcision. RaMBaN assumes that Dinah's brothers intended to rescue her during their enemies' condition after the painful operation, but that after the enactment of the ritual, Simeon and Levi turned the planned abduction into the massacre. After this carnage, Joseph watched his angry father rebuke the two, "You have befouled me, making me stink . . ." But Joseph also heard their retort, "Should then our sister be treated like a whore?" (vv. 30f.). Though Joseph, already fifteen years old at that time, was certain that the brothers' revenge violated God's will, he realized that his father was also wrong not to have taken any initiative of his own.

7) JACOB'S PILGRIMAGE TO LUZ-BETHEL

The events in Shechem had a purgatory impact upon Jacob; he opened up to God's summons to fulfill his vow, made on his flight to Haran (cf. 28:20ff.). Joseph heard his father call upon "his household and all who were with him, 'Rid yourselves of the alien gods in your midst [not only those mentioned 31:19, 34], cleanse yourselves and put on fresh garments. We will go to Bethel where I shall build an altar to God Who appeared to me [cf. 28:13ff.], when I was in distress, and Who has been with me wherever I have gone.' They handed [them] over . . . and Jacob buried them" (35:2ff.). After this pilgrimage, Jacob surely told them about God's revelation to him, confirming him as *Yisrael* and blessing him and his offspring (cf. 35:9-12). The father may then have disclosed more fully to Joseph his other experiences of "the deity" in vision and dream (cf. 28:13; 31:11ff.; 32:25ff.), whereas to his fathers (to Abraham: cf. 12:7; 17:1; 18:1 and to Isaac cf. 26:2, 24), "YHWH" had appeared in greater intimacy.

8) DEATH OF JOSEPH'S MOTHER, GIVING BIRTH TO BENJAMIN

Soon after God had revealed Himself and blessed Jacob, the whole clan resumed traveling, going south to reach Isaac in Hebron whom Jacob had not seen for thirty years (see expos. on 46:27). Rachel was already pregnant in Shechem, and the strain of traveling seems to have been too hard for her. "They set out from Bethel; but when they were still some distance short of Ephrath, Rachel was in childbirth, and she had hard labor. . . . Thus, Rachel died. She was buried on the road to Ephrath. . . . Over her grave Jacob set up a monument, the same monument that is Rachel's grave to this day" (35:16ff.). The son was called Benjamin. (The Torah says nothing about the grief of Jacob and Joseph. Only shortly before his death does Jacob vent his sorrow to Joseph). After Rachel's burial, the observance of the mourning rites and the erection of the monument, the clan moved on, camping "beyond Migdal Eder." There, "Reuben went and lay with Bilhah, his father's concubine, and Israel found out" (35:22b).[4]

9 THE ARRIVAL OF JACOB'S FAMILY AT HEBRON

After thirty years, Jacob returned to his father, who, by then, no longer lived in Beer Sheba (cf. 28:10), but in Hebron (cf. 35:27), where Isaac had buried Abraham (cf. 25:9) and Rebekah (cf. 49:31). It must have made an indelible impression on Joseph to see his father re-united with Isaac, but the Torah says nothing about it, leaving it, as so often, up to our imagination.

Interpretation of the Narrative

GENESIS: 37[1]

1   Jacob lived in the land of his father's
               sojourning, in the land of Canaan.

After his twenty year stay with Laban, Jacob had returned
to Canaan ten years (see *Appendix 3*) before his reunion
with his father in Hebron. The Torah contrasts Canaan, "the
land of his father's sojourning," with "the hill country of Seir"
(36:8). The Fathers were to live in Canaan merely to "sojourn" there (cf. 17:8; 23:4; 26:3; 28:4). But Esau and his
descendants settled in Seir as "the land of their possession"
(36:43). Not the Fathers, but their offspring would live in
Canaan as their "eternal possession" (17:8; 48:4).[2]

V. 2 appears to be a "torso" (von Rad, *Genesis*) until its
immensely condensed five parts are carefully scrutinized:

2a   *Eleh toledoth*—this is the History of—Jacob.

When, as here, *toledoth* is preceded in Genesis by *'eleh,* it introduces a new chapter in the pre-history of the Israelites.[3]

2b   Joseph was seventeen years old.

The report that follows this verse gives an account of what
preceded Joseph's mission, at seventeen years of age.[4] The
Torah inserts v. 2b here to intimate that *'eleh toledoth Ya-
'aqov* (v. 2a) begins with Joseph's mission. It marks the
fifth and last phase of the Israelites' pre-history, preceded by
the emergence of "Heaven and Earth," of Adam, of Noah and
of Shem. Joseph's mission was providentially designed (see
below): Jacob's children were already the fourth generation
in Canaan. Lest they be assimilated there to the "Amorites"

(cf. 15:16), God initiated the migration of the Jacob clan to the "land not theirs" (cf. 15:13; B. Jacob), when Joseph was mature enough to remain faithful to his tradition.

2c   *Hayah ro-'eh 'et 'eḥaw batson,*
          'He used to shepherd his brothers at the sheep.'

Hayah used with a participle means "he used to." [5] The sentence does not mean "he shepherded with his brothers . . . ," but "he shepherded (advised) his brothers," [6] after having been an apprentice:

2d   He had been an apprentice with the sons
          of Bilhah and Zilpah, his father's wives.

This is a flashback in the pluperfect, a parenthesis: Bilhah and Zilpah were the maidservants of Rachel and Leah, respectively, before Jacob's wives gave them to him as concubines. If Bilhah became Benjamin's foster mother, it stands to reason that Joseph also stayed with Bilhah and her two sons after his mother's death. He associated with Zilpah's two sons too, perhaps because Leah's Six looked down upon the Four as "servants" (RaShI), and such disdain, in Joseph's eyes, was disrespectful of his father, since the maidservants became "his father's wives" (B. Jacob). Joseph may also have enjoyed the Four's deference to him (S. R. Hirsch).

2e   He brought their evil slander to their father.

What Joseph reported was true. Spreading calumnies requires the verb used in Num. 13:32; Prov. 10:18. Moreover, had—as RaShI assumes—the brothers heard about Joseph's reports, it would have been mentioned. "Now they hated him even more because . . . of his words," refers to something else (see expos. and n. 14 on v. 8c). Nor did the father consider Joseph a talebearer, (see below). As if to caution us not to attribute pettiness to the teenager, the Torah intimates the chivalry and precocity of Joseph, aged six (Cf. *Background* 3). His upbringing (cf. *Background* 5), and later his moral stamina as a slave compel the following speculation: His pride and exultation was that he and his brothers were destined to inherit "Abraham's Blessing" (28:4), provided, as he thought, that they all remain worthy of God's Covenant (cf. 15:18); 17:2ff.) by "keeping the way of the Lord, doing what is just and right" (18:19). Thus it was his ardent concern for the family's future under God which motivated him when "he brought their evil slander to their father." *Dibbatam*—their slander—is remarkably ambiguous. Considering the Narrative's otherwise so masterly stylistic competence, such ambiguities are deliberate and call for all the possible interpretations: "Their slander" can mean the slander *by* or *about* them. Moreover, "them" can refer to all ten brothers, to the sons of Leah and to the concubines' sons. Consequently, the verse seems to say that Joseph reported the defamations of the two "parties" about each other and by all Ten about himself. It was already their guile and massacre at Shechem (cf. *Background* 6) that had appalled him. Yet at that time he was still younger and even the father was stunned. Yet now, all living at Isaac's homestead, Joseph appeals to their father to reprimand and correct them, (see Leqah Tob), lest they forfeit siring God's covenant-people.

3a   Israel loved Joseph of all his children, for
        to him he was *ben zequnim*—a born leader.

"To him" means to "Israel," not to "Jacob." It is noteworthy that the Torah calls Jacob now by his name of honor (cf. *Background* 5) which failed to appear on eight successive occasions after Reuben's vile deed (cf. 35:22). Thus, Joseph's appeal resuscitated "Israel." As "Jacob," he loved all his children, though he felt Joseph's nature most akin to his. Rachel's first-born, moreover, resembled his beloved wife (cf. 39.6 with 29:17), and he wanted to compensate him for her loss, mindful of his own mother's love for him and his father's greater affection for Esau (cf. 25:28; S. Lowenthal). But as "Israel," he could not help loving Joseph alone, "for to him [as 'Israel'] he was a born leader," about to start out in life from the point which Jacob had reached.[7] Of Joseph's great endowments, learning and piety, Jacob had known before. Yet now his son's deep concern for the family's future under God evokes the patriarch's apprehension about their ways after his death, and that makes him decide to make Joseph his successor.

3b   And he had made for him *ketonet*
        passim—a tunic of distinction.

The meaning of this term was already lost at the time when

II Sam. 13:18ff. was written, for to explain it, its author adds, "With such robes were the king's daughters that were virgins apparelled." The writer of the following citation does not list its source, nor does he recall it.[8]

> Reproductions of 4000 years old paintings . . . show that the garb of the Canaanite aristocrats . . . , contemporaries of Jacob, was an ankle-length, chemise-shaped gown with colored, embroidered stitches down the side and middle. Sometimes, sashes with colored, diagonal stripes draped the thighs.

With this ornamented tunic Israel marked Joseph for the chieftainship of the firstborn after his death.[9] Joseph's vanity may have caused Jacob to make the mistake of bestowing such a tunic upon him at so early an age. Or did Providence "blind" his judgment?

Since such a tunic impedes physical work, Joseph seems now to have been relieved from pasturing the sheep and, as legend has it, to have turned exclusively to study with his elders.

Joseph must have been a thorn in the side of the Six even before he received the tunic because of his precociousness, egocentricity and partiality for the Four. Above all, they resented the father's more intimate relationship with him. With the bestowal of the ornamented tunic, the Six found allies in the Four, for it indicated to the Ten the father's selecting him for "Abraham's Blessing," excluding them, as Ishmael (cf. 21:12), Keturah's sons (cf. 25:5f.), and Esau (cf. 28:4) had been barred before them (Abrabanel). In reality, Jacob never contemplated such exclusion. He hoped and trusted that God would fulfill his father's prayer (cf. 28:3), that his offspring would all become a "sacred league of tribes" (see expos. on 48:4).

4   When the brothers saw it was he whom the
     father loved of all his brothers, they hated
     him and could not endure it when he would
     speak toward peace.

In his naive self-centeredness, Joseph was not aware that now they all hated him, though he was puzzled and chagrined that they shunned him. That is why he wanted to "speak toward peace" with them, to talk amiably to them.[10] Only when his attempts to mollify them backfired did it dawn on him that they resented his tunic. Then, one morning, he thought that a change for the better was in the offing, because he had had a dream which seemed to confirm from on high his father's selection of him for chieftainship (*Or haHayim*).

5   Joseph told his brothers that he had a
              dream. Yet they hated him even more.

He was so elated that he had to tell them that he had a dream of great interest to them. "Yet they hated him even more" because of his importunity and would not listen. Then, however, talking to each other, they decided to allow him to have his say if he should again ask them to listen, for dreams were important, assumed to be divine messages (cf. 15:12ff; 20:3,6; 28:12; 31:10f.,24). Besides, the Hebrew word for "told" implies that what he had dreamt concerned them (MaLBYM).

6   [When again] he said to them. "Please hear the
              dream which I have dreamt[, they listened].

7   "Imagine: We were binding sheaves in the field.
              And lo, my sheaf was rising, yea, remained
              upright. Suddenly your sheaves formed a
              ring. Then they bowed down to my sheaf." [11]

Instead of making its message clear that it was Joseph's destiny to attain an exalted position and become his grateful brother's provider, the dream poured oil on the fire.

8a   They said, "Do you really mean to become
             king over us?

8b   "Would you indeed rule over us?!" [12]

Though his dream did not express their exclusion from "Abraham's Blessing," their hatred makes them see the dream as evidence of Joseph's ruthless ambition to dominate them. What makes the brothers even more furious—and that is why they rant about it first—is what they regard as Joseph's megalomania: Having succeeded in becoming their chief, he then expects them to acknowledge him as their lord and master. They assumed that he had fabricated the tale to fit his tunic, for such a "mantic" dream was unheard of. After their outbrust, they sent Joseph away, but they remained together to discuss the matter.[13]

8c   Now they hated him even more for his talk
about his dreams.[14]

"His dreams" is "categoric plural" (F. J. Delitzsch), connoting the genre (see expos. on v. 10). During their discussion they were no longer sure that Joseph had invented the story. This made them more full of hate because if he really had that dream, their "interpretation," provoked by "his talk," made them their own worst enemies, by causing the dream's message to come true.[15] Then, they decided henceforth to hide their feelings from the dangerous upstart. Joseph was indeed deceived. That is why he had no qualms about telling them another dream.

9   When he had a different dream, he told
his brothers about it, and he said,
"I had another dream: The sun and the
moon and eleven stars bowed low to me." [16]

The brothers listened, but to Joseph's bafflement said no word. Then they met secretly and there was a good deal of discussion. "Here is our chance!" they concluded. "Now he has overreached himself. If he dares to repeat this dream before our father, his love for his idol will surely give way to rage. He will defrock this brazen favorite, intent on having the sun, our father, the patriarch, bow before him!" As they had already agreed, however, they decided to be polite to Joseph; for only thus would they be able to persuade him to tell this "interesting" dream to the father also. Joseph, naturally, was only too glad to oblige and felt flattered that they were willing to hear it all over again.

10   When he told it to his father and his brothers,
the father rebuked him: "What kind of dream is
it which you dreamt? Are we actually to come,
I and your mother and your brothers to bow down
to the ground before you?!"

The exposition on v. 5 mentioned the kind of dreams of the Patriarchal period which were messages from God, in which He would demand, command, warn or promise. They were not "mantic" (see expos. on v. 8ab). That is why Jacob "questions" the genuineness of Joseph's dream. In reality, the three sets of dreams in the Narrative, of which Joseph's are but the first, indicate the remoteness of God. Moreover, the somewhat secular mold, in which the Narrative is cast, is altogether new. It is in poignant contrast with the immediacy of God's communication with the Patriarchs. Though throughout its course, it reflects Providence, nowhere do any of its *personae*—God Himself included (yet see expos. on 39:2)—use the word YHWH, connoting His intimacy with man. "Natural causes" replace "miracles."

The Torah adds in the next verse that, actually, Jacob takes Joseph's dream seriously. But, intercepting the Ten's look of hatred as they gaze upon Joseph and recognizing rebellion welling up, he goes on to "debunk" the dream. He ridicules it by pointing out that "the moon" can only refer to Joseph's mother who is already dead. To show his "anger," he even misquotes Joseph, who did not say, ". . . bow down *to the ground.*" Yet, the brothers see through the father's pretense of anger and are furious that he can produce nothing but sputtered protests when told that he, the patriarch, would pay homage to his son. "This is an outrage that cannot be brooked!" they may have thought, as once they said it before setting out to take revenge for their sister's defilement (cf. 34:7).

11   So his brothers envied him.
            The father pondered the matter.

Now, they *know* that Joseph had those dreams, because no son would otherwise dare to tell his father about it. That is why to their thrice mentioned *hatred*, "envy" is now added. They now fear Joseph and decided to tolerate the situation no longer.

12   His brothers left: "to pasture the
            sheep of their father in Shechem."

This translation is guided by two MT markings, complementing each other, but disregarded by those who translate the verse, "The brothers went to pasture the father's flock in Shechem."[17] The first MT marking connotes a period after *wa-yeleku 'ehaw* —his brothers went—i.e. they "left." The second intimates that "to pasture the sheep . . ." was merely their claimed intention, whereas in reality, they "left for good," they seceded from the father's homestead.

13   Then Israel said to Joseph, "You know that your
        brothers are pasturing in Shechem. I wish to
        send you to them." "I am ready," he replied.

Jacob's sons had stayed away for so long a time that "Israel" became apprehensive. Adding up the signs of their restiveness, which he had failed to take in earnest, he now begins to realize the seriousness of the rift between them and Joseph and becomes fearful for his family's future. Joseph also had pondered why the brothers had left in such an ominous way. He knows that the father's purpose in sending him to them is to bring about a reconciliation, not merely to learn how they and the flocks were faring (cf. v. 14). For otherwise, he would send one of his men, not a seventeen year old lad, on such a long and perilous trip. Joseph's *hinneni*—I am ready—said to his father is the same that Abraham said to God. Yet, whereas Abraham said it before he was told what to do (cf. 22:1), Joseph said it after he was told. Besides, the "sacrifice" there was to be Isaac, not Abraham. Here, Joseph says about himself *"hinneni."*

14   And he said to him, "Go, please, find out how
        your brothers are and how the flocks are
        faring, and bring me back word." And he sent him
        off from the valley of Hebron, and he came to
        Shechem.

Why does the Torah report, "he sent him off from the valley of Hebron"? Is it merely because again a father and his son "walked together," as Abraham did with Isaac (cf. 22:6,8), then ascending (cf. 22:2), but now descending?[18] It is because in the "valley of Hebron," Abraham (cf. 25:9), Sarah (cf. 23:19), and Rebekah (cf. 49:31) lay buried. The patriarch wanted to impress upon his Joseph the presence of the sacred place before he left on his mission.[19]

Whereas Israel thought that "he sent him off" he, in reality, acted unwittingly to initiate the fulfillment of God's prediction to Abraham, "You must know that your offspring shall be strangers in a land not theirs, to be enslaved and oppressed (15:13).[20] Joseph's eagerness to reach his brothers is intimated by the fact that only two Hebrew words are spent on his four day trip along the road north of Shechem through the central hill country west of the Jordan.

As Joseph travelled in solitude, it might have dawned on him how much his brothers had suffered from their father's favoring him and how he himself may have contributed to their resentment. For once, he may have realized that he had never acted "brotherly," that his interest in them was merely critical, that he had censured their conduct in his mind and before their father. He may even have thought of Esau: how he must have cringed, perceiving his brother's greater endowments.

15   A man met him wandering in the open country and
         the man asked him, "What are you looking for?"

Joseph knew the place, for hardly more than two years ago, his family had lived there for a long time. In fact, his father had bought a piece of land there on which he erected an altar-monument (cf. *Background* 5). The "man" occurs twice in the verse. Was he the "man" who had wrestled with his father (cf. 32:25), or was he simply one of his herdsmen? He seems to have known Joseph and his brothers:

16   "I [myself] seek my brothers. Tell me,
         please, where they are pasturing."

It seems that Joseph had rehearsed all the old stories of brotherly quarrels and hostility, for he uses for the pronoun "I" the emphatic word *'anoki* which is not required here, but in Cain's horrible answer to God (cf. 4:9), *"hashomer 'aḥi 'anoki"* —Am I my brother's keeper? Thus Joseph's *'anoki*-sentence seems to echo Cain's words, implying that, when he becomes the chieftain, he wants indeed to become "his brothers' keeper."

17   The man said, "From this they departed, for I
         overheard them say, 'let us go to Dothan.' "
         So Joseph went after his brothers and found
         them in Dothan.

18a   They saw him from afar.

"From this" instead of the expected—but actually superfluous —"from here" is strikingly interpreted, "from your concept of brotherliness, they removed themselves." In this homily,[21] the thrice occurring "man" is naturally an angel (cf. 32:25f.), "I overheard them say" (Abrabanel) seems more correct than "I heard them say." Dothan, close to Samaria in the valley of Jezre-el, is located on the same route as Shechem, one long day's trip north of it. Although Joseph was tired from traveling, he did not for a moment consider giving up or postponing his search. He "went after his brothers" instead of "after them" shows his anxiety to make his father's desire his own. He "found them in Dothan," presumably as they were about to take their meal (cf. v. 25) on top of a hill. Since he was looking for them and saw ten people against the sky, he recognized them before they, overlooking the caravan road, recognized the approaching lad by his tunic (cf. v. 23). We wonder why he donned it after he saw them, since he knew how much they resented it. Was he not determined now to do his part toward a cordial relationship with them? The answer seems to be that he wanted the "peace" on his own terms: Whereas the issue of the birthright had been evaded in the case of Isaac's half-brothers and of Esau by their exclusion from "Abraham's Blessing" (cf. expos. on v. 3b), the birthright issue had become inescapable for Jacob's sons because they were all destined to father the covenanted people. Joseph naively hoped that, after he had apologized for having had a wrong attitude toward them in the past, they would recognize the birthright as his by the father's choice and God's confirmation. Nothing was further from his mind than the possibility that by thus impiously hastening what was to be in God's own time, his brazen assertiveness would soon see him in the "pit." (Chaninah Maschler). The Torah does not disclose why the brothers left Shechem for Dothan, and whatever they had planned in Dothan, will be cancelled with Joseph's arrival. Why, however, Shechem was mentioned at all, becomes clear in the next verse in which its memory reverberates in such a ghastly way.

18b	Before he came close to them,
18c	*wa-yitnaklu*—they conspired the plot—
	'oto le-hamito—that [this time] it
	should be he who would be put to death.

The Hebrew words allude to the massacre at Shechem (ch. 34). Though *wa-yitnaklu*—they conspired a plot—does not explicitly occur there, it is implied in the words "speaking with guile" (cf. 34:13).[22] And what the brothers now plan against Joseph recalls Shechem, as is expressed by the accusative ending of *le-hamito*, following *'oto*—him. *Oto* sticks out as a seemingly double accusative, unless it shows that this time they plotted that "it should be he who would be put to death," as once they had done with the Shechemites. What fanned the brothers' fury must have been the sight of the ornamented tunic. The decision to kill him was, however, not unanimous.

19   One said to his brother, "Lo,
       there comes the master dreamer."

"One said to his brother" is the literal translation. Since all could not possibly have spontaneously made that sarcastic exclamation, it seems preferable to "they said to one another." In 49:5, Jacob says, "Simeon and Levi are brothers." Presumably, he means "cronies" in violence, referring to 34:25. It is, therefore, noteworthy that TJ actually paraphrases "one said to his brother" by "Simeon said to Levi." *Ba'-al ha-halomoth*—the master dreamer—is translated by B. Jacob, *"Der Herr Traeumer"*—that Mister Dreamer. It could also mean "he who in his dreams sees himself already as the lord and master" (Chaninah Maschler), or "the one empowered to prophetic dreams" (von Rad).

20   "Now [is our chance;] let us kill him and throw
       him into one of the wells and say, 'a savage
       beast has devoured him.' Then we shall see
       what comes out of his dreams."

The intent of the speakers was first to kill him and then to throw the corpse into a pit. They no longer doubted that God had imparted his dreams (see expos. on v. 11), but now, they deride and defy God's plan.

21   Reuben listened. He tried to save him from
       them and said, "Let us not smite a life."

Being the oldest, Reuben might have had more reason to eliminate Joseph as his rival, but, though tempestuous (cf. 49:4), he was less given to hatred. Twenty-one years later (cf. 42:22), Reuben reminds his brothers that he had added, "Do not sin against the child" and "But you would not listen."[23] This explains why the Torah's next words are "And he said to them," though he was not interrupted. Whenever two or more *wayomer* —he said—follow each other in this way, it indicates that the speaker scrutinizes the effect of his words before he continues (B. Jacob).[24] Their refusal to listen made Reuben ponder how else to "save him from them," and it came to him: "Did they not speak of a well, the pit into which they would throw the body of Joseph? If I can only persuade them to throw him into it alive, if I can only steer their fury, all may still end well" (J. Horovitz).

22   And Reuben said to them, "Shed no blood!
                  Cast him into that pit in the wilderness,
                  but lay no hand upon him" to save him
                  from them and to restore him to his father.

Reuben is the only one to think of the father who may, in the end, hold him responsible, being the eldest. He may also redeem himself in the father's eyes from his offense with Bilhah (cf. 35:22). This time, Reuben succeeded because the brothers agreed that letting a person die by himself is "better" than outright murder (Or Hahayim).

23   When Joseph reached his brothers, they
                  made Joseph take off his tunic, the
                  ornamented tunic that was on him.

There was no greeting. Just one word: "Undress!" *Wa-yafshitu* is the causative verbform, "they made Joseph take off" (Ibn Ezra, RaLBaG). The use of "Joseph" instead of "him" reminds us of a king having to remove his crown (Chaninah Maschler).

24   And they seized him and they cast him into
                  the pit. The pit was empty; there was no water
                  in it.

Twenty-one years later, the brothers will recall, "We looked at his anguish, yet paid no heed when he pleaded with us" (42:21). The pit was the well Reuben had suggested. He knew "it was empty; there was no water in it." There, they left him to die. It stands to reason that such a cistern was in the valley and that the brothers, having noticed Joseph from the camping site on the hill, returned there now, the well out of their sight.

25   They sat down for their meal and, looking up,
            they saw an Ishmaelite caravan coming in from
            Gilead on the way down to Egypt, their camels
            carrying gum tragacanth and balm and myrrh.

"Ishmaelite" here is not an ethnic designation (B. Jacob), but refers to nomadic merchants (cf. Jud. 8:24). Their merchandise, identifiable at a distance by its characteristic packaging, indicated both their origin and their destination.[25] "Egypt!" That gave Judah an idea. All along, he was horrified by his brothers' cruelty toward Joseph, but his protest would have been overruled. Now the sight of the caravan makes him conceive what might sway his brothers. As the Narrative will show more and more, Judah is the most decent and intelligent. He is able to reason with the others and to gauge their view before addressing them (B. Jacob). His use (cf. v. 26) of the word *bets'a* —profit—as equivocal in Hebrew as it is in English—is a good example: He appeals to the nobler instincts of some and the baser of others.

26   Then Judah said to his brothers, "What profit if
            we were to slay our brother by covering his blood?"

"Covering blood" is a Hebrew idiom for causing death without shedding blood, "indirect" killing.[26]

27   "Let us [rather] sell him to the Ishmaelites.
            Then our hand would not be against him. For
            he is our brother, our own flesh." The
            brothers listened.

"The brothers agreed" is incorrect. They only "listened," for the same Hebrew word also occurs in v. 21 where it certainly cannot mean "agreed." B. Jacob gives elaborate proof that, without added explicit expression of consent, this verb always means either disagreeing or having reservations: Some of the brothers insisted that only Joseph's death would relieve them of their fear of his future lordship over them. They may have been those whose overweening pride in belonging to "Israel" (cf. 34:7), led them to violate all tenets of "Israel" with their savagery. But for others Judah's proposal[27] was even better than

Reuben's because it suggested "fratricide" just the same. In addition, some of these were intrigued by making a "profit." At last, Judah's suggestion was accepted. During the long debate, Reuben remained silent, in great tension. (The following is a novel speculation to make the enigmatic v. 29 intelligible:) When at long last the brothers made their decision, he rose and vigorously, without opposition, insisted that the sale of Joseph to the Ishmaelites was his prerogative as the eldest. Naturally, the brothers had no inkling that he planned "to restore him to his father" (v. 22) and never to return to his brothers! So he left the camping site and descended toward the cistern.

28a	But Midianite traders passed by and pulled Joseph up out of the pit.
28b	They sold Joseph for twenty pieces of silver to the Ishmaelites.
28c	And they brought Joseph to Egypt.

Rabbi Shmuel ben Meir, RaShBaM (1085-1174), RaShI's grandson, was the first to suggest that "they pulled . . . and sold . . ." refers to the "Midianite traders," the new subject, not to the brothers.[28] Otherwise, what point would there be in mentioning them? No conflict should be seen between this view and 45:5, where Joseph, after his self-disclosure, says to his brothers, "Now then, be not grieved and angry at yourselves that you sold me here . . .," for Joseph (v. 8) continues, ". . . It was not really you but God Who sent me here" which indicates that "you sold me here" is a tactful and foreshortened phrase: He did not want to say "you flung me into the pit to die there" and merely states that they caused his being brought to Egypt as a slave, which was providentially planned (J. Horovitz). Moreover, eleven years *before* that scene he told the butler, "I was stolen" (kidnapped) (40:15; Horovitz), and thirty-nine years *after* it (cf. *Appendix* 2), he told his brothers, ". . . You meant evil against me" (50:20), clearly implying that they had no chance *to do* it (J. Z. Meklenburg). Though Joseph will say, "I was stolen," Providence actually caused a "theft" without a "thief":

a) The *Brothers* intended to sell Joseph, but Providence interfered lest they commit the horrible crime.

b) The *Midianites* sold Joseph. But they had saved his life, and, therefore, they thought they "owned" him.

c) The *Ishmaelites* bought Joseph, but slave-trading has
   been practiced till quite recently even by "gentlemen."

The three brief and somberly rhythmical Hebrew sentences
of v. 28 mark the turning point in Joseph's life. That is why his
name occurs thrice as three times he becomes the object of
strangers (Chaninah Maschler). It dawns upon the Israelites
reading the Narrative that what v. 28 reports is also the turning
point in the life of their ancestors.[29] Entering Egypt from Canaan is usually expressed by "descending" (the opposite move
is "ascending"), because Egypt lies so much lower than Canaan.
But the verb *b–'*, used here causatively, is of solemn significance:
B'o, 'coming in' and *yts'o*, 'getting out' are "scissor-words" in
regard to slavery (see Exod. 21:3). Whenever the Torah
speaks of entering bondage, *b'o* appears (46:7f.; 27; 47: 1,5;
Exod. 1:1 etc.). Conversely, being liberated from bondage is
expressed by the stem *yats'o* (cf. Exod. 20:2; 21:3, etc.). With
Joseph's being "brought" to Egypt, Israel enters the "House of
Bondage" (Exod. 20:2; B. Jacob). For a trained slave, older
than twenty years, the price is thirty shekel (cf. Lev. 27:5).[30]

29   Reuben returned to the pit. But lo! There was
       no Joseph in the pit. He rent his clothes.

While the brothers camped on the hill for their meal, they
could not see the Midianites who, hearing Joseph's cries for help,
pulled him up from the cistern and sold him to the Ishmaelites
who happened to pass by. That is why Reuben did not find
Joseph in the pit, to which he returned with his brothers' consent
(see expos. to v. 27). Rending one's clothes was the reflex action of a horror-stricken person. (V. 34 will mention "tearing
one's garments," a mourning ritual.)

30   Then Reuben went to his brothers and he said, "The
       child is not in the well! And I, where shall I go?"

Dazed and numb with despair, he returned at last to the
brothers and tells them that Joseph must have become the victim
of a wild beast that had carried him away and devoured him.
No path now seems open to Reuben: He had not wanted to
return to the brothers, and to the father he cannot go without
Joseph. His brothers may have wondered about his utter con-
sternation and his words, "And I, where shall I go?" It is quite

possible, though, that then and there, he revealed to them that he had intended to restore the "child" to his father. Though they were not as stunned as Reuben was, Joseph's disappearance and apparent death bewildered them just the same. Now that he would no longer threaten their future, they decided to leave Dothan and return to the father's homestead. But the very thought of facing him in his anguish terrified them. Then they "bettered" their original plan: Instead of "We will say a wild beast devoured him" (cf. v. 20), they will say nothing. Joseph's tunic will speak for them.

31   They took Joseph's tunic, slaughtered
        a kid, and dipped it in its blood.

32   Then they had the ornamented tunic taken to
        their father, and they said, "This is what
        we found. Please examine it. Is it or is
        it not the tunic of your son?"

Had they spoken directly to their father and had he replied to them, both would have said "Joseph's tunic," whereas v. 32 has "the tunic of your son" and v. 33, "my son's tunic" (RaLBaG). This indicates that the brothers found a way to have villagers show it in the neighborhood, pierced to simulate the tooth-marks of wild beasts (RaMBaN), when it should reach their father before they arrived themselves.

33   Recognizing it, he said, "My son's tunic! A savage
        beast devoured him! Torn to pieces is Joseph!"

Toraph—torn—is the shepherd's language; his lamb, his Joseph, is torn! (B. Jacob).

34   And he tore his garments, put sackcloth on his
        loins, and mourned his son for many days.

Jacob performs the mourning rites (cf. II Sam. 1:11; 3:31; 13:31; Job 1:20) for the dead, like tearing one's garments and putting on sackcloth, a girdle of rough and prickly fabric (Sforno). That "he mourned him for many days" seems to mean that he continued to conduct himself as a mourner beyond the traditional span of time (BT *Megillah* 17a; *Genesis Rabbah* 84:20). Upon their delayed return, the brothers naturally kept their secret from everyone, pretending utter surprise and dismay when they "learned" what had happened, and expressed their condolence to the desolate father.

35   Then all his sons and daughters stood up to
console him, but he refused to be comforted,
saying, "I will go down mourning to my son in
Sheol." Thus his father wept for him.

When the family realized that the patriarch would not cease observing the mourning rites, they met in council (S. R. Hirsch) and prevailed upon the Ten to take them all to him. Thus they "stood up" and went to him, hoping that the sight of "all his sons and daughters" would sooth his anguish (Or ha-Hayim). "Daughters" includes daughters-in-law (cf. Ruth 1:11f.; 2:2; etc.). The Ten may even have tried to give their father some glimmer of hope that Joseph could still be alive. By then, they were all seized by deepest regret for what they had done to their father, and henceforth, they would never say anything resentful about Joseph, making only sad references to him who is "gone." The father's "refusal to be comforted" was perhaps also caused by his sense of guilt for having sent Joseph on the perilous trip. Jacob insists that he will mourn Joseph for the rest of his life until he himself will "go down . . . in Sheol."[31] With this, the Torah parts for a long time from Jacob and his family.

36   The Medanites had sold him to Egypt; for Potiphar,
a courtier of Pharaoh, the chief executioner.[32-36]

In the pivotal verse 28, Joseph's name was thrice mentioned. In the above last sentence of the chapter, his name is painfully missing as if Joseph as a slave has become a mere object, his humanity lost. Actually, however, the Joseph whom the Midianites had pulled from the pit had just attained a humanity he did not have before: The Joseph who had displayed himself in his ornamental tunic as he approached his brothers no longer existed. It was in the pit, "in the valley of the shadow of death," that he experienced a transfiguration. "Until the time that His decree had come to pass," the author of Ps. 105:19 reflects, viz., that the brothers had flung him into the pit, he was not yet worthy of God's companionship and help. He must have become worthy of it after "His word had purged him," as the Psalm continues. The pit was his "crucible of affliction" (Isaiah 48:10). Therein he reflected in amazement—even stronger than his fear

—upon his brothers' outburst of hatred and fury, blotting out all prudence, humanity, and filial terror, and experienced a radical moral stocktaking.[37] Lying half naked in the pit, Joseph recognized his sin of brazen assertiveness, of impiously revealing what his dreams had been meant to intimate to him alone, his future elevation in God's own time (Chaninah Maschler). From then on Joseph grows in humility and humanity, in constancy and diligence, in charity and, above all, in wisdom and 'emunah—steadfast loyalty to God.

GENESIS 39

Chapter 37 begins by reporting that Jacob settled at last in Hebron at his father's homestead. It comes to a close with the information about the fulfillment of the first phase of God's prediction to Abraham (cf. 15:13f.) that his descendants would be "strangers in a land not theirs" before their "return" to Canaan. This "land not theirs" is Egypt, and Joseph is the first of the Jacob clan to enter it. The opening verse of ch. 39 resumes where ch. 37 had left off, before ch. 38—omitted in this exposition—interrupted the Narrative. The first verse adds nothing new, except the seemingly redundant remark that Joseph's master was an Egyptian:

1   When Joseph was taken to Egypt, Potiphar, a
        courtier of Pharaoh, the Chief Executioner,
        an Egyptian, bought him from the Ishmaelites
        who had brought him there.

If the "new king," mentioned in Exodus 1:8, who later "arose over Egypt," and "who did not know Joseph" was of the native Egyptian dynasty, having come to power after the reign of the Hyksos invaders, if, in other words, the king who was reigning when Joseph was brought down to Egypt was not himself an Egyptian, then the Torah's thrice calling (vv. 1,2,5) Joseph's master, Potiphar, an Egyptian, would, of course, not be superfluous (J. H. Hertz), since the high officials under the Hyksos must, for the most part, themselves have been Hyksos, i.e. of north-west semitic stock.[1] Yet, however tantalizing the Hyksos question may be to the modern historian, what matters to the Torah is that Providence brings Joseph, enslaved, face to face with Egypt's court as represented by Potiphar, the "Egyptian." The three verses that emphasize Potiphar's being an Egyptian all contain Joseph's name with equal emphasis, as if to intimate that Joseph prefigures the enslaved "Children of Israel" as

Potiphar prefigures the Pharaoh (see expos. on 37:28c; Chaninah Maschler).

2   YHWH was with Joseph; so he was a man of
            success; and he stayed in the household
            of his Egyptian master.

"YHWH" appears only in this chapter where it is *the Torah* that speaks.[2] None of the *personae* in the Narrative uses "YHWH," only *'elohim*—the Lord. Even God Himself, speaking to Jacob (cf. 46:2f.), avoids "YHWH." This striking "eclipse" of "YHWH" in the Narrative manifests it as a "prelude to Exodus" (see expos. on 37:10). Only with Moses does YHWH reemerge after the interval of the Narrative which separates the patriarchal epoch from the Exodus (B. Jacob). Eight times in this chapter (five times in vv. 2-5 and three times in vv. 21ff.), the Torah emphasizes that "YHWH was with Joseph." It seems that he became worthy of YHWH's "being with him" after the brothers flung him into the pit, where he had a "rebirth" (see expos. on 37:36). YHWH was "with him" not to protect him *from,* but *in* adversity (von Rad). That "YHWH was with Joseph" was mainfested not only by his becoming "a man of success," but already by his not having been sold in the rural regions where he would have disappeared without a trace, but to Potiphar, a courtier of Pharaoh who even employed him in his home.

3   And his master saw that YHWH was with him and
      that YHWH lent success to everything he undertook.

Joseph must have so endeared himself to Potiphar through his virtues that the master inquired about his slave's background. This is how he learned from Joseph about his God.[3] That his master "saw that YHWH was with him" means that he saw how Joseph *had YHWH with him* (see RaShI). Joseph "walked with God" in *'emunah* (see expos. on. 37:36). Potiphar also recognized "that YHWH lent success to everything he undertook," that Joseph's deity helped him to excel in morale, industry and faithful service in the Egypt of the Egyptian gods.[4]

4   He became fond of Joseph, made him his
            personal attendant. [Then] he put him
            in charge of his household and entrusted
            to him all his possessions.

The repetition of "Joseph" shows that Potiphar wanted him close to himself, making him his personal attendant and controller of the household and estate.

5 And as soon as he had put him in charge of
  his household and over all that was his,
  YHWH blessed the Egyptian's house for
  Joseph's sake so that YHWH's blessing was
  on everything he owned, inside the house
  and outside.

Now Joseph was completely on his own. He no longer had to follow instructions, and it became obvious to his associates that not only Joseph's own undertakings, but Potiphar's entire estate became blessed by God for Joseph's sake.[5]

6a,b He left everything in Joseph's hand and with
  him [around] he did not know anything except
  the bread he ate.

Joseph has now become Potiphar's overseer, no longer expected even to give his master an account. To ascertain the meaning of the seemingly simple words "anything except for the bread he ate," we have to compare them with the way Joseph paraphrases them in vv. 8ff., "Lo, with me [around], my master knows nothing . . . nor has he withheld anything from me *except yourself* . . ." (emphasis added). "The bread he ate," then, is a euphemism for sexual intercourse.[6]

Why then, having attained such a high position of independence, did Joseph not send word about his wellbeing to his lamenting father in Canaan? The *midrash* answers that he did not attempt it "lest he should have to explain his presence in Egypt and, thus, betray his brothers":[7] Jacob would find out who had sold Joseph to Potiphar and, thus, learn about the Ten's crime. So, though his father would rejoice at regaining one son, he would lose ten others, for, having heard about their crime, he would have to disinherit them; and the "House of Israel," Joseph's hope and prayer, would become an impossibility (see expos. on 41:51, answering why Joseph did not contact his father after having been elevated to regency).

6c Joseph was beautiful of form and fair
  to look upon.

Nowhere else in Scripture is a male thus described (cf. 29:17).

7   It was then that his master's wife cast her
      eyes upon Joseph and said, "Sleep with me."

The literal translation of the beginning of v. 7, "It was after these things," is a phrase which always introduces a turning point (cf. 22:1,20; 40:1; 48:1, etc.; B. Jacob). The *Midrash* sees a causal nexus between vv. 6ab and 6c, also between vv. 6c and 7:

> Free from anxieties, he turned his attention to
> his external appearance. He painted his eyes,
> dressed his hair, and aimed to be elegant in his
> walk. But God spoke to him saying, "Thy father
> is mourning in sackcloth and ashes, while thou
> dost eat, drink and dress thy hair. Therefore
> I will stir up thy mistress against thee. . . ." [8]

Thus, the midrash makes Joseph responsible for the woman's advances to him. The Torah seems to have postponed mentioning Joseph's charm to indicate that only after he had attained his high position did Potiphar's wife "cast her eyes upon Joseph."[9]

8   But he refused. And to his master's wife he
      said, "Lo, with me here my master knows
      nothing as to what is in the house, having
      given into my hand all he has."

It is noteworthy that *wayema'en*—he refused—has a rare Masoretic cantillation mark which indicates sustained deliberation (cf. 19:16; 24:12, etc.).[10]

9   "He wields no more authority in this house than
      I and withheld from me nothing except yourself,
      you being his wife. How then could I commit
      this great wrong and sin against God!"

Tactfully Joseph says "my master" instead of "your husband" and does not mention the wrong she would do. It is obvious that he attempts to dissuade her by speaking her language, calling merely the breach of trust, not adultery, a "great wrong and sin against God."

The prohibition of adultery is one of those Divine Laws already obeyed in patriarchal times. Though an Israelite was permitted more than one wife, intercourse even with a person merely engaged to someone else was considered adultery, a sin and pollution so severe that both the adulterous woman and her paramour had to suffer death.[11] Though extra-biblical wisdom and priestly texts show that adultery was also considered abhorrent by the gods of other Near East nations, the Babylonian Code of Hammurabi, the Assyrian and the Hittite Laws give the husband the right to pardon his adulterous wife and her paramour, thus rendering adultery merely a crime, a proprietary misdemeanor, a matter of private litigation between the insulted husband and the adulterer.[12] Though for Joseph it is, above all, the sin of adultery he abhors, he knows enough about "the practices of the land of Egypt" (cf. Lev. 18:3), not to expect his mistress to be overly concerned with *her* "fear of God."[13]

10   Although she spoke to Joseph day after
             day to lie beside her, to be with her,
             he would not listen to her.

After Joseph had refused what originally she had asked him to do, viz. "sleep with me"—lit. "lie with me"—she then reduced her request, imploring him, "Lie beside me"; lastly, "Be with me." But Joseph refused. He managed never to be alone with her, lest he be seduced.

11   One day he came as usual to the interior
             of the house to do his work, and none of
             the household was inside there.

Joseph had no inkling that he would find the woman waiting for him in that chamber where he would "do his [administrative] work."[14] "On that particular day, the domestics were all drawn away to a religious observance, which the mistress pretended not to be able to attend because of illness."[15]

12   She seized him by his coat: "Sleep with
             me!" But he left his coat in her hand,
             fled and walked out of the house.[16]

The "coat" was a long shirt tied about the hips, worn inside the house, actually his undergarment. He did not pull it away from her by force since she was his mistress (RaShBaM). But he swiftly divested himself of it as she held it, in order to elude her grasp (J. Z. Meklenburg). Joseph thus fled completely undressed, at once disgracefully and honorably (von Rad). "Out of the house" does not mean into the street, but from the living quarters into the courtyard which they surrounded (B. Jacob). The Torah emphasizes that after he "fled" from the chamber, "he walked out of the house": Once outside, he resumed his normal gait to avoid unwelcome questions (Sforno). Furious that Joseph had rejected her, the woman's passion turned into hatred.

13   When she saw that he left his coat with
            her and had fled out of the house .

"She saw that . . . he had fled out of the house." Mistakenly, she assumed and feared that Joseph had kept on running and had divulged to the returning domestics what had happened. With great presence of mind, she turns the tables by accusing him (see RaMBaN).

14   She summoned her domestics and told them:
            "Look, he had to bring us a Hebrew fellow
            to sport with us! He came to me to sleep
            with me, but I called out loud!"

The Hebrew text has merely "he brought us," but the above NJPS's "he had to bring us," emphasizes her disrespectfully calling her husband and their master "he" in her sarcastic remark about Potiphar's intention. She toadies to the domestics by disparaging their master and places herself on their level by saying "us." She also makes them feel superior to Joseph, telling them that the upstart is but one of the impure Hebrew pastoral people (cf. 43:32; 44:34), whose very admission to their race-pure Egyptian home by their master had been an insult, not to mention the master's intention to have him toy with them and her.[17] Thus, to avenge the slight, and to anticipate the possibility of an accusation by Joseph, she resolves to accuse him and calls the servants forthwith to be "witnesses."[18] As we recall, she had feared that Joseph was seen running in the courtyard. The reason she will soon report that "he walked out of the house" must be that she now learns Joseph was seen "walking" unclad.

15   "The moment he heard me scream, calling
           [for help], he left his coat with me,
           fled and walked out of the house."

With great cunning, she turns the coat into evidence, implying that Joseph had just begun to undress, but fled when she screamed without even taking time to grasp his coat. Once outside, she adds, this shrewd villain stopped running and walked as if nothing had happened. Having thus procured "witnesses" for Joseph's crime, she waits for Potiphar.

16   She placed the coat at her side
           until his master came home.

She put Joseph's coat on her couch to make it appear that she kept "the scene of the crime unchanged" (J. Z. Meklenburg) and pondered what words to use when "his master" should return that would cause him to punish his ungrateful, wicked slave.

Throughout Genesis, we find striking "measure for measure" retribution—as well as compensation (see expos. on 42:38)—on the part of Divinity:[19] As Joseph had humiliated his brothers by wearing his "coat" of distinction, so will he now be humiliated through a "coat." And as the brothers used his coat as circumstantial evidence for his death, so the woman is about to use it to "prove" his crime.

17   Then she told him the same story: "The
           Hebrew slave whom you brought to us to
           make love to me came to me."

In the Hebrew text her words are deliberately ambiguous: She makes her husband guess whether she insinuates that he intended to have his slave make love to her or that this was the slave's own fiendish plot. To the domestics, she had said, "to toy with us," in order to incite them. She does not now repeat "to sleep with me," lest Joseph be provoked to defend himself, if accused of such a capital crime.

18   "But when I screamed and called [for
           help], he left his coat at my side
           and fled out of the house."

Since Potiphar had not been present, she switches again to "he . . . fled out of the house," as if Joseph had run away lest he be caught by the domestics.

19   When his master heard as his wife kept on
    talking, "Such and such did your slave do
    unto me," his wrath was kindled.

Against whom was "his wrath . . . kindled?" Against Joseph? This is our first thought and the impression Potiphar wanted to give the public (see below). Yet, according to Egyptian law, Joseph would at least have been mutilated, had Potiphar actually believed her.[20]

20   And Joseph's master took him and placed
    him in *bet-hassohar,* the place where the
    royal prisoners were jailed. And there
    he was in *bet-hassohar.*

Potiphar's trust in Joseph's character was not shaken. The Hebrew verb for "he took him" always expresses careful concern (B. Jacob).[21] He knew what to expect from his wife whose overly verbose and defensive talk only confirmed his distrust of her. But he had to "save face" for his family and to part from his faithful servant. Yet, he merely transferred him to *bet-hassohar,* a fortress-like round wing of his large residential complex in which those who had failed to pay crown-tax levies were jailed at hard labor.[22] Henceforth, I shall call *bet-hassohar* "the Tower."

21   And YHWH was with Joseph. He caused
    affection for him and disposed the
    chief jailor favorably toward him.

"YHWH was with Joseph" implies also (see expos. on v. 3) that Joseph maintained his trust in God even when he was not only demoted from his unique advancement as a slave, earned by years of faithful service, but also had the stigma of criminality attached to him.

Chs. 40/41 will show that precisely this adversity was for the sake of his salvation. God's being with Joseph is now emphasized even more than at the outset of Joseph's enslavement: 1) "He caused affection for him" in the hearts of the prisoners

(NaTsYB). Though such usually tough-minded men were not given to appreciate a foreign slave, God made Joseph endear himself to them.²³ 2) He "disposed the chief jailor favorably toward him." The prisoners' affection for Joseph influenced the chief jailor.²⁴

22   Then the chief jailor put Joseph in charge
         of all the prisoners in the Tower; and
         whatever was done there, he was the doer of it.

As in Exod. 32:35, the Torah here considers the initiator of an action its executor (S. R. Hirsch). Again, as in Potiphar's house, Joseph attains an overseer's position. He had acquired such standing before in his father's household (Chaninah Maschler). Now, he was the administrator not of an estate, but of a prison.

23   Since YHWH was with him, the chief jailor
         did not himself supervise anything in his
         charge whatsoever, and whatever he under-
         took, YHWH made it prosper.

In v. 6, Potiphar did not "know"; here, the chief jailor does not "supervise," lit. "see." There, it was "not . . . anything"; here, it is "not . . . anything . . . whatsoever." In v. 3, "the master saw that YHWH was with him . . ."; here, "YHWH made it prosper." The jailor himself did not attain such conviction about YHWH as Potiphar had done.

GENESIS 40

1   Some time after this, the cupbearer and
            the baker of the King of Egypt gave of-
            fense to their lord, to the king of Egypt.[1]

The exposition of 39:7 explained that the Hebrew for "some time after this" introduces a turn of events. The Torah expresses "gave offense" by (lit.) "sinned" as if to contrast those who really "sinned" with Joseph, who was in the Tower because he refused to "sin" (cf. 39:9; B. Jacob).

2   Pharaoh was angry with his two courtiers,
            with the chief cupbearer and with the
            chief baker.

Chief cupbearers held an important office in Pharaoh's court and were actually trusted advisors to the king.[2] The word "with" is repeated, indicating that the offense of each may, as in fact it will, be judged differently (B. Jacob).

3   He had them put in custody in the house
            of the chief executioner, into the Tower,
            the place where Joseph was confined.

4a   Now the chief executioner appointed Joseph
            to be with them, and he waited on them.

Knowing Joseph's winsome personality, Potiphar released him from his previous duties and appointed him "to be with them" as a companion of Potiphar's unfortunate colleagues (B. Jacob), taking the edge from their miserable plight (NaTsYB). That "he waited on them" was not Joseph's duty, but a voluntary kindness. As if to underline that they were not his superiors, the Torah adds in v. 7 that they "were with him in custody in his master's house."[3] Had Potiphar, as most translations have it, "assigned Joseph to wait on them," the text would have been *wa-yifkod 'oto lesharet 'otam,* in which case Joseph would, indeed, not only have been demoted from having all prisoners under his supervision (cf. 39:22), but would also have been incomprehensibly audacious when familiarly questioning the courtiers (cf. v. 7).

4b   They had been in custody for about a year.[4]

5   Then both of them, the cupbearer and the baker
          of the king of Egypt, confined in the prison, had
          a dream, each as if his dream was foretelling.

The literal translation of the enigmatic v. 5b is "each man according to the interpretation of his dream."[5]

6   When Joseph came to them in the morning,
          he looked at them. They were distraught.[6]

It seems that Joseph kept on spending the night with the prisoners he used to supervise.

7   So he asked Pharaoh's officials, who were
          with him in custody in his master's house,
          "Why do you appear so downcast today?"

Since Potiphar had made him their *companion* (see expos. on v. 4a), *not their servant,* he feels at liberty to inquire how he can help them out of their obvious trouble.

8a   And they said to him, "We had a dream,
          but there is no one to interpret it."

They are sure that their dreams forecast their fate (see v. 5). What distresses them is that in the Tower, no "professional" is available to them, mastering the "science" of dream-interpretation.[7] By then, Joseph was already twenty-eight years old (cf. 41:1 with 41:46), and since dreams had become fascinating to him ever since he had his own dreams, he was well acquainted with Egyptian oneiromancy which he rejected in spite of its fame.

8b   Joseph said to them, "Surely, God can
          interpret! Please tell me [your dreams]."

For Joseph, dream interpretation is not a science of men, but an inspiration of God to those who commit themselves to Him Who imparts dreams. He implies that God endowed him

with his gift. We can assume that just as Potiphar learned from
him about his God (see expos. on 39:3), so had he previously
told the courtiers about Him. Now Joseph attempts to persuade
them to trust him and his interpretation.

9   Then the chief cupbearer told his dream
    to Joseph. "In my dream," he said to
    him, "there was a vine in front of me."

The baker hesitates to confide in Joseph. He may have felt
something ominous about his dream. Only after Joseph has
auspiciously interpreted the cupbearer's dream will the baker
also hope to receive a favorable interpretation.

10   "And on that vine there were three branches. It had
    barely budded, when out came its blossom,
    and its clusters ripened into grapes.[8]

11   "Pharaoh's cup was in my hand; so I took
    the grapes, pressed them into Pharoah's
    cup, and placed the cup in Pharoah's hand."

We may assume that the grape juice became wine with the
lightning speed of the preceding stages (reminding one of modern time-lapse films). This is in contrast to the cupbearer's own
heedful scrutiny. He appears, unostentatiously, only in the second part, not at the outset as does the baker (cf. v. 16). The
cupbearer's thrice speaking of "Pharaoh" indicates to Joseph
his deep sense of responsibility and devotion (B. Jacob).

12   Then Joseph said to him, "This is what it
    means: The three branches are three days."

The only contingent element in the dream, which otherwise—
because of the self-interpretative coherent sequences of its
phases—predicts rehabilitation, is the three branches. Because
of the rapidity of the dream-phases, Joseph concludes that
"three" stands for the shortest time span, hence "three days"
(B. Jacob), after which Pharaoh's birthday, as Joseph knows,
is to be celebrated (Ibn Ezra).

13   "In three days Pharaoh will pardon you
    and restore you to your former station
    when you were his cupbearer, and you
    will be handing the cup to Pharaoh." [9]

14   "Except that you retain me in your memory,
            when all has become well with you, to do
            me the kindness of mentioning me to
            Pharaoh and get me out of this house."

Ki 'im—except—nowhere introduces a sentence in Scriptures. One should, therefore, assume that what preceded it, is left out and that it refers to a reward which Joseph declines to accept.

15a   "For kidnapped, yes kidnapped, was
           I from the land of the Hebrews."

This seems to be the first time that Joseph speaks about his misfortune (B. Jacob), sensing it providential that he has met the cupbearer. His expression "kidnapped" should not be taken literally: As we saw (see expos. on 37:28), the Midianites did not actually "steal" him (the literal translation of what is rendered here as "kidnapped"). What he wants to express is merely that his being a slave is not a consequence of birth and/or war, but of crime. "Kidnapped" is another proof that the Midianites (see expos. on 37:28), not the brothers, pulled him from the pit (B. Jacob). "The Hebrews," an appellation on the lips of foreigners (cf. 39:14,17; 41:12)—or of Israelites speaking, as here, to or about foreigners (43:32)—does not connote a distinct people but itinerant clans, typically found in Canaan.

15b   "Nor have I done anything here that
           should have put me into the pit."

He does not disclose his case, but wants the cupbearer to know that he lost his former high position with Potiphar because of a miscarriage of justice which only the king can annul. It was needless for the Torah to add that the cupbearer gave Joseph his promise.

16   When the chief baker saw that he had inter-
           preted auspiciously, he said to Joseph,
           "The same with me! In my dream, imagine,
           there were three wicker baskets on my head." [10]

As mentioned before, the baker had hesitated to tell Joseph his dream because it seemed ominous to him. Now that Joseph had assured the cupbearer that he would be pardoned, the baker attempts to receive such a favorable interpretation (considered causative for its realization, see expos. on 37:8b) by claiming that his dream was a precise analogy of the other.

17   "And in the uppermost basket there was of all
                  pastry for Pharaoh; and the birds were
                  eating them out of the basket on my head."

For "pastry" see n. 2 in expos. on v. 2. Joseph was not deceived: Had this dream been "the same," it would have shown grain growing, ripening, harvested, made into pastry . . . all before the baker placed it before his king. In his dream, however, he does not appear before Pharaoh who is only casually mentioned. Besides, he carries the king's pastry in the "uppermost," i.e. unprotected, basket, and is unable to drive away the birds (cf. 15:13). His is a "prevented (neglectful) action."[11]

18   Then Joseph replied, "This is what it means:
                  The three baskets are three days."

See expos on v. 12: Here, for the same reason, "three baskets" indicates "three days."

19   "In three days Pharaoh will lift your head—
                  off you, and have you impaled on the stake;
                  and birds will be picking off your flesh."

As Joseph begins his interpretation, the baker is made to hope that his dream also foretells reinstatement, for the words are the same, including "lift your head." But then, with horrible irony, Joseph corrects the baker's impression, showing that he merely employed "lift your head" as a pun, adding "off you," i.e. he will be beheaded. It seems that Joseph resented the baker's attempt to force his hand. He was quite sure of this forecast also which would have cost him dearly had he been wrong.

20   And so it happened: On the third day, when
                  Pharaoh gave a banquet for all his officials
                  —for it was his birthday—he had the head
                  of the chief cupbearer and the head of the
                  chief baker lifted from among his officials.

See expos. on v. 2: As there the word "with" is repeated, so here the words "the head of," to prepare us for the possibility that either case may turn out quite differently. The celebration of a Pharaoh's birthday included appointments, proclamations, and amnesties.[12] This verse has "head-lifting" in the meaning of "roll call."[13] It seems that by using again this equivocal idiom, the Torah wants us to realize how the fate of each man hangs in the balance up to the last moment (Chaninah Maschler).

21   And he restored the chief cupbearer
        to his cupbearing so that again he
        placed the cup in Pharaoh's hand.

It seems that Providence tipped the balance in his favor so that he could inform Pharaoh in his hour of need of Joseph's ability to interpret dreams. In fact, the two courtiers' dreams seem to have been providentially caused merely for Joseph's sake, because, except for giving the cupbearer a chance to prove his art, they lacked the intrinsic purpose of the other dreams to induce action in accordance with their message.

22   But the chief baker he had impaled
        —just as Joseph had foretold them.

The violation of the corpse was a specially grievous punishment for the Egyptians who took such pains with the remains of the dead.

23   Yet the chief cupbearer did not keep
        Joseph in mind, and he forgot him.

L'o zakar, usually literally translated as "he did not remember," makes "he forgot him" redundant. Yet, as in 8:1; 30:22 and Exod. 2:24 *z-k-r* means "planning to do something at a given time" (B. Jacob). The "given time" would have been Pharaoh's birthday. Because the chief cupbearer failed to make this resolution, he forgot about Joseph. Though Joseph's (and the reader's) hope is, therefore, dashed, it will be recognized that man's failure can serve the design of Providence. Had the courtier remembered, Joseph might have been freed and returned to his father; but the Divine plan to have Jacob and his house come to Egypt because of Pharaoh's gratitude to Joseph would not have come to pass. As will be seen, by God's design the cupbearer will have to recall Joseph.

GENESIS 41

1   At the end of two whole years, it
     was Pharaoh who had a dream. He
     was standing beside the Nile.

Pharaoh had a dream during the night preceding his birthday,
two years after the one mentioned in 40:20.[1-3] He sees himself
standing beside the Nile.[4]

2   Suddenly, out of the river came
     up seven cows, handsome and
     sturdy, and grazed in the reed grass.[5-8]

The Nile symbolizes the fertility of Egypt. Water cows, coming up from it, are nothing unusual.

3   But, lo, right after them, seven other
     cows, ugly in appearance and gaunt, came
     up from the Nile and stood on the bank
     of the Nile beside the [other] cows.

4   And the ugly cows ate up the seven hand-
     some cows. Then Pharaoh awoke. But he
5   feel asleep and dreamed again. This time
     seven ears of grain, healthy and goodly,
     came up upon a single stalk.[9]

6   But, suddenly, right behind them
     sprouted seven other ears, thin and
     scorched by the east wind.

Such "scorching" is caused by the sirocco wind, blowing from
the south-eastern desert. It can last fifty days from which it is
called *hamsin*—fifty. For its dreaded effect, cf. Isa. 15:5ff.

7   And the seven thin ears swallowed up
     the seven solid and full ears. Then
     Pharaoh woke up: it was a dream!

That it took Pharaoh some time to realize that both events were but a dream convinced him that something dreadful was bound to happen.

8   In the morning his spirit was agitated,
            and he summoned all the magicians of
            Egypt and all its sages. Pharaoh
            recounted his dream to them, but
            none could interpret them to Pharaoh.[10]

Egyptian oneiromancy claimed the ability of specially trained semantic skill to divine from a person's dreams what will happen to him. The singular in "his dream" indicates that Pharaoh himself realized that his second dream merely reiterated his first dream in different terms. "None could interpret them," however, shows that Pharaoh's experts saw in the two dreams two different portents (Hizquni).[11] The Torah is about to contrast the fallacious heathen magic and Egyptian "wisdom" with true wisdom inspired by God (cf. also Exod. 8:14; Dan. chs. 2 and 5).

9   Then the chief cupbearer addressed Pharaoh:
            "I must make confession of my sins today."

He may have included his "sin" against Joseph. But "sins" in the plural can also be understood in an abstract sense (E. A. Speiser).

10   "Once, when Pharaoh was angry with his ser-
            vants, he placed me in custody in the house
            of the chief executioner—me and the chief
            baker."

RaShBaM and Ibn Ezra remind us that Pharaoh is never addressed in the second person or by his own name.

11   "We both dreamt in the same night, I and
            he; each as if his dream was foretelling." [12]

12   "A young Hebrew was there with us, a
            slave of the chief executioner; and when
            we told him our dreams, he interpreted
            our dreams for us, he interpreted each
            according to its particular meaning."

Out of respect for the king, the cupbearer limits himself to the essentials. Yet, precisely because the courtiers' dreams seemed identical, "he interpreted" is reiterated to indicate what matters most, that Joseph gave each dream a different interpretation (see expos. on 49:28c; B. Jacob).

13   "And just as he told us, so it turned out: I
     was restored to my post, and he was impaled."

Though it would be offensive to public opinion for Pharaoh to consult so despised a person as a slave, a Hebrew and a youth to boot, the open-minded monarch accepted the cupbearer's implied suggestion.

14   Pharaoh sent for Joseph to be rushed
     from the pit who [first] had his
     hair cut and put on fresh clothes.
     Then he came before the king.

S. R. Hirsch contrasts "rushed" with "had his hair cut and put on fresh clothes. . . ." All in his own good time, he "comes" to Pharaoh, fully aware of the weight of his personality and the importance of his mission.

> In the eyes of *Semitic* people the beard was a mark of dignity, long hair an ornament of warriors and heroes, and only prisoners and slaves were shaved as sign of humiliation and dishonor. The *Egyptians* had an exactly opposite view, and the first thing every Egyptian of better upbringing was anxious to do, as soon as he came of age, was to deliver his head and face to the razor of the barber. He only grew beard and hair when mourning for a near relative. Thus Joseph wanted to appear before Pharaoh not as a barbarian and in foreign garb, but as a dressed and well-shaven perfect Egyptian gentleman. (A. S. Yahuda, *The Accuracy of the Bible,* 8)

Twice, Joseph was put into a "pit" (cf. 37:24 and 40:15). Now he leaves "the pit" and appears before Pharaoh and the splendor of the court.

15   And Pharaoh said to Joseph, "I have
     had a dream but none to interpret
     it. Yet about you I have heard:
     You listen to a dream to [make it]
     interpret it[self]!"

Pharaoh was told that Joseph understands dream-language
(A. B. Ehrlich).[13]

16a   "It is not I," replied Joseph to Pharaoh.

Joseph refuses the compliment and says that a human's innate
gift as such is as incapable of interpreting Pharaoh's dream as
is professional oneiromancy. Then Joseph, as he has done before
(cf. 40:8b), refers to God:

16b   "May God answer for Pharaoh's welfare."

With the courage of faith, yet with courtly deference, Joseph
dares to proclaim his God as the Lord of Egypt and of its king,
revered as a deity: It is God Who sends the dreams and whom-
ever He deigns He inspires to interpret them. Joseph implies
that this inspiration will be granted to him (RaShI), as he expressed it to the two courtiers. Joseph hopes that through him
God will "answer" (cf. Jer. 23:35; Micah 3:7) the king's request for his highest good. Pharaoh marvels at the slave's inner
freedom, boldness, and ability to establish personal contact with
him at once. Instead of the Torah's objective report, Pharaoh
will now give his subjective account, colored by his "agitated
spirit" (cf. v. 8), his feelings of fright, horror and helplessness.
His description is more personal and drastic. He was less impressed by the good cows and ears, but he adds adjectives
when he speaks of the bad ones (B. Jacob).

17   Pharaoh then reported to Joseph,
      "In my dream, lo, I was stand-
      ing at the bank of the Nile.

18   "Then suddenly out of the Nile came
      up seven sturdy and well-formed cows
      and grazed in the reed grass."

"Handsome and sturdy" (v. 2) now becomes "sturdy and
well-formed," emphasizing their functional rather than their
aesthetic value.

19a   "But, imagine, after them came up
       seven other cows, scrawny, exceed-
       ingly ill-formed and emaciated."

"Ugly in appearance and gaunt" (v. 3) now becomes

"scrawny, exceedingly ill-formed and emaciated." Pharaoh omits "from the Nile," but adds v. 19b to express his horror (B. Jacob):

19b   "Never have I seen their likes for
          hideousness in all the land of Egypt.

20   "And the seven lean and ghastly cows ate
          up the first seven cows, the sturdy ones.

21   "They disappeared within them, yet
          one could not tell that they had
          consumed them, for they looked just
          as bad as before. And I awoke."

In v. 21, Pharaoh adds, again as in v. 19b, his own comment, expressing the incomprehensibility of the horrible process.

22   "And in my dream, I saw seven ears of grain,
          full and goodly, growing on a single stalk."

It is noteworthy that Pharaoh leaves out "I dreamed a second time" (v. 5) because he felt himself that he had had but *one* dream (see expos. on v. 8). "Full" now replaces "healthy" (v. 5) because after he had dreamed the sequence, "full" is a more apt contrast, as he sees it, to what follows:

23   "But right after them sprouted seven ears,
          shriveled, thin, and scorched by the east wind."

As in the description of the ugly cows (cf. v. 19a), to depict his horror, Pharaoh uses three adjectives instead of the two in v. 6.

24a   "And the thin ears swallowed the
          seven good ears."

As in v. 20, Pharaoh uses only one adjective to describe the latter (cf. v. 7).

24b   "I have told the magicians, but
          none had the answer for me."

At first, Pharaoh told Joseph simply that he had found "none to interpret" his dream (v. 15). Now, having gained confidence in Joseph, Pharaoh tells him that his "magicians" failed. In reality, Egypt's sages (v. 8) had also disappointed him. But he may still need them and so he does not want to antagonize them.

Joseph's reply (vv. 25-36) is the first long speech in the Narrative. It shows remarkable clarity, conciseness, certitude, and precision. The key-words are "Seven," "Egypt," "Pharaoh," "Famine," and "Abundance"—repeated twelve, ten, six, and four times respectively (B. Jacob). Vv. 25-33, his first speech, makes four points; the second speech (vv. 33-36) is his fifth and last point. I indicate these points by the numbers in parentheses.

25a   Then Joseph said to Pharaoh:
        (1) "Pharaoh's dream is [but] one."

Joseph assumes that when Pharaoh found "none to interpret it," it was because its two *parts* were considered to be two *dreams* (Sforno). Whereas the two courtiers' dreams seemed to be identical (cf. 41:9-11; 16f.), but actually were different, Pharaoh's seemingly *different* dreams were actually identical. In fact, Joseph reasons, Pharaoh himself sensed this, for why else should he speak of his "dream" in the singular?

25b   (2) "God has foretold to Pharaoh
        what He is about to do."

God has privileged the king to receive a message, warning "for Pharaoh's welfare" what "He is about to do" to Egypt. At once Joseph recognizes the fundamental difference between the king's dream, on the one hand, and those of the courtiers and his own, on the other. While the latter show the dreamer involved, predicting what will happen to him, Pharaoh's dream shows what will happen to Egypt, for the king is merely a spectator in his dream.

26   (3) "The seven good cows are seven years,
        and the seven good ears are seven
        years; it is the same dream."

"Good cows" and "good ears" are not only metaphors for bounty (as lean cows and ears stand for famine), but are "scissor symbols" for the annual "ploughing and harvesting" (cf. 45:6; RaMBaN), so that "seven" of each stand for "seven years."

27   (4) "The seven lean and ugly cows that
followed are seven years, as are the
seven empty ears scorched by the
east wind; there will be seven years
of famine.

28   "This is what I have meant to announce
to Pharaoh: What God is about to do
has He made Pharaoh see."

God's first purpose for sending Pharaoh the dream is predictive, announcing the famine. (For its second, hortatory, purpose, cf. vv. 33ff.). Joseph leaves it open whether other countries will also suffer famine.

29   "There will [first] come seven years of
great abundance throughout the land of
Egypt."

Joseph knows that only Egypt will be blessed with seven years of bounty, because the good cows emerged from the Nile, the symbol of Egypt, and because they grazed on the reed-grass bordering the Nile (RaShBaM).

30   "But following them there will rise up
seven years of famine, and all abundance
in the land of Egypt will be forgotten;
and famine will ravage the earth."

That the famine will immediately follow the years of abundance Joseph derives from the fact that both the emaciated cows (cf. v. 19a) and the shriveled ears (cf. v. 23) came up "right after" the good ones (RaMBaN). "All abundance in the land of Egypt will be forgotten" interprets v. 20 (RaShI).

31   "No trace of the abundance in the land
will be left because of the famine
thereafter, for it will be very severe."

This is the interpretation of v. 21 (RaShI).

32   "And the duplication of Pharaoh's
dream means that God has made the
matter irrevocable and God
has decided its imminence."

The dream-duplication indicates the irrevocability of the events to come. The imminence of the events is shown by the two dreams taking place in the same night (Ibn Ezra).[14] With this remark, Joseph concludes the fourth and climactic point of his first speech. Its decisive element is "God," Whose herald Joseph is. He speaks of God in the preamble (v. 16), in vv. 25 and 28, and twice at the conclusion (v. 32), five times in all (B. Jacob). Even though the name of "God" does not occur in it, it is Joseph's second speech which convinces Pharaoh of his God.

33   (5) "Now then, Pharaoh should select a
man, discerning and wise, and set
him over the land of Egypt."

With v. 33, Joseph's second speech begins. It must not be understood as his own practical suggestion (RaMBaN on v. 4), but as the interpretation of the dream's hortatory meaning (see expos. on v. 28): Had God merely intended to warn Pharaoh that Egypt's abundant harvests would be followed by famine, the dream would have shown only seven good cows and ears followed by the bad ones. Joseph now interprets the swallowing up of the former by the latter, that part of the dream which horrified Pharoah the most. Joseph sees in this "swallowing up" the exhortation to take emergency measures to enable Egypt to "swallow up" the surplus of the abundance during the famine. This calls for a "discerning and wise" plenipotentiary: The "wisdom" of the "sages" is not enough. Though it may provide the knowledge how to store all produce without spoilage, "discernment" is required for the collection and the husbanding (cf. v. 35).

34   "Pharaoh should [authorize him to] appoint over the land overseers to take
a fifth of the yield of the land of
Egypt during the seven years of abundance.[15, 16]

35   "They shall [buy and/or] gather all [avail-
able other] food of the good years and
pile up and keep under Pharaoh's authority
all grain for food in the cities."

Abrabanel holds that "all food" means more than grain and

that it was to be purchased by the crown. Yet it seems that Joseph would leave it up to the farmer either to sell or to store in the royal city-granaries all produce not needed for immediate consumption. The levying of the grain tax without antagonizing the farmer, the buying of the grain by the crown without causing price rises, and the subsequent equitable allocation of the rations require "discernment" of the man in charge of hiring and supervising his agents to do these things (RaMBaN).

36   "This food shall thus be a reserve for
         the country against the seven years
         of famine which will come upon the
         land of Egypt so that the land may
         not perish in the famine."

With these words, Joseph concluded his interpretation.

37   The speech pleased Pharaoh and all
         his courtiers.

Pharaoh is glad that Joseph has relieved his agitated mind. He trusts him fully, not merely because of the cupbearer's testimony, but also because Joseph's interpretation reminds him that he himself had actually dreamed the interpretation, but had forgotten it (Abrabanel). The Torah seems to imply that the "magicians" and "sages" had left before Pharaoh assembled his courtiers for consultation. What pleased them was, perhaps, not only the self-evident truth of the interpretation of the young Hebrew slave, whom Pharaoh had been so wise to interview, but also Joseph's solving—through the produce-tax to be levied upon the wealthy lords—the problem of supporting the entire population without expense to the crown. Still, some officials may have cautioned Pharaoh to wait and see whether the next crop would, indeed, turn out to be as abundant as Joseph predicted. But others, hoping to be chosen for the new appointment, obviously recommended that Pharaoh proceed at once. Before the king discloses his decision, he prepares the assembly for the stunning effect he knew it would have.

38   And Pharaoh said to his courtiers,
         "Could we find a[nother] man like
         this, endowed with the spirit of God?"

The Courtiers were all deeply impressed by Joseph's combining his unique interpretive gift with the practical sagacity of a statesman. But Pharaoh's acknowledgment of Joseph's God must have startled them. This Pharaoh is the Torah's image of a good monarch. He is the opposite of both "the Pharaoh of the Oppression" (cf. Exod. 1:8), "who did not know Joseph" and his successor who speaks of YHWH in defiance except in extreme straits, but never in sincere submission (cf. Exod. 5:2ff.). The Pharaoh of the Narrative not only "knows Joseph," but also has learned to know God through Joseph.

39   Then Pharaoh said to Joseph, "Since God
        has made all this known to you, there
        is none as discerning and wise as you."

Pharaoh refers to Joseph's own words (cf. v. 33) and implies his disillusionment with the proverbial "Wisdom of Egypt." Joseph had convinced him that true wisdom is but the fruit of faith in God. Grateful to Him for having sent him His servant, Pharaoh wants Joseph to serve him also.

40a   "You shall be in charge of my palace."

Joseph will call this position "father of Pharaoh" (see expos. on 45:8).[17]

40b   "Under your authority shall my
        people be provided for." [18]

With these words Joseph is assigned the position which he himself had suggested to the king, saying "Pharaoh should select a man . . . and place him over the land of Egypt . . ." (cf. v. 33f).

40c   "Only with respect to the throne shall
        I outrank you."

Joseph's occupying this highest position in the government had been prefigured by his status with Potiphar (B. Jacob). As his former master "outranked" him only in respect to his wife (cf. 39; 6, 9), so Pharaoh is now superior to Joseph "only with respect to the throne," being the "king."

41   And Pharaoh said to Joseph, "I herewith in-
        stall you over the whole land of Egypt." [19]

The repeated "Pharaoh said to Joseph" (cf. v. 39) introduces official action (B. Jacob). Pharaoh does not specify Joseph's rank. The Torah calls him "the *Shallit*" (cf. 42:6).[20] V. 44 indicates that he was given military control of Egypt besides having authority over Pharaoh's personal estates (cf. vs. 40a) and heading the ministry of agriculture (cf. 40b).[21]

42   With that, Pharaoh removed the signet ring
          from his hand and put it on Joseph's hand.
          He then had him dressed in robes of fine
          linen, and put the Gold Chain about his neck.

Such formal investiture required the three mentioned insignia.[22]

43   He [also] had him ride in his two-seated
          chariot, and they cried before him,
          "*Abrek!*" Thus he was installed
          over the whole land of Egypt.[23, 24]

Both vv. 43 and 45 anticipate what followed the day of Joseph's installation, while v. 44 follows the investiture.

44   Then Pharaoh said to Joseph, "I am Pharaoh:
          Without your approval no one in all the
          land of Egypt shall lift up hand or foot." [25]

The repetition of "Pharaoh said to Joseph" indicates that this was a private talk after the termination of the assembly. "I am Pharaoh" conveys that it is as Pharaoh, that is, with his authority and guarantee of sanctions, that he is about to speak.[26] That no one may do anything against Joseph's will or without his consent is expressed by the idiomatic "lifting up hand or foot." This is the language of the absolute ruler (B. Jacob), giving a minister dictatorial powers.

45a,b   Then Pharaoh named Joseph Tsaphenat-
          paneah and gave him in marriage Asenath,
          daughter of Potiphera, priest of On.

Pharaoh gave Joseph a new name and a wife from the elite of Egyptian nobility to signify both his naturalization and his elevation. The city of On, seven miles northeast of Cairo, on the eastern bank of the Nile, is Heliopolis in Greek. It is *Bet Shemesh*—Sun-House—in Jer. 43:13, the great cultic center of the sun-god Ra. "Potiphera" is the fuller form of "Potiphar" (cf.

37:6) and is Egyptian for "he whom Ra gave."

45c   And Joseph shone forth over the land of Egypt.[28]

46a   Joseph was thirty years old when he stood
        before Pharaoh, the king of Egypt.

"Standing before (an authority)" indicates authorization.[29] "The king of Egypt" is added, for now Joseph is the king's minister and no longer Potiphar's slave (B. Jacob). The listing of Joseph's age at his installation is expected.[30] Thirteen years after his arrival as a slave in Egypt, Joseph not only has been elevated to the highest rank, but also is now the son-in-law of the revered priest in On, thus a member of the most prestigious nobility.

46b   After Joseph had left Pharaoh's presence,
        he travelled throughout the land of Egypt.

"Left Pharaoh's presence," lit. "went out from before Pharaoh," following his investiture, refers to his respectfully walking backward, facing the king (cf. 47:10). A disrespectful parting from a king is expressed by omitting the word "before" (cf. Exod. 8:8,26; 9:33; 10:6,18; 11:8; NaTsYB). Joseph seems at once to have enacted the novel produce-legislation, appointed officials, initiated granary construction (see RaDaQ), all requiring repeated inspection tours (cf. I Sam. 7:16; Sforno).

47   During the seven years of plenty, the
        land produced in abundance.

48   And he made all [available] food in
        the land of Egypt during the seven years,
        gathered up and had the food stored in
        the cities: The food of the fields
        around each city he had put therein.

This work was done under Joseph's agents (see expos. on v. 35).[31] RaMBaN assumes that the rationing began in the first year of abundance to prevent all wastage. As in v. 35, "food" is repeated here three times, perhaps to include other produce besides grain.

49   And Joseph laid up corn as the sand of the
        sea, very much, until it had stopped
        being measured, for it was beyond measure.

Since only this verse speaks of "grain" and only now Joseph's name reappears, it seems that it refers to the grain, levied as tax (see expos. on v. 34), and that Joseph himself supervised its accumulation in centrally located granaries.

50   Before the [first] year of famine set in,
          Joseph became the father of two sons whom
          Asenath, daughter of Potiphera, priest
          of On, bore to him.

RaDaQ assumes that "before the year of famine set in" means that both sons were born during the last year of plenty, when Joseph was 37 years old (cf. v. 46). The seeming redundance of "whom Asenath . . . bore to him" may intimate both parents' determination to bring up their sons according to the father's mores (S. R. Hirsch). Jewish tradition derives from this verse the obligation of sexual abstinence during times of calamity like famine (BT *Taanith* 11a).

51   Joseph named the first-born *Menasheh,* meaning
          "God has caused me *nashoh*—to forget—all
          my hardships and all my parental home." [32, 33]

Joseph wanted those around him to understand that his reason for calling his firstborn *Menasheh* is that his bitter toil as a slave, his anguish of having been wrongly suspected of a crime and, above all, his having been torn away from his father, the rest of his family and from his homeland . . . are all "forgotten" now, thanks to God, Who has caused his elevation and crowned it with the joy of married life and paternal bliss.

Yet, it seems that underlying Joseph's words, there is also an esoteric soliloquy, the understanding of which requires the following reflection. The exposition on 39:6b showed that he did not contact his father after having become Potiphar's overseer "lest he would have to explain his presence in Egypt and thus betray his brothers." Yet, why did he still remain silent after having become able through his elevation to the regency to prevent his father from learning about the Ten's crime? The answer seems to be that although originally he had seen in his dreams merely a prediction of his future rise, a prediction which enabled him to maintain his morale in all adversities, his realization that Pharaoh's dream had a hortatory as well as predictive meaning (see expos. on v. 35) was reflected back on his own dreams: Though his "sheaf was rising" had been fulfilled with his elevation, he should do nothing about communicating with his father and family until the bowing of his brothers' sheaves before his should be fulfilled by the Ten bowing before him after the famine had also engulfed Canaan (J. Z. Meklenburg). It is this hortatory meaning of his dream which he now expresses in the words, "God has caused me to forget," meaning, "God wants me to act as if I have forgotten," until the time is ripe. This thought came to him as he contemplated sending word to his father after his elevation, but he expressed it only after Manasseh's birth.

52   And the second son he named Ephraim
      —Double-Fruitfulness—meaning,
      "God *hiphrani*—has made me fruitful,
      in the land of my affliction."

Again, Joseph expresses his gratitude to God. "The land of my affliction" can refer to his past afflictions, or mean that Egypt will always remain his "affliction," i.e. "exile" from his Fathers' land (cf. 50:25; Abrabanel).

53   The seven years of abundance that was
      in the land of Egypt came to an end.

54a   Now the seven years of famine set in,
      just as Joseph had predicted.

V. 54a anticipates that the first year of famine in Egypt was followed by its other six years. "As Joseph had predicted" refers to both Joseph's prediction of abundance in Egypt (cf. v. 29) and the immediately succeeding famine in Egypt (see expos. on v. 30).

54b, c   [Also] in all [adjacent] lands, there was
         famine, but in all the land of Egypt,
         there was bread.

That "just as Joseph had predicted" precedes v. 54b confirms that Joseph did not explicitly predict the famine in the adjacent countries. "All lands" means "adjacent lands."[34] "In all the land of Egypt there was bread" means plenty of grain, not only stored and locked by the government in the cities and metropolitan granaries, but also stocked all over Egypt by the farmers themselves.

55a   Now the whole land of Egypt felt the
       hunger [to come] and the people
       cried out to Pharaoh for bread.

The people knew about the masses of grain piled up in the royal silos, but Joseph withheld permission to have them opened. That is why the people became panic-stricken and protested to Pharaoh.

55b   But Pharaoh said to all the Egyptians,
       "Go to Joseph; whatever he tells you,
       you shall do."

Pharaoh may have foreseen what drastic decisions Joseph would have to make in the future (cf. 47:16ff.) and determines not to interfere. That is why he declares that as Joseph in his wisdom "told" that the famine would come and how to prepare for it, so the people must trust that his wisdom will "tell" them how to be saved from starvation (B. Jacob). The next verse seems to say why Joseph waited.

56a   [Only] when hunger had spread over
       all of the land did Joseph open up all
       [granaries] in which there was [grain].[35]

RaShI interprets "all of the land" to mean even the wealthy, "the upper strata."[36] It seems that Joseph wanted first to have all grain, still in private hands, used up.

56b   And he rationed for Egypt, for the
       famine was severe in the land of Egypt.

"He rationed" implies free distribution to the poor, selling to the other Egyptians and to people of other lands (cf. v. 57).[37]

57   And all [adjacent] countries came to
       Egypt, to Joseph, to obtain rations;
       for famine had gripped the entire world . . .

". . . Came to Joseph," because he was in charge of ration distribution.

Chapter 41 is epitomized in Ps. 105, already referred to in expos. on 37:36:

A king, a ruler of peoples, had him unfettered and set him free. He made him a lord of his household and steward of all his estate [, and YHWH caused him] to enthrall his courtiers with his person, that he impart wisdom unto his elders (vv. 19b-22).

GENESIS 42

Not until 47:13 will the Narrative return to developments in Egypt, for the text which now follows resumes the story of Joseph's family. Twenty-one years[1] have passed since Jacob cried out "Torn to pieces is Joseph!" (cf. 37:33). Meanwhile all of Jacob's sons had established families (cf. 46.9ff.) and by now not only Rachel but also the other three mothers were dead: Leah was buried in the family sepulchre at Hebron (cf. 49:31), and neither Bilhah nor Zilpah is among the House of Jacob that enters Egypt a year hence.

1   Jacob saw that there were rations in Egypt,
     and Jacob said to his sons, "Why do you keep
     staring at one another?"

"Jacob" occurs twice, obviously to indicate that after his many years of gloom and indecision following the "death" of Joseph, it was fear for his family's starvation that re-kindled his initiative. Jacob "saw" caravans returning from Egypt with grain (cf. 41:57). What made his sons procrastinate (Sforno) was their dread of Egypt whereto they had planned to sell Joseph.

2   And he said, "I hear that there are rations
     in Egypt. Go down there and procure for
     us from there that we live and not die."

"And he said" is repeated to indicate that his reproach was of no avail to stir them from their perplexity, each expecting advice and initiative from the other.

3   Then ten of Joseph's brothers went down
     to get grain rations in Egypt.

4   For Benjamin, Joseph's brother, Jacob
     did not send with his brothers, as he
     said, "lest harm befall him."

That Benjamin is explicitly called "Joseph's brother" underlines the reason for Jacob's fear. For Joseph perished "on the
way," as had their mother also (Abrabanel; cf. 35:19; 48:7).

5   Thus *Bene Yisrael*—the sons of Israel—
     arrived among those that came to obtain
     rations, for the famine extended to the
     land of Canaan.

Except for two merely anticipatory historical glosses (cf.
32:33; 36:31), the appellation *Bene Yisrael* appears here for
the first time. Compared with "the sons of Jacob" (cf. 34:7,13,
25, 27; 35:5, 22, 26) *Bene Yisrael* is as pregnant with
meaning as is "Yisrael" (see expos. on 37:3) compared with
"Jacob." By first calling them "his (Jacob's) sons" (v. 1), then
"Joseph's brothers" (v. 3) and now *Bene Yisrael,* the Torah
seems to intimate the master-motif of the whole Narrative, the
progression from "his sons" via "Joseph's brothers" toward *Bene
Yisrael* (Chaninah Maschler). "His sons" is merely the natural
affinity of consanguinity, the condition for the unique people's
advent. At the outset it was only Joseph who envisioned the additional need for "brotherliness" (see expos. on 37:16). But instead of promoting it, his naive egocentricity had, on the contrary, only caused his brothers' natural rivalry to progress from
resentment to hatred, envy, fury, and intent to destroy him altogether. With the resumption of the story of Jacob's family the
Torah will show how the Ten, "his sons," having become in
truth "Joseph's brothers," will, together with him and Benjamin,
mature to become the germ-cell of God's people, *Bene Yisrael*—
The Children of Israel.

6a   As to Joseph, he was *ha-Shallit*—the regent—
     over the land of Egypt, [though] he [also]
     administered the dispensation of rations to
     the entire population.

The Torah's purpose in emphasizing that Joseph was also
ha-Shallit—the regent—is to explain how, among the multitudes
to be provided with grain, Joseph happened to meet his brothers:[2] All other responsibilities Joseph had delegated to staffs of
agents. In order to encounter his brothers (see expos. on
41:51), as his dream had predicted, he personally discharged
the *Shallit's* function, part of which seems to have been to pro-

tect Egypt against hostile infiltration.[3] With the start of the famine this office implied also allocation of rations to foreigners who crossed the northeastern border. It was there that Joseph expected the "sheaves" of his brothers, i.e., his brothers petitioning for food during the famine. The *Shallit* had left word with his agents that when a large number of brothers, "sons of Jacob," arrived from Canaan, they should be brought before him for investigation.

6b   When Joseph's brothers arrived, they
            bowed low to him, face to the ground.

The brothers, we read, "were among those who came to procure rations" (v. 5). While these latter were not dealt with by the regent himself, the brothers were ordered *to appear before him*. This so filled them with apprehension that they prostrated themselves before him.

7a, b   When Joseph saw his brothers, *wayakkirem*
           —he recognized them—*wayitnakker*—but he
           made himself into a stranger.

As the punned Hebrew words (von Rad) show, Joseph's first concern was to hide his identity as soon as he recognized them. The reason must be that he recalled that in his dream they (their sheaves) did not bow before him but to his sheaf, i.e., his person unknown (Abrabanel). It is important to note that *wayitnakker* also puns with *"wayitnaklu*—they conspired a plot —that [this time] it should be *he* who would be put to death [as once they put to death the Shechemites]." (See expos. on 37:18). With this second pun the Torah informs us that Joseph plans to turn the tables, plotting against the erstwhile plotters.[4] As soon as they prostrated themselves, he recognized that all (see expos. on 41:51) of his first dream had come true.[5]

7c   He spoke to them harshly and said,
          "From where did you come?"

Had he merely wanted to ask "Where do you come from?" he would have said *me'ayin 'attem* (cf. 29:4) instead of *me'ayin b'atem* (NaTsYB). Besides, since they entered Egypt at the northeastern border, wearing Canaanite garments and speaking its tongue, "Where do you come from?" would have been superfluous. Moreover they must have registered their name and homeland at the point of entry. Thus, "From where did you come?" is "spoken harshly," implying that before having arrived at the regent's office and after having left Canaan they may already have reconnoitered something at Egypt's border (NaTsYB). The reason for Joseph's "speaking harshly" is that his second dream showed also "the moon," his mother already dead. Now he thought, "what if by now also 'the sun' and the 'eleventh star' are no longer alive? What if the Ten, who had blotted out their love and reverence for their father and their compassion for him, had eliminated also Benjamin, the favored wife's second son? What if their baseness had precipitated the father's death even if he first survived the shock of her firstborn's disappearance?" Joseph is thus about to spy on them (Suzanne Lowenthal) by accusing them of espionage. They sense his suspicion:

7d   They replied, "from the land of
          Canaan, to procure food."

They asseverate that nothing but "to procure food" is the purpose of their trip.

8a   Joseph recognized his brothers.
8b   They had not recognized him.

9a   And Joseph recalled the dreams
          which he had dreamt about them.

At first sight, there seem to be three redundancies:
1) Does not "Joseph recognize his brothers" simply repeat v. 7a?
2) Is not "They did not recognize him" superfluous? They had not seen Joseph for twenty-one years, he was Egyptianized in appearance, rank, speech (cf. v. 23), and name (cf. 41:45). At any rate, their anxiety prevented them from scrutinizing his face (Abrabanel).
3) Was not "Joseph recalled the dreams . . ." obvious when they prostrated themselves?
Yet, as already mentioned in *Preface* C, such seeming redundancies in the Narrative turn out to be singular intimations if duly examined: In v.8, the Hebrew for "recognize" also means "understand, know" (cf. Job 24:13,17; Neh. 13:24). If thus v. 8a means, "Joseph understood his brothers" and v. 8b means, "They had not known him," then these sentences make it possi-

ble to understand why, after Joseph heard their voices (cf. v. 7d), he, for the first time, "understood his brothers" and realized that in the past "the brothers did not know him": Joseph recognized that the Ten had resented his precociousness, pertness and egocentricity just as much as the father's favoring him. It dawned on him that their resentment had become hatred when he received the tunic and that their hatred had increased when he told them his first dream. While to him, it meant the confirmation from on high of his father's destining him to become the chieftain, to them it reflected his ruthless ambition to dominate them. While to him their sheaves forming a ring around his sheaf and bowing had previously meant that they would acknowledge him as their chief, he now sees it as meaning that though they would plot against him before, in the end, they would be grateful to their "keeper" and provider. What caused their misinterpretation, he now knows, was their hatred and their projecting on him their overweening pride (see expos. on 37:12).

As for the third redundancy, the emphasis in "Joseph recalled the dreams which he had dreamt about them" is on "about them." Before he compared what he dreamt about the Ten in his two dreams, it occurred to him that while Pharoah's dream-couplet actually meant the same event (see expos. on 41:25a), his own dreams, having occurred on separate nights, foretold two different events (see expos. on 41:32). Now he ponders that in his second dream the Ten bowed "before me," his identity known, whereas in his first dream they are not yet to know that he is Joseph. This can only mean that whereas he had failed to accomplish his father's desire, God now wants him to bring about his reconciliation with his brothers. Thus it dawns on him in fear and trembling that it is up to him to cause his brothers— once he knows that both his father and Benjamin are still alive— to repent of their sin before he can unmask himself and reconciliation follows. So far he had merely "made himself into a stranger," turned the tables, plotted against the erstwhile plotters and "spoke harshly to them," implying their evil intentions. Only now does he conceive his plan fully:

9b   Then Joseph said to them, "You are spies.
        You have come to see the nakedness of the land."

Accusing them explicitly and persistently of espionage, Joseph now realizes, will not only compel them to disclose sooner or later whether or not the father and Benjamin are still alive but will in the end also enable him, if they are, to compel the Ten to bring Benjamin, required in his now finalized plan. That a band of ten men, crossing the eastern border, should induce suspicion was not unusual in ancient Egypt. Its defenseless spots, "the nakedness of the land,"[6] required fortification and special garrisons. The regent accuses them of being professional spies, having just returned from an exploratory trip.

10   "But no, my lord," they said to him. "Really
      your servants have come to procure food."

In this sentence they deny the second accusation: They have come directly from Canaan to buy food.

11   "We are all of us sons of the same man. We
      are forthright. Your servants have never
      been spies."

If their arrival as a group caused the suspicion that they are a gang of professional spies, the regent's first accusation, their coming *together,* on the contrary, proves them to be harmless, for they are brothers. What father would risk all his sons' lives for hazardous espionage? Besides, how can a single family plan to invade a whole country? Would not an "invading" people select one spy from each tribe? (Arama). "We are forthright" seems to imply being "well-known as reputable people" about whom it would be easy to obtain information (RaMBaN). (As for their unwittingly including Joseph in "we are all of us sons of the same man," the Midrash aptly points to the poignant effect which their words had upon him.[7]) Nevertheless, intent upon their disclosing information about his father and Benjamin, Joseph brushes off their desparate attempts to clear themselves and reiterates his second accusation.

12   And he said to them, *"l'o kee*—nay—you have
      come to spy out the nakedness of the land."

Lo' kee, lit. "no but" is also used in 18:15 as an emphatic reassertion of a denied accusation. Their following reply was induced by his added demand (see expos. on 43:7; 44:19) to tell him more about their claim to belong to the same family, perhaps by sarcastically pointing to their dissimilar facial features.

13   They said, "Your servants are twelve, we are
         brothers, sons of the same man in the land of
         Canaan. As to the youngest, he is with our
         father; another one is gone."

With their repetition "sons of the same man" (c. 11), they explain that their dissimilarity is due to the fact that their father took several wives, their mothers. Still, having the same father, they are brothers. Joseph witnesses the dark shadow of the "lost" but unforgotten brother strike their emotions (von Rad). Though they were apprehensive that the regent would pursue inquiry about that strangely "missing brother," they did mention him. This proves to Joseph that they are "forthright" and that he can trust their assertion that both his father and Benjamin are still alive. What elates him also is that they have just included him and Benjamin, calling all of them what he never before heard them say, "brothers." In the past, only he had thought and spoken thus as in "It is my brothers whom my self is seeking" (see expos. on 37:16). He delicately refrains from inquiring about their "missing" brother, for he would not tax them more than they could bear without lying. Yet he persists in his accusation, except that he now offers them a way to prove their innocence.

14   Now Joseph said to them, "as to what I told
         you, that you are spies,

15   "this is how you shall be probed: By the life
         of Pharaoh [I swear that], unless your youngest
         brother comes here, you shall not go from here.

16   "Send of you one to bring your brother while
         [the rest of] you remain imprisoned. Thus shall
         your words be probed whether there is truth in
         you. If not, by Pharoah's life, you are spies."

The peculiar phrasing in v. 16, "send of you one" instead of "send one of you" suggests that in v. 15 the regent had at first decided to send an agent to Canaan with a note by their hand to fetch the youngest from the father and bring him to Egypt, a proposal which the brothers would not agree to, whereupon (v. 16) the regent changes his mind, allowing one of the brothers, whom they are to choose, to be their delegate. In 44:19ff. we learn that again the brothers refuse to comply, declaring of Benjamin, ". . . Only he is left of his mother, and his father dotes on him. . . . The boy cannot leave his father for . . . he would die."

These words stab Joseph so keenly that he almost drops his mask, all the more because they show the Ten's compassion. But he swiftly rehearses his task and persists, for at stake is not his but God's forgiveness, requiring their radical repentance. Besides, would not his own forgiveness, if declared now, fix them in their hatred against him, their "lord" (Chaninah Maschler)? Instead, Joseph now embarks upon an amazing and protracted strategy of "testing" them, i.e., to actualize through their true repentance their potential brotherliness. That is why Joseph decides to purge them first with a "show" of anger, God's anger and God's retribution. While the brothers assume that the regent's "probing" is to ascertain their veracity, his plan is to discipline and chasten them so that they will become conscience-stricken. That is why he disregards their second refusal.

17   He herded them into the guardhouse
      for three days.

He wanted to give them three days time to change their minds (cf. 22:4; Ezra 10:8), knowing that they will consent and choose their delegate, lest the father, Benjamin and all their families starve to death. There can be no doubt, however, that Joseph never intended to persist in his order that only *one* of them return to Canaan. By exposing them for three long days to the excruciating pain and dilemma of whom to choose as their delegate, he compels them to review each brother's part in the crime and to ponder not only who would best be able to persuade the father to entrust Benjamin to him but also who would most deserve the chance to save his own life by leaving for Canaan. Joseph hopes that their agony will cause these headstrong men, who had never before suffered the pain of being wrongly suspected, imprisoned and threatened with death, to correlate their desperate plight with the suffering they had inflicted upon Joseph and thus fathom God's retribution.

18   On the third day Joseph said to them, "Do this
      and you shall stay alive, for I fear God.

19   "If you are forthright men, you will let one of
      your brothers be held in your place of detention,
      while you go and bring home rations for your
      starving households.

20   "But you must bring me your youngest brother,
      that your words be verified and that you may
      not die." They consented.

Assuming that the three days of affliction have had the effect he expected, Joseph then visits them with his interpreter (cf. v. 23) who informs them that his master has changed his mind: Though his "fear of God" still holds him bound to his duty to the crown, wherefore he must insist on the youngest's appearance to exonerate them, it also urges him to prevent their and their families' unnecessary suffering.[8] Thus, on second thought, all that he needs to insure the arrival of the youngest is to retain but one hostage, again of their choice, while the other nine may leave with provisions for their families. The brothers who had already resigned themselves to the original condition were naturally very glad about its modification and, lit., "made [the] Yes [sign]" (cf. Speiser on 29:28). Thereupon the interpreter was dismissed and the regent stayed on, ostensibly to wait for their selection of the hostage.

21   They said to one another, "Alas, we are being
      punished for our brother, since we looked at
      his anguish, yet paid no heed when he pleaded
      with us. That is why this anguish has come
      upon us."

Assuming that the regent cannot understand their tongue, they are much too excited to restrain themselves in his presence. Prior to v. 21 they may have said, "This regent fears God though he is an Egyptian. He is compassionate even with our far-away families. We, however, brought up in our father's fear of God and also in Abraham's tradition of compassion for sinners (cf. 18:17-32), what have we done!"[9] "This anguish," naturally, is the retribution for "his anguish." Joseph witnesses their confession of sin (though, so far, it has been under duress). Moreover, he hears not only Reuben's following speech, but also other words of Reuben that must have preceded it since the text has *wa-ya-an Reuven*—then Reuben replied. As to the omitted words the Torah invites the following speculation: When the brothers had decided to choose their delegate, Reuben may have persuaded them that he be it, being the eldest. When, however, the regent reversed his decree, the Nine may again have chosen him, for the eldest must bear the responsibility, i.e., be the hostage. This is what incensed Reuben and to which he "replied" (Ehn Shelomoh):

22   Then Reuben replied to them, "Was it not I
           that warned you, saying, 'Do not sin against
           the child?' But you would not listen. Now
           comes the accounting for his blood."

These words of Reuben were omitted between vv. 21 and 22 in chapter 37. He now reminds his brothers that he attempted to persuade them how foolish their fear of Joseph was since he was a mere "child" (RaShBaM), that he was the only one who had wanted to save him, wherefore singling him out to be the hostage would only aggravate their guilt. This guilt, he continues, was not merely their mercilessness, as they now "rationalize," but their hatred which caused Joseph's death. "Now comes the accounting for his blood" is in accordance with God's law to Noah and mankind, "He who sheds the blood of man, by man shall his blood be shed" (9:6). After the brothers expressed their feeling of guilt, it is Reuben who is the first to imply "God," from Whom "comes the accounting of his blood."[10]

23   They did not know that Joseph understood for
           there had been an interpreter between them.

Joseph had remained with them as if he were waiting for their decision whom to choose as the hostage. Yet he did not intend to let it come to their resolution of this terrible dilemma, for it would cause them irreparable discord. What he now heard hit him harder than he anticipated.

24a   He turned from them to cry.

Except that he "pleaded" (v. 21), we do not read that Joseph cried when his brothers seized and flung him into the cistern. Neither did he cry when he was sold as a slave or, when through the calumny of the woman, he lost the high position he had earned and was put into prison. Nor did he cry when the cup-bearer forgot to free him. But from now on, Joseph will cry on seven occasions.[11]

What finds vent in Joseph's first tears is a turmoil of feelings: His gratitude to God for His gracious guidance up to the moment; his awareness of his brothers' remorse for their past sin and the realization that Reuben at least had not hated him. But above all, it is pity for the Ten, for Benjamin and especially for his father upon whom he would still have to inflict so much anguish, before the Ten could become true *ba-'ale teshuvah*— masters of return (to God). Joseph's wisdom knows that everything falls short of true repentance which does not prevent committing the same sin again.[12] So far he had merely "probed" the Ten, finding out their potential for becoming *ba-'ale teshuvah*. Their "repentance," so far, was merely "prison repentance," and the love they had evinced was only for their father. What Joseph plans is to bring about "the same situation," this time with Benjamin, the other son of their father's favored wife, as the touchstone of their brotherliness. Only if they had become *ba-'ale teshuvah* could they pass the test.

24b   Then he returned to them, spoke to them and
       picked Simeon, whom he had bound before their
       eyes.

"He returned to them" with the interpreter. What he said to them was not only what they were to report to their father (B. Jacob, cf. v. 34), namely that once they are exonerated, they may "move freely in the land," but what is more important, why he would rather pick the hostage (see expos. on v. 23) than leave the choice up to them. He did not take the eldest, Reuben, because of what he had just overheard. Simeon was next in age. Yet the real reason for taking him may possibly be that, during the brothers' vehement discussion, he had overheard that Simeon was among those who had plotted his death (cf. 37:18, 20) and together with Levi had perpetrated the massacre at Shechem (*Sefer haYashar*). In this case, Simeon's seizure must have added greatly to the brothers' fathoming God's mysterious retribution.

25   Then Joseph ordered [1] that they fill their
            containers with grain, [2] that the coins of
            each be placed into each one's sack, and
            [3] they be given provisions for their
            journey. And he did this for them.

The first order, being part of the purchase, was carried out by the granary workers. "He did this for them" refers to Joseph's trusted steward (cf. 43:16; 44:1; S. Dubno). Secretly, the steward put (2) the money-bags into the fodderbags. Yet under the eyes of the brothers, he (3) put provisions for their journey into their saddle-bags, perhaps as a compensation for what they had gone through (B. Jacob). Presumably, Joseph reimbursed the crown. B. Jacob thinks he wanted to be his family's provider from the outset and to prevent them from running out of cash for another purchase. Yet would Joseph not have foreseen the frightening effect of their discovering it? It is more probable, therefore, that the shock was actually intended to make them relate also this mystery to their guilt, furthering their repentance even before their return to their father. In the expos. on 44:13, another reason for having returned this money will be suggested.

26   They loaded their asses with their rations
            and departed.

These rations were in "their containers" (v. 25), which the brothers themselves loaded on their pack animals. Their riding asses each carried saddle-bags, hanging down on either side and containing personal belongings and a "sack" for fodder (B. Jacob).

27   When one of them opened his sack at the
            night encampment to give fodder to his
            ass, he saw the money. There it was
            at the top of his bag.[13]

28   And he said to his brothers, "My money has
            been returned: It is right in my bag!"
            They exchanged terrified glances at each
            other and said, "What is this that God
            has done to us?" [14]

43:18-22 will report the brothers' terror that, upon their return to Egypt, they will be charged with embezzlement. At this moment they all thought, "Now comes the accounting for his blood" (v. 22), and for the first time, they all utter the word "God," the thought of Whom they had so far suppressed. With this acknowledgement, they reach the second rung toward real repentance. The first rung had been reached when they exclaimed, "Alas, we are being punished . . ." (v. 21; B. Jacob).

29a   They came to their father Jacob, to
            the land of Canaan.

All the way back "to the land of Canaan," to which they were given permission to return, their minds were occupied with "the fear of God" and their anxiety about the anguish which their report would cause to their father. They decided to tell him only what was essential to explain why Simeon had not returned and to obtain permission to bring Benjamin to the regent so that Simeon would be released. They seem to have decided also to keep the father ignorant about the money matter until he had given his consent.

29b   They told him all that had befallen them:

With the following report they pretend to have told him "all" (see expos. on 45:28a).

30   "The man who is the lord of the land spoke
            harshly to us and accused us of spying on
            the land.

31   "We said to him, 'We are forthright; we have
            never been spies.

32   ' There were twelve of us brothers, sons by the
            same father; but one is no more, and the youngest
            is now with our father in the land of Canaan.'

33   "But the man who is lord of the land said to us,
            'By this I shall know that you are forthright:
            leave one of your brothers with me, and take
            [provisions] for the hunger of your households
            and be gone.'

34   " 'And bring your youngest brother to me, that I
            may know that you are not spies but forthright.
            I will then restore your brother to you, and you
            shall be free to move around in the land.' " [15]

What they omitted was a) the regent's "third-degree-treatment," b) his original demand that they choose one delegate while the others remain in custody, c) that they were incarcerated for three days, d) that then the terms were reversed, and e) that finally it was the regent who took Simeon and had him fettered before their eyes. Having finished their report they hope that it has reassured the father that Simeon will return after Benjamin's appearance before the regent, and they wait for his consent. Jacob says not a single word, not because he disbelieves their strange story; not yet. It is because he is dismayed about their having volunteered, as he thinks, the information about his two other sons. Only later in 43:6 will he reproach them for it, saying, "Wherefore dealt you so ill with me as to inform the man whether you had another brother!" But now he remains silent. For the brothers there was nothing else to do but to unpack their luggage.

35   As they were emptying their sacks, lo, in each
          one's sack there was his money bag! As they
          saw their coin-bags, they and their father were
          in fear.

V. 27b implied that they had all found their coin-bags. What they now fear is the effect the regent's foul play will have upon the father. What he fears is his sons' foul play! He becomes suspicious:

36   Then their father Jacob said to them, "You
          bereave me: Joseph is gone, Simeon is gone,
          and [now] you would take away Benjamin. All
          [that I can bear] has [already] come upon me!"

After having been tormented by the regent's acrimony and suspicion, by the torturing suspense during their three days in custody and the shock over their replaced money, the brothers are now horrified that the father suspects them about Joseph, about Simeon and about Benjamin.[16] What tortures them most is that the father's suspicion may now doom Simeon. Yet they do not dare to speak.

37   But Reuben said to his father, "You may kill
          my two sons if I fail to bring him back to
          you. Leave him in my care, and I will return
          him to you."

Reuben breaks the silence not only because he is "tempestuous like [boiling] water" (49:4), but also because he is the eldest son and because he wants to redeem himself and regain the father's forgiveness for his sin with Bilhah (cf. 35:22).[17] B. Jacob compares Reuben with Lot (cf. 19:8). In both cases, their ingenuous overstatement expresses their incapacity to tolerate the alternative. Reuben would rather have his father kill his own two sons than see the father lose Benjamin. Yet Reuben's words only exacerbate Jacob's grief: What inanity to console him for the loss of his second Joseph by offering him two grandsons to slay. With this well-meant, but foolish, importune and rash offer Reuben forfeits whatever leadership he may have had.

38   Yet he said, "My son shall not go down with you,
    for his [own] brother is dead, and he alone is
    left. If he would meet disaster on the journey
    you are taking, you will send my white head down
    to Sheol in grief."

"My son" is the last son of Jacob's beloved, mourned Rachel (Sforno). "His own brother," Joseph, never returned from his journey. Though Reuben may have abated the father's suspicion, Jacob insists (see expos. on v. 4) that Benjamin stay with him. Neither Jacob nor his sons utter the name "Benjamin," the second "Joseph" (B. Jacob). The whole family remains in trepidation.[18] None of the brothers says anything further. Judah may have proposed leaving the father alone: If the famine continues, the father will be compelled to give in (*Midrash Tanhumah*). Until then, Simeon will have to remain in prison.

Chapter 42 reports how Joseph has goaded his brothers to acknowledge God's "measure-for-measure retribution: He makes his brothers suffer in analogy to what they had made him suffer. In v. 21 they already speak of retribution. In v. 22 Reuben implies God is the Judge. Finally, the Nine articulate it (cf. v. 28b). Yet in reality all this is Joseph's own devising. A measure-for-measure retribution by God Himself is, however, traceable through the whole Torah.[19] Abrabanel, moreover, also finds the following ten "measure-for-measure *compensations*" in the Narrative. He compares *Sidrah* X and XI. "There" refers to *Sidrah* X, "here" to *Sidrah* XI:

1) *There* Joseph was hated and despised by his brothers.
   Here he is loved by strangers (in jail), by Pharaoh and the Egyptians.
2) *There* he was hated because of his dreams.
   Here he is *loved* because of dreams.
3) *There* the brothers make him disrobe himself of his tunic.
   Here Pharaoh has him dressed in robes of fine linen and puts the chain of gold on his neck (cf. 41:42).
4) *There* the brothers throw him *into* the pit.
   Here Pharaoh sends for him and he is rushed *from* the pit.
5) *There* he was sold.
   Here he sells: 'All the world has come to Joseph in Egypt to buy grain' (41:47).
6) *There* 'Joseph went after his brothers. . . . And before he came close to them, they conspired the plot. . . .'
   Here he plots against his brothers (cf. 42:7).
7) *There* he was separated from his brothers.
   Here they are reunited.
8) *There* he was 'brought down' to Egypt (39:1), an idiom of degradation.
   Here he is 'installed' 'over the whole land of Egypt.'
9) *There* his master's wife wants to seduce him to commit adultery.
   Here he marries Asenath in joy and in obedience to the commandment 'Be fruitful.'
10) *There* the cupbearer did not keep Joseph in mind.
    Here—because of the Pharaoh's dream—the butler remembers and praises him to the king.[20]

GENESIS 43

1   The Famine was severe in the land.

The dry brevity of the three words in Hebrew portray the in-
difference of time, another year, to the mounting anxiety and
lamentation of Jacob's family (B. Jacob).

2   When they had used up the grain which they
      had brought from Egypt, their father said
      to them, "Go again and buy a little food
      for us."

There must have been some food left from the past. Otherwise
their families could not have survived the next few weeks. The
longer the brothers hesitated to buy new provisions, the more
Jacob became convinced that he had wrongly suspected them
(see expos. on 42:36). At last he timidly asks that they again
procure "a little food," realizing that this would require taking
up the painful issue of Benjamin which he had so vehemently
dismissed.

3   But Judah replied, "The man plainly forewarned
      us, 'You may not come before me unless your
      brother is with you.' " [1]

44:23 will confirm that Joseph made such declaration. None
of the Ten understands the father's fears so well and has so
deep compassion for him as Judah. Again, as once before (see
expos. on 37:26) the others recognize his insight, and from now
on he becomes the brothers' spokesman. To spare his father
more fear than necessary, he paraphrases the regent's oath, using
the legal phrase he-'id,[2] 'forewarned' instead. Originally the
brothers called the regent "the lord of the land" (cf. 42:30, 33).
From now on he will simply be called "the man." (B. Jacob).

4   "If you consent to send our brother with us,
      we will go down and get your food."

"Our brother" is to convey that they all share the father's concern for Benjamin and that they will all watch for his safety. "Get you food" expresses that if he overcomes his objection he will become the provider for all.

5   "But if you will not send [him], we will not go
        down, for the man told us 'You may not come
        before me unless your brother is with you.' "

Judah is not being repetitious, for in Hebrew such reiteration is required to mark one's decision as irrevocable (cf. Num. 32:29f). Judah refrains from mentioning Simeon lest the father be made to feel that Benjamin's life is being risked to liberate Simeon.

6   Then Israel said, "Wherefore did you treat me so
        ill as to inform the man whether you had yet
        a[nother] brother?"

This is the first time "Israel" recurs after its "eclipse," following "Israel's" fateful dispatch of Joseph on his mission (cf. 37:13). Just as Joseph's words (see expos. on 37:3) had caused "Israel's" re-emergence, so does the terrible present crisis. At last the patriarch vents what he had suppressed ever since his sons' return, and he reproaches them for their seemingly foolish indiscretion in volunteering their disclosure about Benjamin (cf. 42:32).

7   They replied, "The man kept on asking
        us about ourselves and our family, 'Is your
        father still alive? Have you another
        brother?' We told him accordingly. How
        could we have known that he would say,
        'Bring your brother down'?"

It follows from 44:19 (see expos. on 42:12) that they spoke the truth.

8   Then Judah said to his father Israel,
        "Please let the boy go together with
        me, and we will arise and depart, that
        we may live and not die, both we and
        you and our children."

After the brothers' outburst Judah, having sensed the resurgence of "Israel," calmly resumes his point:[3] Benjamin will live if the father sends him, but if not, he will die in Canaan from starvation.[4] Judah now changes "send off" (cf. v. 4) to the more tender plea "Please let go," and instead of "our brother," he affectionately says "the boy," another "Joseph" (cf. 37:2). Finally, instead of the more common " '*immi*"—with me—he says more emphatically " '*itti*"—together with me—(B. Jacob).

9   "I myself will go surety for him; you shall
        hold me accountable for him: If I fail to bring
        him back to you and set him before you, I shall
        be banned from you forever."

Judah voluntarily pledges his own person as surety.[5] "I shall be banned from you" is the rendition according to BT *Makkot* 11b, though the literal translation is merely "I will have sinned before you." The Hebrew phrase connotes a self-imposed ostracism out of the deepest sense of guilt and shame (cf. Num. 12:14; Ps. 88:9, Job 10:14f.; B. Jacob). Judah wants to show the agonized father his deep compassion and tender love, for after vv. 1 and 3, followed by the definitive ultimatum and the father's oblique yielding (cf. v. 6), Judah's self-immolation was actually no longer needed. V. 9 is a parenthesis after which Judah resumes and concludes his argument.

10   "Had we not lingered, we could have been
        back twice over."

Judah implies that had it not been for the father's delay, he would also have been relieved of his anxiety for Simeon long ago (RaShI). Judah's mild reproof hides his deep emotion.

11a   Now their father Israel replied, "If it be
        so, then do this":

"Their father Israel" intimates how his sons' explanation (v. 7) and especially Judah's loving kindness have rekindled the patriarch's affection for them. Though he still cannot utter the words, "Benjamin may join you," he now energetically takes the reigns and turns to the practical preliminaries of the precarious journey.

11b   "Take in your baggage, as a gift for the
        man, some produce for which our country is
        famous: a little balm, a little honey, gum
        tragacanth, myrrh, pistachio nuts, and
        almonds."

37:25 has already given the information that gum tragacanth, balm and myrrh were export items. Jacob adds pistachio nuts, almonds, and honey.[6] Bringing gifts to a high official is no more than a sign of good breeding (von Rad), not a tribute for appeasement, such as Jacob once sent to his brother (cf. 32:14-22; 33:8-11).

12   "And take with you double the money,
immediately restoring the money that was
replaced, at the top of your bags; perhaps
it was a mistake."

"Immediately," lit. "in your hands," indicates the returning of the money before being told about it (NaTsYB). Jacob actually does not seem to have been as upset about the matter as his sons were (see expos. on 42:35). He may have assumed that the silo workers discovered their mistake too late (RaShBaM).

13   "Take your brother too. Now be off and
back to the man!"

Only after all has been prepared does Jacob utter with heavy heart the decisive "Take your brother too" and speed them on their way. "Jacob gazes upon his sons and asks, 'Why do you stare at me; is there anything else you need?' They reply, "Father, it is your blessing!'"[7]

14a   "May *El Shaddai* dispose the man to mercy
toward you that he release to you your
brother left behind and Benjamin."

El Shaddai is one of God's appellations.[8] After having given instructions to his sons (cf. vv. 11a-14a) Jacob resumes with "As for me" his plaint, v. 6, and he laments:

14b   "As for me, if I am to suffer bereavement, I shall suffer bereavement."

These words express not only his resignation to God's decree if He refuses his entreaty; they also release Judah from his pledge and, above all, rescind explicitly his bitter accusation, "you [my sons] bereave me" (42:36). Israel thus acknowledges that God had caused his loss of Joseph and that his sons are guiltless about Simeon.

15   So the men took the gift, and double the
      money they took in their hand—and Benjamin;
      and they arose and went down to Egypt and stood
      before Joseph.

This time it is Joseph's brother who goes down to Egypt with a "caravan . . . on the way to Egypt which carries gum tragacanth, and balm, and myrrh" (cf. 37:25) and other products. They "stood before Joseph," in line with many others who waited their turn, hoping that soon the regent would nod to them to display their gifts before him. The Torah compresses into one sentence their bidding farewell to their loved ones, their departure, the long journey and their arrival in order to indicate their eagerness to redeem Simeon. But eleven verses separate their arrival from their actual interview with Joseph.

16   Joseph saw Benjamin with them.

The regent pretends to be too pre-occupied to notice him (ShaDaL).

16b   He told his house steward, "Take these men
      home. Have a meal prepared of freshly
      slaughtered animals, for the men are to dine
      with me at noon."

Joseph sets in motion his pre-conceived plan: Simeon has to be released and the brothers have to be given satisfaction for wrongly having been suspected of espionage. Above all, he wants to have Benjamin seated next to him, hear his voice, speak and laugh with him and rejoice in their reunion after so many years though, before he can permit himself to shed his mask, he would shill have his brothers undergo the severest test. He orders his "house-steward" to bring the men to his home.[9] This man seems to be the same whom Joseph had told to secretly replace the brothers money (see expos. on 42:25). He has earned his master's confidence and is briefed to release Simeon, kept in the regent's home, and to amicably settle the anticipated coin-bag issue before the regent's arrival with other invited guests for the festive meal.

17   The man did as Joseph told him and took
        the men toward Joseph's house.

18   Being taken to Joseph's house the men were
        afraid and thought, "It is because of the
        money, replaced in our bags, that we are
        taken, to hurl charges at us, fall upon us
        and seize us as slaves and our asses."

They fear that they have been refused permission to see the regent and are being marched off to the regent's quarters to suffer there the fate of embezzlers. Instead of the hoped-for release of Simeon and their return with new provisions to their starving families, they dread becoming the regent's slaves and having both their animals and money confiscated.

19   They turned to Joseph's steward and spoke
        to him at the entrance of the house.

They refused to enter the house, attempting instead to persuade the steward that they are victims of an error.

20   "Please listen, my lord," they said. "It
        was after our first visit to buy food:

21   "When we reached the night encampment and
        opened our bags, alas, each one's money was
        at the top of his bag; it was our money by
        its weight. Now we have brought it back in
        our hands."

22   "And with it we brought money to buy food.
        We do not know who had put our money in
        our bags."

To avoid resentment they no longer say that their money was "put back" (see expos. on 42:28; 43:12, 18), insinuating a frame-up, but simply say "put" (B. Jacob).

23ab   He replied, "set your minds at rest; do not
        be afraid. It was your God, the God of your
        father, Who hid treasure for you in your bags.
        I did receive your payment."

As he had done with others (see expos. on 39:3,9; 40:8;

41:16,25,28,32) so must Joseph have conveyed his faith in God to his steward, who knows about the deeper reasons for the brothers' anxiety. With dark ambiguity the Torah makes this outsider touch upon God's concealed guidance, the innermost mystery of the Narrative (von Rad). The brothers shiver as they compare the steward's gracious reply[10] with their own, "What is this that God has done unto us" (42:28b).

23c   Then he brought Simeon out to them.

Seeing Simeon unfettered (cf. 42:24) and free, they know that the regent has no further charge against them and feel, at last, that all is well with them.

24   Now the man brought them into Joseph's house.
He gave them water to bathe their feet and
provided fodder for their asses.

25   Then they prepared their gift for Joseph's
arrival at noon, for they heard that they
were to dine there.

"To dine" is "lit. "to eat bread" (cf. 18:5). While the regent's servants are busy "preparing the meal" (cf. v. 16b), the brothers use every minute before his arrival to arrange their gifts according to etiquette in the anteroom, before their reception in the parlor.

26   When Joseph came home, they presented him
in the parlor with the gifts in their hands
bowing to the ground before him.

27   He greeted them, and he said, "How is your
father, the 'aged one,' as you said? Is he
still alive?"

44:20 will evince that they had indeed called their father "aged." The regent refers to their plea before their incarceration (see expos. on 42:16). Joseph's question is not a mere matter of courtesy. He trembles at the thought that the brothers' return was so long delayed because his father had refused to be parted from Benjamin, so that Benjamin's arrival became possible only after the father's death.

28   They said, "Your servant, our father, is well;
he is still alive." And they bowed low and
prostrated themselves.

They perform the ritual of giving thanks to God Who has kept their father alive (Siftheh Cohen; cf. 48:12), and/or to the regent for his thoughtful inquiry (RaShI). Now that Joseph is relieved of his anxiety about his father, he guardedly turns his attention to his beloved Benjamin.

29a　　Now he looked and saw Benjamin his brother,
　　　　his mother's son.

He only pretends to notice him for the first time, for had he not (cf. v. 16) seen him at the brothers' arrival he would not have instructed his steward to bring them to his home. The Torah intimates with "his [own] mother's son" his deep, pent-up feelings for Benjamin, whose mother had died giving birth to him (cf. 35:18) who was not yet two years old (see *Appendix 7b*) when Joseph had last played with him.

29b　　And he said, "Is this your little brother,
　　　　of whom you told me?"

There is a bit of irony in the regent's use of "little," for actually Benjamin is no longer the little boy the brothers had made him out to be.[11] At the same time "little" expresses how Joseph himself used to think of him. Apprehensive that he might lose his self-composure, he does not wait for the brothers' reply and, turning directly to Benjamin, his voice choking in his throat, he quickly merely adds:

29c　　"God be gracious to you, my son." [12]

His first word to his brother Benjamin is "God." The Ten understand that with these affectionate words the regent wants to make up for all the contumely he had inflicted on them.

30　　With that, Joseph hurried out, for his
　　　　emotion for his brother was seething. He
　　　　wanted to cry, entered the chamber and
　　　　wept there.

At Joseph's first encounter with the Ten the Torah did not say why "he turned from them to cry" (see expos. on 42:24a). Here the Torah intimates his reason for crying: "His emotion for his brother was seething." This phrase implies not only Joseph's love for Benjamin but also his compassion for him.[13] He must not unmask himself until he has put the Ten to the crucial test on the following day. He wept: "Tears extinguish the heart's burning coals" says the *Midrash*.

31   Then he washed his face, came out and in
       control of himself gave the order, "Serve
       the meal."

32   They served him by himself, and them by them-
       selves, and the Egyptians who ate with him by
       themselves; for the Egyptians cannot eat with
       the Hebrews, for that is detestable to the
       Egyptians.

Being the regent, he was served apart from the other Egyptions (ShaDaL). That "the Egyptians cannot eat with . . ." means that they "might not eat with . . ."[14]

33   When they were seated by his direction [15] the
       oldest in the order of his seniority and the
       youngest in the order of his youth the men
       turned in amazement to one another.

The "amazed" men can, and therefore does, refer to both the Egyptian guests and to the brothers. The Egyptians marveled at the regent's unusual hospitality to Hebrews, which was not extended to any other foreigners (Minhah Belulah). The brothers were amazed that the regent could know their ages though most of them had been born within only six years. Each guest was seated singly at a small table (von Rad). The host's seat seems to have been at the apex of a triangle, the brothers placed on one side, the Egyptians on the other.[16] This arrangement enables Joseph to be inconspicuously seated next to Benjamin (RaShI). *Sefer Hayashar*[17] intriguingly adds that during their *tête à tête* Joseph told Benjamin that he was Joseph, but that he must keep it a secret until the brothers had been tested by the forthcoming plan involving the goblet.

34a   Portions were served them from before him.

The portions were first brought to the host who would assign them to each guest individually (Hizkuni).[18]

34b   Benjamin's portion was five times larger
       than that of all the others.[19]

34c   And they feasted and drank freely with him.

It seems that after dinner only the brothers stayed on "with him," their anxiety relieved. Imbibing with him they felt at ease in the presence of the strange Egyptian lord. Though Joseph had already planned what would happen to them after their departure early the next morning, he allowed himself a period of delight with all his brothers cheerfully seated around him and with Benjamin at his side.

GENESIS 44

1   He had ordered his house steward, "Fill
the men's bags with as much provision as
they can carry and put each man's money at
the top of his bag."

This order was given on the day of the banquet, for the
brothers left early next morning. Not mentioned are the purchased rations. They were "in containers," loaded on pack animals (see expos. on 42:25). "The men's bags with . . . provisions" and fodder for the journey were put in saddle bags on
riding asses (see expos. on 42:25f). "Each man's money" was
"double the money" (43:15) of the Ten. Benjamin's money
is mentioned separately in the next verse. Since this time the
Ten were not amazed to find their money returned to them (cf.
v. 11), they must have been told about it before leaving.

2   "And put my goblet, the silver goblet, at
the top of the bag of the youngest one,
together with his ration-money." And he
did according to Joseph's word as he had
spoken.

In 42:25 the Torah reports "he did this for them," and in
43:17, "the man did as Joseph had said." S. R. Hirsch, therefore, assumes that "and he did according to Joseph's word as
he had spoken" expresses the steward's bewilderment, obeying
his master's order concerning the youngest "under protest," as
it were.[1]

3   At daybreak the men were sent off and their asses.

This time not only the pack animals (see expos. on 42:26),
but also the riding asses, were loaded for the brothers, enabling
them to leave as early as possible. The brothers are grateful for
the courtesy. "The men . . . and their asses" seems to allude to
"us and our asses" (43:18), contrasting their horror *then* and

their cheerful mood *now*. All their anxieties are dissipated: Not only is the regent's suspicion against them gone, Simeon released and Benjamin safe, but they have also been invited and entertained as the regent's honored guests, who, having showered presents upon them, ordered gifts of silver and "all the provision they can carry" to be loaded for them. Having been sent off in this kindest way, they anticipate the father's happiness upon their return.

4 Before they had gone far from the city,
   Joseph said to his steward, "Go at once
   after the men, and when you catch up with
   them say, 'Why have you repaid good with
   evil?"

By now the steward had been told all about the purpose of the plot. He was also instructed how to address them, using the plural "you," impeaching them all, but avoiding the words "theft," "thief" and "goblet" when provoking their protestations to his mystifying innuendo (cf. v. 5). To avoid public scandal he was to overtake them swiftly so as to be back while the regent would still be at home. V. 5a and 5b have been rendered differently by different exegetes. It seems however, that these interpretations need not exclude each other, the text being intentionally ambiguous. Three different renditions are here selected:

5a (1) "It is the one from which my master drinks.
     That is why in it[s theft] he sees a very
     bad omen."

The steward conveys that it is not the monetary value but the fact that it is the regent's personal drinking goblet. Even had it merely fallen from his hand, it would be a bad sign, more so, if it had broken. But its theft augurs the worst for him.[2]

5a (2) "It is because my master drinks from it,
     he had ordered a thorough search for it
     through divination." [3]

5a (3) "It is the one from which my master drinks,
     and which he uses for divination." [4]

That Joseph actually practiced such heathen cup-divination seems excluded (see expos. on 41:50). Whatever the meaning of the innuendo, the brothers know that the goblet's theft is *lese majesty*.

5b   "You have done a base thing."

The brothers will not understand this sentence as merely a repetition of the steward's initial words that they have "repaid good with evil." They rather see again three meanings:

1) "You did commit a base crime in the past."
2) "You have now undone what you had hoped to accomplish, to convince the regent of your honesty" (Or ha-Hayim).
3) "You committed your crime very crudely" (Minhah Belulah).

6   When he caught up with them, he spoke these
          words to them.

"These words" repeat exactly what the regent instructed the steward to say (cf. vv. 4b-5b); but v. 10 will show how much the regent left to the steward's own discretion. His terrifying though restrained harangue, presumably, caused the brothers' swift secretive huddling around Judah, their spokesman (cf. v. 14; see expos. on 43:3).

7a   They remonstrated with him, "How can my
          lord say such things?"

Judah retorts to "Why did you repay . . .," protesting against the indictment as such and its riddlesome language (B. Jacob).

7b   "Far be it from your servants to act in
          such a way!"

8   "Remember the silver we found at the top of
          our bags! We brought it back to you from
          the land of Canaan. How then could we have
          stolen silver or gold from your master's house?"

This is legal argumentation (see Abrabanel) with an *a fortiori* inference: There is a difference between an "object" and "money." The law does not require the return of money to its loser. (But even an object need not be returned if, after a considerable time, the owner has given up hope for its recovery.) In spite of this they returned the money. Having thus proved to be gentlemen, they deeply resent their all being suspected of complicity, even if one of them had committed "theft." They are sure, however, that none of them stole the object, just as their father had been when he and his group were suspected of theft by their grandfather Laban (cf. 31:30).

9   "Whosoever be found with it of your servants,
he shall die. We, moreover, shall become
slaves to my lord."

To the death penalty which their father had proposed for the thief (cf. 31:32), they add the punishment of enslavement for the rest of them.

10   He said, "also now it shall be according to you
words: 'Whosoever be found with it' shall be
my slave; [the rest of] you shall be exonerated."

The steward concedes that he was wrong to have suspected them all, for they had indeed proved their honesty. That is why he releases them from their voluntary offer of collective liability.[5] Then he takes them at their own words, "Whosoever be found with it," refusing the others the right to contest mere circumstantial evidence. On the other hand, he mitigates their proposed death penalty for the thief, since his master had decreed that if the thief be found, only he "shall be my slave."[6] Now the brothers are horrified at how shrewdly the steward had pinned them down to their rashly delivered declaration, because they fear a frame-up which this time would not be resolved as it was with their replaced coin-bags (cf. 42:27f.; 43:18ff.). They are so excited that they cannot bear the suspense of first returning before having their extremely heavy luggage (cf. 44:1) unloaded (B. Jacob).

11   Each man quickly lowered his bag to the
ground, and each opened his bag.

They do not even help each other. Their frenzy gives them augmented strength.

12   He searched, beginning with the oldest
and finishing with the youngest, and
the goblet was found in Benjamin's bag.

The steward was instructed to proceed with the search in the order of their age (cf. 43:33), starting with the oldest. This was to prevent their suspicion that he had known where the goblet would turn up. When all but Benjamin's luggage had been searched, they are already relieved, for he certainly has not stolen. Neither do they fear a trumped-up charge against him, for he has just enjoyed the regent's particular favor. Besides he was innocent of their crime. But "the goblet was found in Benjamin's bag."

13   At this they rent their garments; then each
          man reloaded his pack animal, and they re-
          turned to the city.

They are too stunned to speak. The idea of forsaking Benjamin (cf. v. 10) to reproach[7] or even to ask him does not occur to them. "They rent their garments," for what will happen to Benjamin will strike them all. His loss will be theirs, as Joseph's was the father's who "rent his garments" (cf. 37:34), crying out, "Torn to pieces is Joseph" (cf. 37:33).

Joseph was waiting in great anxiety for the outcome of his test. He had exacerbated whatever erstwhile hatred and jealousy his brothers may have had against the other son of his father's favored wife by ordering that "Benjamin's portion was five times larger than all others" (43:34b; Sforno). Just now he had also given them a perfect excuse to abandon the "thief," after having been exonerated themselves (cf. v. 10), tempting them to continue their journey back home with the urgently needed provisions. On the other hand, their experience with the coin-bags (see expos. on 42:25) was to forewarn them that Benjamin had been framed. Above all, they were given the strongest motivation to intercede for Benjamin by making it the condition for sparing the father the heartbreak of losing another "Joseph." Four things give Joseph hope:

    1) The Ten had proved to be "forthright" (see expos.
       on 42:13).
    2) They had shown compassion for their father (cf.
       expos. on 42:16 with that on 44:21f.).
    3) Fearing for their lives, i.e. under duress, they had
       reached the first rung of repentance (see expos.
       on 42:21f.).
    4) Reuben at least had not meant to do him any
       harm (see expos. on 42:22).

What Joseph does not know is that:

> 5) They had reached the second rung toward repentance when they found their money returned (see expos. on 42:28b).
>
> 6) Judah had offered himself as surety for Benjamin (see expos. on 43:8ff.).

14a   Joseph was still in the house when Judah
and his brothers came in.

The steward quickly informs his master that though he suggested to the Ten that they continue their journey, they insisted on returning with the youngest, who, it seems, was immediately marched off on their arrival.

14b   They threw themselves on the ground before him.

15   Joseph said to them, "What a thing for you
to have done! You must have known that a
man like me *nahesh yenahesh.*"

The last two words repeat the steward's ambiguous words in v. 5a, meaning either "sees a very bad omen," "orders a thorough search [if his goblet is stolen]," or "uses [it for] divination." At this moment it may have dawned on the brothers that the regent divined their ages by means of his goblet, (see expos. on 43: 33),[8] and perhaps even their past. (The regent does not upbraid them for ingratitude as the steward had done; cf. v. 4b). They think that he uses the plural "you," as the steward had done (cf. vv. 4, 5, 6), because their all bowing low to him makes him assume that they are all accomplices.

16a   Then Judah said, "What can we say to my
lord? How can we plead, how try to prove
our innocence?"

They cannot "say" in behalf of Benjamin what the Ten did say for themselves (cf. v. 8) because Benjamin was not with them on the first trip (Or haHayim). Neither can they "plead," because the steward has warned them that they must not plead that the "thief" was framed. Lastly, "how try to prove our innocence," since in fact only Benjamin is innocent.

16b   "God has found your servants' guilt."

This is the fifth time that the word "found" appears (cf. vv. 8ff.): What was looked for is one thing, yet what was "found," uncovered by God, is their guilt about Joseph (B. Jacob), for so mysterious a misfortune as theirs can only be His punishment for it. RaShI adds, "The Creditor has found an opportunity to collect His debt (from the Ten through the regent)."[9] *With this confession of their sin, as if to God, the Ten have reached the third rung* (cf. expos. on 42:22, 28) *toward true repentance* (B. Jacob).

16c   "Here we are, [ready to be] my lord's slaves,
       we ourselves as well as the one with whom the
       goblet was found."

They intimate (cf. v. 16b) that not the youngest but all the others had committed a sin in the past. Therefore they ought at least to share his punishment.

17   He replied, "Far be it from me to act
       thus! The one who was found
       with the goblet shall be my slave,
       but [the rest of] you go up to
       your father in peace."

Now the brothers recognize that the regent no longer sees in their prostration the proof of their collective guilt but their abject surrender to his punishment for a previously committed crime. Instead of refusing as inequitable their offer to share the youngest's fate by all becoming his slaves when he says, "Far be it from me to act thus!" he could have said instead, "Am I in the place of God?" (cf. 50:19). He concludes the scene with the stabbingly "kind" words[10] "But you go up to your father in peace" to induce them to pass the test by having one of them offer to suffer vicariously for Benjamin (see Abrabanel).

When the Hebrew text was subdivided in chapters, it would have been more appropriate to end chapter 44 at this point, where the *Masorah* concluded the second *sidrah* of the Narrative.

The regent has spoken; their plea is rejected. Judah arises with his brothers who had made him their spokesman. None of them has as passionate a love for the father and none is as alarmed as Judah who has gone surety for Benjamin and had prevailed upon the father to send Benjamin with them. He is now about to appeal to the regent's "fear of God" which had not only prompted him to change his original demand that the Nine remain as hostages until the tenth had brought the youngest before him (cf. 42:18) but has just made him also refuse as inequitable the brothers' plea to share the punishment of Benjamin. Judah wants to appeal to this humaneness of the regent: to evoke his empathy with the father's sorrow over the lost son; his old age; his sorrow for the death of the two sons' mother; his protective love for the remaining youngest, "the son of his old age"; and with the Ten's anguish, particularly his own, since he has gone surety for the youngest.

18   Now Judah stepped forward to him and said,
      "Let your servant, I beg, please have a
      word in private with my lord. Do not be
      angry with your servant for you are as
      Pharaoh."

Standing against each other are Joseph in terrifying power, and Judah in purified and total self-commitment. In the background are Benjamin—the innocent victim of a mysterious intrigue—his helpless brothers, and the father who is in danger of also losing the last son of his youthful love (von Rad).

The "word"[11] Judah wants to have with the regent is his final plea in v. 33 to accept him as a slave, a substitute for Benjamin (RaMBaN). Vv. 18-32 are a long preamble, giving the reasons why, even if the law requires the punishment of the youngest, the regent should accept Judah's vicarious enslavement. He begins his preamble by acknowledging that once a judgment had been issued, it is final so that his appeal is improper. But as the king can revise a decree so can the regent, "because you are as Pharaoh" (NaTsYB). The literal translation of the Hebrew, rendered "Let your servant . . . have a word in private . . ." is ". . . speak a word in the ears."[12] In spite of the seemingly humble wording of the preamble, Judah is actually the plaintiff. Pervaded by the deep but restrained emotion, he reviews what has led to the present situation. Most poignant for Joseph is Judah's omission that it all originated in the regent's accusation that the Ten are a gang of spies. Underlying Judah's speech are the following penetrating questions: Why was not our assurance, viz. that we had come together because, as sons of the same man we, as brothers, belong together, sufficient to dismiss the suspicion as preposterous (see expos. on 42:11)? When the regent nevertheless irrationally persisted in his accusation, was it pertinent for the *Shallit* to pump them for further information about their family? And when they mentioned their little brother, what was it that made the regent insist that he be brought before him? Would it really prove, as the regent averred, that they are "forthright" and not "spies"? And is his decree, making the youngest his slave, what he had in mind with his promise about him? The more Judah stings him with the bitter innuendoes in his long speech, the more Joseph loves his noble brother for his valor, spirit, wisdom and delicacy of presentation.

19   "My lord asked his servant, 'have you
        a father or a brother?' "

This must have been after the regent had so emphatically reasserted his suspicion following the brothers' asseveration of their forthrightness (see expos. on 42:12).

20   "We said to my lord, 'We have an aged
        father, and there is a little son of
        his old age; his [full] brother is dead,
        and only he is left of his mother so that
        the father dotes on him.' " [13]

Joseph must have pondered why Judah now calls the other brother "dead" though the brothers had first called him "missing" (cf. 42:1). Then he may have realized that Judah became convinced of his death, because when the Ten were told that Nine of them would be kept as hostages, Reuben exclaimed, "Now comes the accounting for his blood" (cf. expos. on 42:22).[14]

21   "Yet you said to your servants, 'Bring him down
        to me that I may set my eyes upon him.' "

Judah subtly cites (what was not mentioned but must have been said by the regent) "that I may set my eyes upon him." This expression derives from language of the court and means "to show someone special favor" (TJ; cf. Jer. 39:12; 40:4), as initially the regent had actually done (see expos. on 43:29c, 34b). According to RaShBaM, Judah implies that once "a man like me" (cf. v. 15), the regent, had explicitly made such a promise, he would have to live up to his word even if that person had turned out to be a real thief.

22 "We told my lord, 'The boy cannot leave his
   father; for if he should leave his father,
   he would die.' " [15]

23 "But you declared to your servants, 'Unless
   your youngest brother comes down with you,
   you shall not come before me.' "

With this Judah reminded the regent of what essentially preceded the brothers' return to Canaan. What he left out is how the regent made them suffer during their three days in custody, (see expos. on 42:17-22) and that Simeon, "bound before their eyes" (cf. 42:24b), was retained as the hostage. Judah now turns to the events that followed the brothers' departure from Egypt. Aside from what was already reported to the steward (cf. 43:20-22) nothing had been related about it to the regent except that their father was still alive (cf. 43:27), for during the banquet there was only banter and pleasantries. The most important thing in what is to follow now should naturally have been Judah's contesting the mystifying supposed evidence of Benjamin's "thievery." Nothing in Judah's speech is as eloquent as his complete silence about it.

24 "When we returned to your servant my father,
   we reported my lord's words to him."

By leaving out the word "all" before "my lord's words" Judah hints that the father was spared learning of the agonies they had suffered, except that Simeon would be released as soon as "the son of his old age" should appear before the regent.

25 "Our father said to us, 'Go back and bring
   us some food.' "

26 "Then we told him, 'We cannot go down; only if
   our youngest brother is with us, can we go; for
   we shall not be allowed to see the man if our
   youngest brother is not with us.' "

Now Joseph realizes that it took the brothers so long to return to Egypt with Benjamin because the father would rather have

Simeon linger in prison than consent to send Benjamin to Egypt, had the famine in Canaan ceased.

27   "But your servant my father said to us,
       'You know that my wife bore me two sons.' "

During the brothers' first visit Joseph had already learned about four of the Ten's six purgative phases (see expos. on 44:13). They had since shown their solidarity with Benjamin by returning to Egypt with him. Moreover, they confessed their sin of the past. Yet what convinces Joseph even more of their radical repentance is Judah's citing his father's words, "My wife bore me two sons." These seemingly simple words express not merely that the father considered only Rachel his "wife"—as if the other mothers were only his concubines (Ba-al Haturim; Abrabanel)[16]—but also show Joseph to his amazement and joy that Judah cites them without resentment. This is proof for Joseph that the brothers have overcome their grudge about the father's having favored Rachel over their own mothers, and, after having realized the tragic aspect of it all, had accepted the father's compensatory transferrence to Rachel's orphans of his affection for them.

28   "One left me, and I said, He must have been
       torn to pieces! Neither have I seen him
       since!"

These words inform Joseph that his father never told his family that he had sent him off (see expos. on 37:14), for he said "One left me." Was it because, when Joseph did not return, his father felt guilty at having asked him to go alone on that perilous trip to Shechem to bring about his reconciliation with his brothers? Joseph now also learns that they never reported having met him in Dothan and never confessed their guilt to their father, for Judah cites "I said, 'he must have been torn to pieces!' " Instead, the brothers must have pierced and bloodied the tunic which they had made him take off and had it brought before the father, who recognized it. Then, however, Joseph ponders the enigmatic sequential "Neither have I seen him since." It excites him, for how could the father have expected to see him again after having been "torn to pieces," unless he had regained hope that he was still alive. Was it because of

Joseph's dream, foretelling his future rise? Perhaps it gave the father the thought that it was *Joseph* who tore and bloodied his tunic to convince the father that he was dead and not to attempt to search for him? Does not "One left me" perhaps even imply his later wondering whether Joseph may not have given up all hope of fulfilling the father's desire that he attempt a reconciliation with the Ten and have instead gone into the wide world, trusting his dream that the time would come for the attainment of his destiny?

29   "If you take this one from me as well, and
      he meets with disaster, you will send my
      white head to Sheol in grief."

At Judah's next words, "Now then, if I . . .," spoken in the singular, Joseph expects that Judah is coming to the "word" (see expos. on v. 18), to his final plea to the regent. Yet Judah cannot tear his thoughts from his father (B. Jacob), not yet. In three hectic, long and climactic verses he makes the regent visualize the father's immediate death when he returns without the youngest.

30   "Now then, if I come to your servant my father
      and the boy is not with us—whose very life
31   is so bound up with his—(31) when he sees
      that the boy is missing, he will die, and your
      servants will have brought down the white head
      of your servant, our father, to Sheol in grief;
32   (32) for your servant has gone surety for the
      boy to my father, saying 'If I fail to bring
      him back to you, I shall be banned from you
      forever.' "

Instead of saying "you will have brought . . . our father . . . to Sheol . . .," Judah tactfully asserts that the patriarch's sons would have caused his death (RaMBaN). "*For* your servant has gone surety . . ." gives the reason: When the "surety" returns without the youngest, the father will immediately assume the boy's death (Sforno). In the next verse Judah will at last utter his presaged "word," his intercession that the regent accept *him* as his slave (B. Jacob).

33   "Now then, please, let your servant remain
        as a slave to my lord instead of the boy,
        and let the boy go up with his brothers."

34   "For how can I go up to my father if the boy
        is not with me? I could not bear to witness
        the evil that would overtake my father!"

Because his heart is bursting with pain, Judah fails in v. 34 to observe "protocol" and omits "your servant" before the words "I" and "my father" (B. Jacob). Judah uses the word most sacred to him, "father," fourteen times in his plea for his brother, and it is his final, climactic word which gathers into itself all the pathos of his appeal.[17] With all his ardent wish that he might change the regent's mind, Judah cannot know the almost unbearable agitation he has caused in the regent: At last Joseph has found his brothers (see expos. on 37:16). As long as he had to test them, he could "control himself" (cf. 43:31) and conceal his turbulent feelings, as he did when he overheard his brothers' confession, culminating in Reuben's speech (cf. 42:24) and when he greeted Benjamin (cf. 43:29f.). Yet he no longer needs the strength to curb himself, because his most fervent hope that his brothers would pass his harrowing long protracted ultimate test is now fulfilled.

All through Judah's speech the reader has been charmed, fixing his gaze upon the speaker's lips, letting it wander only to the powerful man opposite to read what is on his face. We know the outcome and still tremble. Thus does the Torah know how to make one forget (B. Jacob). One can conceive of no scene simpler and yet more powerful (Otto Procksch).

GENESIS 45

1a   Then Joseph could no longer control himself,
        Before all who stood by him he called out,
        "Have everyone withdraw from me!"

Joseph is so excited that he cannot help disregarding his courtly bearings: Instead of telling his attendants that he wants to be left alone with these brothers from Canaan, "he called out" (B. Jacob).

1b   There was no one else about when Joseph
        made himself known to his brothers.

Having escorted the Egyptians from the hall, the servants do not return, realizing that their master wants to be alone with his brothers (NaTsYB), obviously to tell them what had been rumored (cf. 40:15) that Joseph had been "kidnapped" from their land. What they did not know was that these brothers had a hand in this crime, and it was to remain a secret lest his brothers be put to shame (RaShI) and to protect his own honor and that of his father and Benjamin, (see RaMBaN).

2   When he lifted his voice, he was crying. The
        Egyptians heard it, and Pharaoh's household
        learned about it.

His incapacity to control himself not only had caused him to "lift his voice" so that he "called out," but also made the people hear him cry while they were still present (B. Jacob).

3a   Then Joseph said to his brothers, "I am
        Joseph! Is my father still alive?"

Though the brothers have already told him (cf. 43:28) that the father is still alive, Joseph now repeats his question because he yearns to say the wonderful word 'avi—my father (B. Jacob).

Besides, he wants to "break the ice," enabling his brothers to say something (Abrabanel).

3b But his brothers were so dumbfounded at
his presence that they were not able to
answer him.

Joseph realizes that their shock, shame and fear have stunned them, and he now drops all etiquette to put them at ease.

4a He said to them, "Please come closer to me."
They did so.

Now their fear is removed that some people behind the door may be able to hear what Joseph is about to say (Arama).

4b He said, "I am Joseph your brother,"

Joseph now adds "your brother" to "I am Joseph (cf. v. 3a) to express more warmth of feeling for them, particularly because he has to add:

4c "Whom you sold into Egypt."

Only by showing that he knows their secret does he prove his identity beyond doubt.

5 "Now then, be not grieved and angry at
yourselves that you sold me here. For
it is God Who sent me ahead of you as
an instrument of survival." [1,2]

He leaves it up to them to ponder why he made them suffer so much and so long up to Judah's final words. But he assures them that since in reality it was God Who wanted him to come to Egypt to rescue his father's house from starvation, they should now be relieved both from their fear of his retaliation against them and their self-reproach. Twice more, in vv. 7 and 8, he will turn their minds to God, of Whom he had so far goaded them to think merely as *the Lord of Justice and Retribution*, meting out to them "measure-for-measure" so that they may be chastized and repent; but first he explains his last words:

6 "For there have now been two years of
famine in the country, and there are
still five years to come in which there
shall be no yield from tilling. [3]

7   "God has sent me ahead of you to secure
       for you posterity on earth, and to save
       you alive in extraordinary deliverance." [4]

This sentence contains three significant words: *Le-haḥayoth*
—to save alive—is an obvious reference to the same word in
6:20: God has made Egypt for Jacob's family what the Ark was
for Noah's (B. Jacob). *She-'erith*—posterity, remnant—and *pe-
letah*—deliverance, escape—will loom large in Prophecy (F. J.
Delitzsch). Joseph envisages the "seventy souls of the House of
Jacob" (cf. 46:27; B. Jacob)—the germ cell of the future people
under God, its Savior through the ages.

8   "So it was not really you but God Who
       sent me here, and He has made me a father
       to Pharaoh, and lord over all his household
       and ruler of all Egypt."

Now that they have repented and attained the spirit of true
brotherliness as a result of his "testing" them, Joseph repeats for
the third time that God had made him His instrument to make
them understand what he had recognized under his own affliction
(see expos. on 39:2f.), that *God is also the Savior, even the
Lord of Providence,* and that He will fulfill His covenant (cf.
17:2ff.) with those who are "doing what is just and right"
(18:19). By now Joseph may also have realized that when
"Israel sent" him on his mission to the brothers (37:14), his
father himself had unknowingly been God's tool by initiating the
fulfillment of His prediction to Abraham (cf. 15:23f.) [5] Does
Joseph refrain from explicitly declaring his forgiveness because,
as things turned out, there is nothing to forgive? Or is it because
they did not confess their guilt? Or did he want to spare them
the humiliation inherent in "being forgiven"? (see expos. on
50:19b).

"A father[6] to Pharaoh, and the lord of his household," paraphrases two of Joseph's three titles (cf. 41:40f.) in terms familiar to the brothers. But why does he call *Shallit* (cf. expos. on
42:6a) "ruler of all Egypt" when he renders it in the next verse
as "lord of Egypt"? (The brothers themselves had called him
"the lord of the land"; cf. 42:30, 33). It seems that by calling
himself "ruler over all Egypt" Joseph intimates with a smile

that his dream did not mean what *they* had thought, to wit, that he wanted to become *their* "ruler" (cf. 37:8), but that God would make him *Egypt's* ruler.

Now Benjamin (cf. expos. on 44:14a) enters; gasping for breath he hears:

9   "Make haste and go back to my father and
     tell him, 'Thus says your son Joseph; God
     has made me the lord of all Egypt. Come
     down to me; do not delay.' "

From the assiduous wording of his message, vv. 9-11, the father would at once recognize Joseph as its author, and "God," its first word, would assure him that, though being "the lord of all Egypt"—and therefore too busy to bring him down in person (NaTsYB)—he has remained faithful to his father's way of life (B. Jacob). His brothers are to hasten back not only to give Jacob the good news about Joseph but also to relieve him of his anxiety about Benjamin and Simeon (MaLBYM).

10   "You will live in the region of Goshen—
      being near me, you, your children and grand-
      children—your flocks and herds, and every-
      thing you have."

The regent may invite foreigners to settle in Egypt, though not in a specific region. That is why Joseph says, *we-yashavta*—you will dwell—in the region of Goshen," and not *we-hoshav-tika*—I will settle you—(B. Jacob), confident that Pharaoh will permit his protégé's family of livestock-owners to live on the excellent grazing grounds region of Goshen (see expos. on 47:6). "You will dwell" connotes not merely an invitation for a visit (see expos. on v. 28) but permanent residence in Egypt even after the famine. Goshen is the eastern part of the Nile Delta. Though it is in Egypt, it is apart from its seductive, idolatrous main-stream (RaMBaN). It also is "near" Joseph's residence in the capital.[7] From Goshen, moreover, the Children of Israel could enter the Land of Promise without crossing the Nile (B. Jacob).

11   "There I will sustain you—for there are
      still five years of famine ahead—lest
      you and your family and all that is yours
      become destitute."

The Hebrew word for "sustain" (cf. also 47:12; 50:21) used in the Narrative only in relation to Joseph's family, connotes special solicitude. "Destitute" delicately paraphrases that they survive and not die (cf. 42:2; 43:8; 47:19; B. Jacob), for even if they could perhaps continue to purchase rations, pasturing in Canaan, as the brothers will tell Pharaoh, (cf. 47:4) has come to an end (Sforno).

12   "Thus your own eyes see and my brother
        Benjamin's that it is my mouth that is
        speaking to you."

If Joseph's message should not convince the father that it is indeed his own, the brothers will corroborate it as eye-and-ear witnesses. If the father should still doubt, Benjamin will bear them out that Joseph, in their tongue, had spoken all those words.

13   "Then tell my father everything about my
        honor in Egypt and all that you have seen
        and make haste to bring my father down here."

For the third and fourth time Joseph relishes pronouncing "my father," and urges his brothers to confirm that from what they had seen about his high station, he would surely succeed in obtaining Pharaoh's permission to settle them in Goshen (RaMBaN).

14   Then he threw his arms round his brother
        Benjamin's neck and wept, and Benjamin
        wept on his neck.

Now at last Joseph can vent his emotion in open tears. It is natural for him to approach Benjamin first, for these two full brothers' mutual affection is singular and has never been spoiled.

15   Then he kissed all his brothers and wept
        over them; [only] then did his brothers
        [have it in their power to] talk to him.

Should not his tears and kisses convinced them that he does indeed bear no grudge against them?[8] Anyway, they are now able to "talk to him," bringing him up to date about their families, etc.

16   The news, "Joseph's brothers have come,"
        reached Pharaoh's house and pleased Pharaoh
        and his courtiers.

Inquiries were made as to why the regent was weeping (cf. v. 45:2; RaLBaG) whereupon the regent released the news that the other sons of his illustrious father (about whom Pharaoh's house had heard) had finally arrived from Canaan where he had been kidnapped (cf. 40:15). Just as Joseph's dream interpretation "pleased Pharaoh and all his courtiers" (41:27) because it was for Egypt's welfare, so again they were now "pleased" not only because they shared in Joseph's joy, but also for three other reasons: 1) The public will now learn the noble lineage of Joseph, the former slave (RaMBaN). 2) If a family such as the extraordinary regent's could be persuaded to settle in Egypt, it would be a great asset for the whole country. (B. Jacob). 3) If Egypt became their new homeland, the regent would serve the crown with even greater dedication (Sforno).

17   And Pharaoh said to Joseph, "Tell your
        brothers: 'This is what you are to do.
        Load your beasts and go at once to Canaan.

18a   " 'Fetch your father and your households and
        come to me.' "

Pharaoh, obviously, did not know that Joseph had already invited them himself (cf. vv. 9-13).

18b   "I wish to assign to you the best that
        there is in Egypt where [after the famine]
        you will live off the fat of the land."

"The fat of the land" which occurs nowhere else, seems to mean the most fertile farm land. Pharaoh may have taken it for granted that because of Joseph's expertness in agricultural matters his family are farmers.[9]

19   "And you are instructed [to tell
        them,] 'Do as follows: take at your
        pleasure Land-of-Egypt Wagons for your
        little ones, and your wives, and [to]
        carry your father, and come."

RaShI, following TJ, adds the bracketed words. Knowing that Joseph would do nothing for personal advantage, Pharoah *orders* him to provide his family with crown-vehicles (RaMBaN). That the father is mentioned last signifies that the wagons are sent in his honor (Abrabanel).

20   "And never mind your belongings, for the best
            of all the land of Egypt shall be yours."

They should not delay their departure by taking along all their things.

21   The Sons of Israel did so, Joseph giving
            them wagons with Pharaoh's ordinance. And
            he supplied them with provisions for the
            journey.

Without showing Pharaoh's permit they could not have crossed the border (RaDaQ).

22   To each of them he gave ornate robes; to
            Benjamin he gave three hundred pieces of
            silver and a set of five ornate robes.

The brothers needed new garments since they had torn the ones they had (cf. 44:13). Joseph gave them precious robes as token of his reconciliation (B. Jacob). Again, as in 43:34ab, Benjamin receives special gifts.

23   To his father he sent likewise; [moreover],
            ten asses loaded with Egypt's good things,
            and ten she-asses loaded with grain, bread
            and sustenance for the journey.

Kezoth—likewise—(only here; B. Jacob) seems to refer to what Benjamin received (Abrabanel). *Midrash Leqah Tov* asserts that since the brothers bring only ten and not eleven asses and she-asses with the gifts to the father, only *ten* of them, not Benjamin, returned. Also Abrabanel says apodictically, "Benjamin stayed with Joseph." Though this seems to counter v. 12, it could be that when Joseph was told by the king to provide the brothers with crown-carriages, Benjamin was no longer needed to bear out the Ten's report (see expos. on vv. 21, 27).

24   Then he sent off his brothers and as they
        departed, he urged them "Do not be fretful
        on the way."

"He sent off his brothers," followed in v. 25 by "Then they went up from Egypt" suggests that Joseph escorted them to the border.[10] His admonition, "Do not be fretful on the way" seems to imply his assurance that whatever they may fail to disclose to their father about their past, they need not fear that he will ever tell him what they did to him. Joseph (see expos. on v. 23) enables them to discuss the matter freely, unimpeded by Benjamin's presence.

25   Then they went up from Egypt and came to
        the land of Canaan to their father Jacob.

On their first return the Torah reported "they came to their father Jacob, to the land of Canaan," (cf. 42:29) for at that time their main concern was how their father would react to the regent's demand to see Benjamin. This time "from Egypt" precedes, and "to the land of Canaan" follows it, as if to intimate their concern that soon they may exchange their homeland Canaan for Egypt (see NaTsYB).

26a   And they told him, "Joseph is still
        alive, and it is he who is ruler over
        the whole land of Egypt."

Joseph had emphatically enjoined them (cf. vv. 9ff.) to speak,

   "Thus says your son Joseph, 'God has made me the lord
   of all Egypt. Come down to me; do not delay. You will
   live in the region of Goshen—being near to me, you,
   your children and grandchildren—your flocks and herds,
   and everything you own. There I will sustain you—for
   there are still five years of famine ahead—lest you and
   your family and all that is yours become destitute!

Instead of repeating verbatim Joseph's carefully worded message (see expos. on vv. 9ff.) they simply say "Joseph is still alive . . ."

26b His heart went numb, for he did not
believe them.[11]

How could he have believed them! The "ruler" of whom they speak is obviously the same "lord of the land" of whom they had reported that he suspected them of espionage (cf. 42:30), who had kept Simeon as a hostage (cf. 42:33) to compel the appearance of Benjamin before him (cf. 42:34) whose existence he had pumped out from them (cf. 43:7). How can this man who so cruelly insisted that Benjamin part from his old father, be his Joseph?[12] The brothers' words only reopen his old wound (Abrabanel). When the brothers notice the father's stupor, they comprehend their mistake; and as soon as the father gains his ability to listen they deliver accurately Joseph's message.

27 Yet when they recounted to him all the
words of Joseph which he had spoken to
them, and when he saw the wagons that
Joseph had sent to carry him, then the
spirit of their father Jacob surged up.

As soon as Joseph's own words, "Thus says your son Joseph, 'God has made me . . .,' " come from their lips, they touch the father's deepest chords: Each word, each phrase and their sequence enrapture him because they authenticate the speaker. They prompt him to raise his eyes, and the sight of the Egyptian crown-carriages resolves the conflict between his reasoning that the "ruler" cannot be Joseph and the certitude that these are Joseph's own words: Joseph must be the regent, for none but Pharaoh or he can authorize the use of these wagons abroad.

28a And Israel said, "Enough! My son Joseph
is still alive!"

V. 25 implies that during his sons' absence, "Israel," (see expos. on 43:6) had again become "Jacob" and remained "Jacob" even after their return and first message, "Joseph is still alive" (cf. v. 27). V. 28a shows that as "the spirit of their father Jacob surged up," he became "Israel" again. But this sentence means much more than this resurgence, after regaining his attentiveness. *It expresses an upsurge of revelatory insight* (see

TO and TJ) and "Enough! My son Joseph is still alive" should be understood accordingly.[13] Jacob was about to summon himself to allay his tormenting bewilderment at how Joseph could have dealt with him, with Benjamin and with the other sons with such seeming savagery, when in a flash of spiritual lightning *Israel intuited the whole truth: Joseph is indeed the regent and the Ten had caused his enslavement. That is why he had to test them before he could disclose himself to them!* This interpretation would be in accord with "Once, after Jacob's reunion with Joseph, the father told him, 'Thinkest thou I know not what thy brothers did to thee, because thou wouldst betray nothing . . .?' "[14] (see expos. on 46:30). "All the words" in "they recounted to him all the words of Joseph which he had spoken to them" refer only to vv. 9-11 and neither to vv. 4-8 nor to v. 24b (RaMBaN on 42:29b). Presumably (see expos. on 50:15ff.), they "were not able" even subsequently to confess their guilt to their father. Since, moreover, there is no reason to assume that Joseph ever changed his intention not to tell his father about it (see expos. on 39:6b, 41:51; 45:24), how could Jacob possibly ever have abstained from asking him how he came to Egypt, unless he knew it by his own intuition! This must have happened just now when "the spirit of their father Jacob surged up." *Israel's "enough!" thus implies that since the "spirit" gave him the answer, he will never take up the question with any of his sons!* And then Jacob, who had lamented that in mourning and grief for Joseph he will go down to his grave (cf. 37:35; 42:38; 44:29), exclaims:

28b   "I must go and see him before I die."

Joseph expected his father with his whole family to stay in Egypt for good. But Jacob's words show that he merely wanted to visit Joseph (Sforno)[15] if God would allow him to do so (see expos. on 46:1).

GENESIS 46

1   So Israel set out with all he had and
       came to Beer-sheba and offered sacri-
       fices to the God of his father Isaac.

The Jacob clan had lived at Hebron for about twenty-three
years (see *Appendix* 7e). Before their departure they may all
have visited the sacred sepulchre in "the valley of Hebron" (see
expos. on 37:14; B. Jacob). The patriarch sets out with his
family on a pilgrimage to Beer-sheba[1] and summons them there
to a sacrificial repast, dedicated "to the God of his father Isaac,"
on account of the following incident: "There was a famine in
the land—aside from the previous famine that had occurred in
the days of Abraham—. . . when God appeared to him [Isaac]
and said, 'Do not go down to Egypt . . .' " (26:1f.), as Abraham
had done (cf. 12:10-13:1). "Israel" yearned to visit Joseph,
and what he expresses with his offerings on Isaac's altar (cf.
26:25) is his prayerful trust that though Isaac was not permitted
to go to Egypt during a famine, God would allow it to *him,* to
see his son (see expos. on 45:28b).

2   Then God said to Israel in a vision by
       night and said, "Jacob, Jacob!" And
       he said, "I am ready."

The Hebrew word here for "vision" is in the "intensive
plural," expressing grandeur and importance (F. J. Delitzsch).
Whenever God "appeared" to the Fathers or in dream-visions,[2]
He assured them that He would be with them, lest they be fearful (B. Jacob). Because "Israel" is not a calling name, he is
addressed as "Jacob." (B. Jacob). God's calling Jacob twice by
name expressed His love for him.[3]

3   And He said, "I am the God, your father's
       God. Fear not to go down to Egypt, for
       there I will make you into a great nation."

"I am the God" seems to mean "Abraham's God" (*Tseror Hamor*). "Your father's God" is in response to Jacob's appellation (see expos. on v. 1). God assures Jacob that He is with him as He was with Isaac (Hizkuni), who was not allowed to leave Canaan. Jacob is not merely permitted to see Joseph but is commanded to go to Egypt and to remain there with his whole family (Abrabanel). That in spite of God's assurances in vv. 3f. the Torah in v. 5 calls the patriarch "Jacob," not "Israel" and that he has to be "lifted" to the wagon evinces his dread that Egypt is to be the land "not theirs," which God had foretold to Abraham (15:13), in which his descendants "shall be enslaved and oppressed" (NaTsYB). God intimates that the prerequisite for the growth of his offspring into "a great nation," promised to Abraham (cf. 12:2; 16:18), is that they multiply not in Canaan—where their peoplehood would be dissolved through mixed marriages (see expos. on 37:2b)—but in relative seclusion in the Egyptian region of Goshen where they could retain their group-identity.[4]

4   "I Myself will go down with you to
       Egypt, and I Myself will surely bring
       you up again; and Joseph will put his
       hand upon your eyes."

Because God knows Jacob's great apprehension, in spite of his anticipation of his reunion with Joseph, He gives him in these *last words to the Fathers* a more emphatic assurance of His companionship and protection than they ever received. "You" in "I . . . bring you up again" has a double meaning: It predicts that his remains will be interred with his fathers', and that God will return his offspring once "the iniquity of the Amorite" is "replete" (15:16). "Joseph will put his hand upon your eyes" is usually paraphrased by ". . . will close your eyes,"[5] that is, Joseph will be with him in his last hours.

5   Then Jacob rose up from Beer-sheba, and the
       sons of Israel lifted their father Jacob,
       their little ones and their wives into the
       wagons which Pharaoh had sent to transport
       them.

In this sentence "the sons of Israel" connotes for the last time

Jacob's sons. In v. 8 the whole clan will be so called i.e. *Bene Yisrael* "the Israelites." The wagons were not used for the pilgrimage because Jacob did not then know yet whether he might go to Egypt.

6   And they took their livestock and their
         possessions which they had acquired in
         the land of Canaan. Thus they came to
         Egypt, Jacob and all his offspring with him.

Vv. 1 and 6 seem to indicate that they did not heed Pharaoh's suggestion (see expos. on 45:20). "All his offspring" implies, on the one hand, that none of the family's herdsmen (see expos. on 45:20) emigrated with them. On the other hand, it emphasizes that Jacob was spared what had marred the lives of both Abraham and Isaac, whose descendants except for Isaac and Jacob were excluded from their parental inheritance, since "all his (Jacob's) offspring" remained together (see expos. on 48:4).

7   He brought with him to Egypt his sons and
         grandsons, his daughters and granddaughters
         and all his offspring with him.

"His daughters" may include not only Dinah but also "the wives of Jacob's sons" (cf. v. 26). "Granddaughters" seems to imply not only Serah (cf. v. 17) but also other unlisted granddaughters. "And all his offspring" may refer to Jacob's great-grandsons (cf. vv. 12, 17).

8   These are the names of the Israelites who
         came to Egypt, Jacob and his sons. The
         firtsborn of Jacob [1], Reuben [2].

In this verse Bene Yisrael is no longer translated "the sons of Israel," but "the Israelites" (see expos. on v. 5). Jacob heads their listing. He is the first of the "thirty-three" (cf. v. 15; RaShBaM). In v. 27 he will be included in the "seventy," "the total, . . . belonging to the House of Jacob." Reuben was the firstborn (cf. 29:32; 35:23) in regard to genealogy. Yet cf. expos. on 48:5 and see I Chron. 5:11.

9   Reuben's son: Hanoch [3] Pallu [4],
         Hetsron [5], and Carmi [6].

For the last two sons of Reuben see exposition on v. 27.

10   The sons of Simeon [7]: Yemuel [8],
Yamin [9], Ohad [10], Yachin [11],
Tsohar [12], and Shaul [13], the
son of the Canaanite woman.[6]

11   The sons of Levi [14]: Gershon [15],
Qehat [16], and Merari [17].[7]

12   The sons of Judah [18]: Er, Onan, Shelah [19],
Perets [20], and Zerah [21]. Er and Onan had
died in Canaan. The sons of Perets: Hetsron [22]
and Hamul [23].

For Judah's grandsons see exposition on v. 27.

13   The sons of Issahar [24]: Tola [25],
Puvvah [26], Yob [27] and Shimron [28],[8]

14   The sons of Zebulun [29]: Sered [30],
Elon [31], and Yahleel [32].

15   These were the sons of Leah whom she bore
to Jacob in Padan-aram, also his daughter
Dinah [33] [excluding Er and Onan, v. 12].
Persons in all, his sons and daughters—33
[i.e. 32 without Jacob].[9]

16   [And Zilpah's:] The sons of Gad [1]: Tsiphion [2].
Haggi [3], Shuni [4], Etsbon [5], Eri [6], Arodi [7],
and Areli [8].[10]

17   The sons of Asher [9]: Yimnah [10], Yishvah [11],
Yishvi [12] and Beriah [13]; also their sister
Serah [14]. Beriah's sons, Heber [15] and Malkiel [16],[11]

18   These were the descendants of Zilpah, whom Laban had
given to his daughter Leah. These she bore to Jacob—
16 persons.

19   The sons of Jacob's wife Rachel were Joseph [1]
and Benjamin [2].

20   To Joseph were born in the land of Egypt Manasseh [3]
and Ephraim [4] whom Asenath daughter of Potiphera,
priest of On, bore to him.

21   Benjamin's sons: Bela [5], Beker [6], Ashbel [7], Gera [8],
        Na'aman [9], Ehi [10], Rosh [11], Muppim [12],
        Huppim [13], and Ard [14].[12]

For the strange "fact" that Benjamin, "the son of his (Jacob's)
old age," (44:20) came with ten sons to Egypt see exposition
on v. 27.

22   Thus the descendants of Rachel born to
        Jacob were 14 persons in all.

23   [Bilhah's sons:] The sons of Dan [1]:
        Hushim [2].[13]

24   The sons of Naphtali [3]: Jahtseel [4],
        Guni [5], Yetser [6] and Shillem [7].

Shillem is Shallum in I Chron. 7:13.

25   These were the descendants of Bilhah,
        whom Laban had given to his daughter
        Rachel, that she bore to Jacob, 7
        persons in all.

26   Altogether, all the people who came to
        Egypt, belonging to Jacob—that came out
        of his loins, not counting the wives of
        Jacob's sons [32+16+14+7=69, excluding
        Joseph and his two sons] 66 in all.

Jacob's wives are not listed because they were dead: Rachel
died first. Leah was buried by Jacob in Hebron (cf. 49:31).
Since Bilhah and Zilpah are not mentioned, they must also have
been dead.

27   And Joseph's sons who were born to him in
        Egypt were two in number. Thus the total
        of all persons who came to Egypt, belonging
        to the House of Jacob [the 66 of v. 26 plus
        Jacob, Joseph and Joseph's two sons] was 70.

Concerning Reuben's last two sons, Judah's grandsons and
Benjamin's sons (cf. vv. 9, 12, and 21, respectively) reference
was made to the exposition on v. 27, which may solve the following three riddles:
    1) In 42:37 Reuben tells his father, "You may kill my two

sons." If he had four sons (cf. v. 9), he should have said, ". . . two of my sons."

2) Judah was three years older than Joseph, who was thirty-nine when Jacob's House immigrated (see *Appendix* 4b). V. 12 lists two of Judah's grandsons from Perets whose mother was Tamar (cf. 38:29). Even if Judah married before Joseph was seventeen, Tamar was his second wife. She conceived from Judah after his third son from his previous wife (cf. 38:5) was already old enough to marry (cf. 38:14). When Tamar gave birth to Perets, Judah could thus already have been a grand-father three years before, so that when Perets' first son was born Judah must have been old enough three years before to be a great-grandfather at the age of forty-two! This seems impossible.

3) Benjamin was born less than nine months after Dinah's tragedy (cf. *Appendix* 6). He could not have been more than 16 years younger than Joseph who was 17 when abducted while Benjamin lived at Hebron. Neither could he have been much older, since Dinah, a little less than two years younger than Joseph (cf. *Appendix* 3), was in her 14th year when violated (cf. 34:2; *Appendix* 7b). Hence Joseph was 15 when Benjamin was born, and since Joseph was 39 when Jacob's family arrive in Egypt, Benjamin was only 24 when he is supposed to have come with ten sons.

The wording in v. 27 seems to solve these problems: Though Joseph's sons were born in Egypt, the Torah includes them among the "persons who came to Egypt." This suggests that also among the sixty-six other offspring of Jacob there might have been some sons of Benjamin, Judah's grandsons and two sons of Reuben who were not yet sired but "came to Egypt" "*in* their father!" The cautious wording "belonging to Jacob," v. 26, and "belonging to the House of Jacob," v. 27, instead of "with Jacob" seems to support this assumption.[14]

The Torah's reason for listing, beside Joseph's sons, some other offspring of Jacob as having "come to Egypt" seems to be to reach the sacred number "seventy" as the nucleus of the Israelite people.[15] These "seventy" are "Israel's numbers," correlated with "the divisions of man," the seventy peoples descended from Noah[16] in the sentence: "When the Most High gave nations their homes and set the divisions of man, He fixed the boundaries of people in relation to Israel's numbers." (Deut. 32:8; RaShBaM).

| 28a | He sent Judah ahead of him to Joseph |
| | to point the way before him to Goshen. |

The exposition on 45:10 explains the intent of Joseph in the second sentence of his message to his father: "You will live in the region of Goshen." That is why Jacob would not go any further when arriving in Goshen. The same Judah who once caused Joseph's separation from his brothers (cf. 37:26f.), who later on became their mediator (cf. 43:9), is now made the courier of both Jacob and of Joseph (B. Jacob), announcing to Joseph his father's imminent arrival in Goshen and to his father, in turn, where in Goshen they would meet Joseph and stay (TJ; RaShI).

| 28b | And they came to the region of Goshen. |

They travelled slowly and soon Judah was back with them.

| 29a | Joseph hitched up his chariot and went |
| | up to Goshen to meet Israel his father. |

"Israel," since "Israel" had sent him on his mission of re-conciliation (cf. 37:13). The regent "hitched up his chariot" himself, as Abraham, also of high station (cf. 23:6) "saddled his ass" himself (22:2f.) for his encounter with God. Now Joseph's retinue, about to accompany the regent, watches Joseph himself harness the horses to his splendidly arrayed chariot to show honor to the patriarch (B. Jacob).

29b	As he appeared to him, he flung
	himself on his neck and wept upon
	it continuously.

Joseph "appeared" to Jacob (RaShI) as God had "appeared" to Abraham, (cf. 12:7; 17:1; 18:1) to Isaac (cf. 26:2, 24) and to himself (cf. 35:9). He gazes up at his son, who stands on the chariot. No other human being "appears" in Scriptures (B. Jacob). Joseph dismounts, and Jacob (RaMBaN) embraces him, overcome by deepest emotions while Joseph bends to kiss the father's hand (RaMBaN). Then the patriarch weeps on the neck of his beloved son, after twenty-two bitter years of mourning for him. He wept 'od—continuously—(Ruth 1:14; Ps. 84:5) for a long time, unable to tear himself away (B. Jacob).

30   At last Israel said to Joseph, "Now
     I can die, having seen your face, that
     you are still alive."

Joseph's "appearing," rekindled the spirit of "Jacob" (see expos. on vv. 2, 5) to become "Israel" again. "Now,"[17] having seen Joseph "resurrected from Sheol" (cf. Ps. 30:4; see expos. on 37:35; 42:38; 44:29,31), the patriarch had nothing else to live for, having attained the greatest joy in life (J. H. Hertz). Joseph may well have been anxious that his father would ask him how he came to Egypt. Judah must have told Joseph that the brothers "were not able" to confess their guilt to him (see expos. on 45:24) and Joseph was unaware that his father had intuited it (see expos. on 45:28a). What the Midrash speculates (see same exposition) about the father, telling Joseph that he knows the secret, may have taken place after Joseph had greeted and conversed with his brothers' families.

31   Then Joseph said to his brothers and to
     his father's household, "I will go up and
     inform Pharaoh, telling him 'My brothers
     and my father's household [who were] in
     the land of Canaan, have come to me [now].' " [18]

To Jacob himself Joseph does not speak about this matter, for the patriarch is to be relieved from all tension (see expos. on v. 4b). But Joseph not only is about to brief his brothers on how to speak to Pharaoh but also wants all other members of the household to confirm the brothers' words if questioned.

32   "And the men are shepherds, have been
     keepers of livestock, and they have
     brought with them their flocks and
     their herds, and everything they own."

Ro-'eh means both herdsman and shepherd. Shepherds may be their own herdsmen; yet they can also be "keepers of livestock," as the fathers were, with herdsmen as their servants.[19] Joseph's words are to imply that because they left their herdsmen in Canaan, they will now first have to be shepherds themselves. After the parenthetical vv. 33,34a, he will explain why Pharaoh should learn that they are "shepherds."

33, 34a   [33] "Thus, when Pharaoh calls on you and asks
                 'What is your occupation?' [34a] you shall
                 say 'Your servants have been keepers of
                 livestock from our youth until now, both we
                 and our fathers.' "

With this parenthesis Joseph instructs them not to call themselves "shepherds" but "keepers of livestock," as they actually have been, because it sounds more honorific. In fact, Pharaoh himself owns livestock (cf. 47:6).

34b   "So that you may stay in the region of
                 Goshen, because all shepherds are ab-
                 horrent to Egyptians."

According to A. Dillman, *Genesis,* the Egyptians had an aversion to herdsman whose occupation made them neglect the high Egyptian standards of cleanliness and refinement in care of their bodies. But it seems possible that they refrained from contact with herdsmen simply because the shepherds would eat the animals which the Egyptians at large worshipped (see expos. on 43:32; Exod. 8:22), Joseph hopes that when the king learns about his kinsmen's occupation he will himself suggest that they stay and settle in Goshen where they happen to have arrived. Yet the beginning of the next chapter shows that this hope was not so readily fulfilled and why, for all Joseph's diplomacy, it was not.

GENESIS 47

When Joseph returned from Goshen to announce to Pharaoh
that his family had arrived, he took along his father and a few,
lit. "five,"[1] of his brothers. While the patriarch was seated in an
antechamber of the palace, the brothers entered Pharaoh's hall
together with Joseph, remaining first in the background.

1   Joseph then came and reported to
     Pharaoh saying, "My father and
     brothers have arrived from the
     land of Canaan, with their flocks
     and herds and everything they own;
     they are in the region of Goshen."

Instead of saying, "have come to me" and "the men are
shepherds" (cf. 46:31f.), he now, on second thought, changes
and condenses what he originally had intended to say.

2   He had selected five of his brothers
     whom he presented to Pharaoh.

3   Pharaoh said to the brothers, "What
     is your occupation?" They said to
     Pharaoh, "We your servants are shep-
     herds, as were our fathers."

Having overheard that Joseph tactfully refrained from calling
them "shepherds," they now say it themselves. And having
noticed how Joseph had shortened his intended report, they also
limit their words. Then they pause, hoping in vain that the king,
who had invited them, "come to me . . ." (45:18), will offer
them Goshen to settle in.[2] That is why they had to continue to

talk to Pharaoh and to be more explicit than Joseph had briefed them to be.

4   And they said to Praraoh, "We have
     come to sojourn in this land, for the
     famine is so severe in the land of
     Canaan that there is no pasture for
     your servants' flocks. Pray, then, let
     your servants stay in the region of Goshen."

They explain that even if they were permitted to purchase further rations in Egypt, their herds and flocks would perish, because Canaan has ceased to provide feed, which they would find in Goshen.

5   Then Pharaoh said to Joseph *le'mor*,—as
     follows: "Your father and your brothers
     have come to you."

It seems that LXX adds to MT and makes transpositions in vv. 5-6 because of some of the following puzzles: 1) Pharaoh says no word to Joseph after he has informed him about his family's arrival. 2) Neither does Pharaoh address the brothers after they have answered his question. 3) More surprising is that Pharaoh's subsequent granting of the brothers petition is directed to Joseph, 4) preceded by the seemingly superfluous words, "Your father and your brothers have come to you." 5) Most perplexing is that the Torah introduces these seemingly trite words with *"le'mor"*—as follows—nowhere else introducing Pharaoh's statements in the Narrative.

The answer to these questions seems to be that Pharaoh was taken by surprise when Joseph informed him that his brothers were not farmers, as he had assumed (see expos. on 45:18), and that he was startled when they told him that they were "shepherds," "abhorrent to Egyptians" (46:34). Pharaoh wanted to fulfill Joseph's desire. But was not Goshen—the long narrow valley, leading straight from the heart of the Delta to a break in the chains of the Bitter Lakes[3]—a "weak spot" (see expos. on 42:9b), a "restricted area," not to be settled by foreigners? How then could he offer it to these foreign shepherds? Even a Pharaoh, particularly in a time of national emergency, has to consider public opinion. That is why it took Pharaoh some time to find a way to grant the petition: The word *le'mor* is meant to underline the last word, *'eleka,* to you! Originally it was Joseph who wanted to say (cf. 46:21) that they "have come to me." Yet he suppressed it, lest he appear presumptuous. Now it is Pharaoh who replaces *his* original "come to me" (45:18) by "have come to you": These owners of livestock from Canaan must not be considered rank-and-file "foreigners." They are the very kinsmen of the regent, who wants them to live close to his residence; and since they have livestock, the most natural thing is to offer them a place in the region of Goshen.[4]

6a   "The land of Egypt is before you; settle
         your father and your brothers in the
         best of the land; they may live in the
         region of Goshen."

"Before you" means "at your disposal" (cf. 13:9; 20:15; 34:10 etc. B. Jacob).

6b   "And if you know energetic men among
         them, place them as chiefs over [the
         herdsmen of] my own livestock [there]."

This suggestion of Pharaoh to appoint some of them as royal officers, superintendents of the king's herdsman, is a further sign of his benignity toward Joseph (J. H. Hertz). Perhaps some of the brothers indeed became such "chiefs."

7   Joseph then brought his father Jacob and
         presented him to Pharaoh, and Jacob blessed
         Pharaoh.

NJPS adopts RaShI's "greeted," yet JPS's literal translation "blessed" seems preferable because if Jacob prayed for Pharaoh's long life[5] the king's response becomes more intelligible.

8   Then Pharaoh said to Jacob, "How many
         are the days of the years of your life!"

This is an exclamation with the emphasis on "your," implying the deep impression the patriarch made on Pharaoh: If the years are counted, the days would be numbered only in the life of the select few (S. R. Hirsch).

9   And Jacob said to Pharaoh, "The days
         of the years of my sojourning are
         thirty and a hundred years."

Jacob takes up Pharaoh's "the days of the years" so that it is all the more impressive that he paraphrases "life" by "sojourning," giving it the elegian connotation that for him life on earth is but a sojourn (cf. Ps. 39:13; 119:54; I Chron. 29:15; B. Jacob). It also reflects the Fathers' acceptance of God's will that they are to live in Canaan as "the land of sojourning" (cf. 17:8; 28:4; 36:7; 37:1) before their offspring will inherit it as their "permanent possession," (cf. 17:8). Jacob's unusual placing of "thirty" before "a hundred" may indicate his knowledge of the Egyptian ideal life of 110 years (see expos. on 50:26): Knowing that he looks older than 100, he tells Pharaoh how many years older than 100 he actually is. Lest Pharaoh considers such an age, to him unheard of, as the reward of an exemplary life, Jacob adds:

9b   "Few and hard have been the days of the
        years of my life. They cannot come up
        to the days of the years of my fathers
        during their sojourns."

His grandfather lived to be 175 years old (cf. 25:7) and his father, 180 (cf. 35:28). Feeling his own death approaching (RaDaQ), he knows that his life will be much shorter. Besides, of Abraham it was said that he died at "a good ripe age, old and contented" (cf. 25:8) and of Isaac, "in ripe old age" (cf. 35:29). He will receive no such epitaph, for "few and hard have been the days of the years of my life." [6]

10   Then Jacob blessed Pharaoh and left
        the presence of Pharaoh.

As he greeted the king with his blessing (v. 7), so he bids him farewell with a blessing (cf. I Kings 8:66). He "left the presence of," lit. "he went out from before him" (see expos. on 41:46b).

11   And Joseph settled his father and
        his brothers and gave them land
        holdings in Egypt, in the best of
        the land, in the district of Ra'-meses,
        as Pharaoh had ordered.

Pharaoh had ordered in v. 6a that they receive a section in

Goshen, "in the best of the land." Joseph thus (RaShI) selected "the district of Ra'-meses" [7] in the region of Goshen.

12   Joseph sustained his father, his
      brothers, and all his father's
      household with food, down to the
      little ones.

V. 12, emphasizing that Joseph's relatives were "sustained," given free rations, resumes the account of the famine in Egypt. It was interrupted (42:1-47:12), reporting the travels of his brothers to and from Egypt and the immigration of Jacob with his family.

13   There had been no food [harvest] in
      any country, for the famine was very
      severe; both the land of Egypt and the
      land of Canaan languished from hunger.

This verse recapitulates 41:53-57. The Hebrew word for "languished" appears nowhere else. It seems to connote "being stunned" (Ibn Ezra).

14   Joseph gathered in all the money that was
      to be found in the land of Egypt and in the
      land of Canaan, as payment for the rations
      as they procured them, and Joseph brought
      the money into Pharaoh's palace.

"Into Pharaoh's palace" means to the royal treasury (TJ). Since v. 19 will make it clear that the events reported in vv. 15 and 16 occur in the sixth year of the famine, v. 14 sums up what happened during the first five years. "All the money that was found" includes what the crown had paid for grain during the years of abundance (see expos. on 41:35).

To those who were poor at the beginning of the famine, others were added to receive state-welfare (cf. expos. on 41:37).

15   When the money was spent in the land
      of Egypt and in the land of Canaan, all
      Egyptians came to Joseph demanding "Hand
      out bread to us! For why should we die
      before you; for the money is gone?"

"All Egyptians" refers to the wealthy ones, who, like the

foreigners, had to pay. When the people from Canaan and other foreign countries had run out of money, the rich Egyptians claimed that they too had no more money, yet are, as Egyptians, entitled to free rations as the poor receive them. The emphasis in the wealthy Egyptians' words is on the word "us," for otherwise it would be superfluous as it is missing in v. 19, ". . . give seed . . ." (NaTsYB). The Torah states that the money of the wealthy Egyptians was indeed gone, but Joseph was not so sure about it:

16   Joseph replied, "Hand out your livestock,
            and I will give you [grain] against your
            livestock if [and when all] money is gone."

As much as Joseph felt it his duty to help the poor population, he also intended to weaken the power of the rich. Using their own "hand out" idiom (B. Jacob), he insists that they pay either in coin or barter.

17   So they brought their livestock to Joseph,
            and Joseph sold them food in exchange for
            the horses, the flocks of sheep, the herds
            of cattle and for the asses. Thus he brought
            them through that [sixth] year with bread
            for their livestock.

The reason for exchanging their livestock for bread instead of killing off their animals as a means of feeding themselves may be sought in the existing animal taboo (Speiser; see expos. on 43:32). If the livestock was confiscated and not merely branded as crown property, it is possible that some of Joseph's brothers were indeed appointed as chiefs over their herdsmen (see expos. on 47:6b) "Bringing through" (cf. Ps. 23:3) connotes special solicitude.

18   And when that year was ended, they came
            to him the next year and said to him,
            "My lord, we have concealed nothing
            from you. Really, the money is gone.
            and with the animal stock consigned
            to my lord, there is nothing left at
            my lord's disposal but our mere bodies
            and our farmland."

"That year" is the sixth, in which the crown acquired the livestock, and the "next," lit. "second," is the seventh, as evidenced by the gentry's plea for seed, v. 19 (ShaDaL). Also "we have concealed nothing" is ShaDaL's, following TO. The same men who had reproached Joseph (cf. v. 15) now address him as "my lord" three times. They have, in fact, become so meek that they do not even argue that some of the livestock they surrendered may have exceeded in value the provisions they received.

19   "Why should we perish before your eyes, we
      and our land as well? Take us and our land
      in payment for bread, and we and our land
      alike will be in bondage to Pharaoh. And
      give seed, that we survive and not die, and
      that the soil will not turn into waste." [8]

"Give seed" indicates their awareness that the land has regained its fertility, and "that the soil will not turn into waste," that the weeds are already sprouting, and unless tilling is resumed, their fields become uncultivable. Thus, though they know that they need sustenance for but one more year, they are so downcast that without inquiring how much of their land would be confiscated in return for food, they not only offer it all but are willing to become Pharaoh's slaves to till it for him.

20   So Joseph acquired for Pharaoh all the
      farm land of Egypt, for they sold each
      his field because the famine prevailed
      over them. Thus the land became Pharaoh's.

"The land became Pharaoh's," but not the people.

21   And as to the population, Joseph *he-'evir*
      'oto le-'arim—translocated it city-wise—[9]
      throughout the land of Egypt.

That the translocation was done "city-wise" means that the people who used to live around "their" city (41:48) were resettled in cohesive groups somewhere else where their ties of community remained intact (ShaDaL). This was not a "deportation" but a necessary[10] "translocation" of communities. The Torah seems at any rate to imply that Joseph's emergency measures caused the disappearance of the old feudal nobility.

F. J. Delitzsch writes, "Joseph undoubtedly had in view no less the good of the country than that of the king, when changing the disproportionately divided landed property into uniform parcels of copyhold liable to rent" [11] (cf. expos. on vv. 23 f.).

22   But the land of the priests he did
        not take over, for the priests had
        a fixed allowance from Pharaoh, and
        they lived off the allotment which
        Pharaoh had made to them. That is
        the reason why they did not [have to]
        sell their land.

Much as Joseph may have wanted to abrogate the Egyptian priests' great privileges,[12] he had no power over them; they were the Pharaohs' favored caste, and his father-in-law was a priest! It should be noted that "that is the reason why . . .," occuring in v. 22, re-appears in the following two passages, obviously to impress upon the Israelites how much less privileged their own priests are, compared with the Egyptian: [13]

And to the Levites I hereby give all the tithes in Israel as their share in return for the services that they perform . . . But they shall have no territorial share among the Israelites; for it is the tithes set aside by the Israelites as a gift to JHWH that I give to the Levites as their share. This is the reason why I have said concerning them: They shall have no territorial share among the Israelites" (Num. 18:21-24).
This is the reason why the Levites have received no hereditary portion along with their kinsmen: YHWH is their portion . . . ." (Deut. 10:9; [18: 1f.]).

23   Joseph told the people, "Now that I have
        acquired you [as tenants] and your land
        for Pharaoh, here is seed for you to sow
        the land."

The literal translation, "Herewith I have acquired of today you and your fields for Pharaoh" defines in legal terminology their new status: "I have acquired you"—as the sequence shows —does not imply that they have become Pharaoh's bondsmen, as they had offered to do, (v. 19), but feudal tenants (see RaMBaN, Sforno, NaTsYB).[14] This pronouncement, accompanied by the distribution of seed-corn for just that one year (cf. v. 24), was issued after the completion for the resettlement.

24   "And when the harvests are in, you give
    one-fifth to Pharaoh, keeping four parts
    for yourselves as seed for the field, and
    food for you, for those in your households,
    and your little ones."

"Your little ones" seems superfluous, unless it assures the panic-stricken people (see expos. on v. 25b) that in future years of poor harvests their own needs, including the children's will have priority before turning in the rent-produce. 41:34,49 reported that already during the years of abundance they had paid twenty percent not as rent but as tax. A rent rate of twenty-percent was very low, particularly in a land as fertile as Egypt.[15]

25   They answered, "You have saved our lives!
    May it please my lord that we become slaves
    to Pharaoh."

26   But Joseph made it [cf. v. 24] into an Egyptian land
    law, which is still valid, that a fifth should
    be Pharaoh's; only the land of the priests did
    not become Pharaoh's.

What originally (cf. v. 19) had been their proposition, viz. to become Pharaoh's slaves for obtaining food during the last year of famine, becomes now their petition. But again Joseph refuses to make them Pharaoh's slaves (NaTsYB), except that he dispossessed them of their fields and made them feudal tenants, (see expos. on v. 23). The reason for their persistence and petition seems to be that the fear of famine had such a traumatic effect upon them (see expos. on v. 20) that they hankered after "freedom from starvation," preferring serfdom, so that their need for food in future famines would be taken care of by their lord. Joseph's diplomacy made him refrain from an outright refusal of what would have made Pharaoh the owner of the entire population, except for the priests. He also wanted to spare the people the embarrassment of being admonished that what they requested was a "sin against God." [16]

They praise him (cf. v. 25a) as their savior, who has accomplished the gigantic task of preserving the life of every Egyptian throughout the terrible years of famine (von Rad). This historical achievement condemns the future Pharaoh "who did not know Joseph" (cf. Exod. 1:8; B. Jacob).[17] Now it becomes clear why the text devotes fourteen verses on what apparently is of merely Egyptological interest: Approaching and introducing the Book of Exodus (B. Jacob) from "the House of Bondage" (cf. Exod. 20:2), the Torah impresses upon God's people that to attain "security from starvation" the Egyptians would rather "escape from freedom." But the Torah wants the Israelites to cherish freedom as the highest good, as did Joseph (see expos. on 50:18 f.), the first of them who suffered enslavement. Though Joseph's abolition of private land-ownership for the benefit of the crown and the introduction of feudal tenancy in the interest of the population at large may have tragically contributed to making Egypt "the House of Bondage," neither does the Torah hold him responsible for it, nor should the modern moralist do so.

"That a fifth should be Pharaoh's" may imply that those who should fail to pay the twenty percent produce tax would forfeit their fields (S. R. Hirsch). It is not clear, though, whether uncultivated land, grazing grounds, would belong to Pharaoh also. At any rate, whatever grazing land was allotted to the House of Jacob in the district of Ra'-meses was their outright "possession" (see expos. on v. 11). V. 26b is thus the transition to v. 27: As the Egyptian priests own their fields, so does the House of Jacob own their grazing lands.

27   After Israel had settled in the land of
           Egypt, in the region of Goshen, they
           acquired [further] holdings in it, [for]
           they were fertile and increased greatly.

The Fathers were to live in Canaan only as "sojourners," but God had promised to give it to their descendants as "holdings forever" (cf. 17:8). Besides the field which Jacob bought (cf. 33:19f.; see expos. on 48:22), the Fathers' only "holding" was the field which Abraham had bought for the grave of Sarah (cf. 23:4). It was in Egypt, however, that Pharaoh gave Jacob's family title to land property (cf. v. 11), and v.

27 reports that before Jacob died, they bought (RaDaQ) even more land in Goshen. Exod. 8:18 and 9:26 will show that the generation of the Exodus, moreover, had settled in the whole region of Goshen.

According to MT, v. 27 concludes the third *sidrah* of the Narrative, as 40:23 and 44:17 conclude the first and second, respectively. What puzzles the interpreter of MT is that it does not place the usual gap in the text to mark the beginning of the fourth and last *sidrah*. The reason may be that vv. 28-31 not only introduce the fourth *sidrah* but also are meant to be the colophon of v. 27, inasmuch as Jacob may have feared that the purchase of new land by his sons might cause them to lose their faithful adherence to the Tradition, of considering no land but Canaan their "homeland." Vv. 28-31 therefore describe what Jacob does to make his offspring resist the temptation to assimilate with the Egyptians. The Torah, however, in v. 27, with the plural verb form calls the brothers "Israel" for the first time and thereby seems to assure us that they actually were determined to retain their distinct identity and not to Egyptianize.

When Jacob became certain that it was indeed Joseph who had sent him the message, he said, "I must go and see him before I die" (45:27). And at his reunion with Joseph he said, "Now let me die, since I have seen your face" (46:30) . It is in reference to these two statements that the next verse needs to be understood. (B. Jacob).

28   And Jacob lived on for seventeen years, in
           the land of Egypt, so that the days of Jacob,
           the years of his life came to 147 years.

In Hebrew "living in a land" requires a verb different from the one used here which connotes "to keep on living" (B. Jacob). Not only did Jacob continue to live, as he did not dare hope, but, whereas his whole previous life had been one of suffering, in Egypt he lived happily and in tranquility (Hizkuni). ". . . the days of . . . the years" refers to 47:8. "Seventeen" are

the last years of Jacob with Joseph, as "seventeen" were the
first years of Joseph with Jacob (cf. 37:2).[18]

29   When the time approached for Israel to
die, he summoned his son Joseph and said
to him, "I wish I could claim this favor
from you: Please put your hand under my
thigh as a pledge of your steadfast
loyalty to me, not to bury me in Egypt."

At great or crucial moments of his life, Jacob's patriarchhood
is reinstated by the name "Israel" (see expos. on 37:3,13;
43:6; 11a; 45:28; 46:1,30). This time, though Jacob was not
ill, not only his presentiment of his approaching death but also
the news that his sons had acquired further land-holdings (see
expos. on v. 27) alarmed him and made him feel deeply his
responsibility as the patriarch. He feared that they might want
to stay in Egypt for good, not as "sojourners." He desired all
the more to be buried in Canaan so that his burial place at the
side of his children's other ancestors would remind them that
Canaan, not Egypt, must remain their "homeland." He summons Joseph not only because he is to become the chieftain
after his death, but also because only Joseph has the authority
to fulfill the father's desire. "Put your hand under my thigh"
connotes a ritual to ratify an oath rendered to a person who
makes a testamentary disposition.[19] Jacob knows the extraordinary importance of funerary arrangements for the Egyptians, so that it would indeed require exceptional "steadfast
love" to break with their mores by not burying the patriarch in
Egypt.

30   "When I lie down with my fathers, carry me
from Egypt and bury me in their burial place."
And he said, "I will do as you have spoken."

"Lying down with one's fathers," (cf. Deut. 31:6; I Kings
2:10) or "being gathered to one's fathers" (cf. 25:8) connotes
reunion with one's forebears. The sepulchre of the Three
Fathers is to become the magnet (B. Jacob) for the Children
of Israel toward the Promised Land, their "Eternal Possession."
Being Jacob's son, not his servant as Eliezer was Abraham's
servant, and because of his high position, Joseph may have

refused to perform the ritual (NaTsYB), as also Abraham considered his word sufficient without rendering a formal oath (cf. 21:23 f.).

31   But he demanded, "Swear to me."
            And he swore to him. Then Israel
            bowed on the head of the bed.

Jacob must have explained that the reason he wanted Joseph to render the oath with the ritual was not that he feared that Joseph might not otherwise fulfill the promise, but that even a Pharaoh could grant such a request only if it was the fulfillment of a solemn oath (RaMBaN, cf. 50:6). After Joseph's oath, the father "bowed" to God (RaDaQ) in gratitude to Him. It seems that during the dialogue Jacob was sitting up (see expos. on 48:2) but now, knowing that he could die in peace, he bowed toward the head of the bed (cf. 49:33), and stretched out. (see ShaDaL; B. Jacob). Then Joseph parted from his father, soon to be summoned back to him.

GENESIS 48

1   Some time afterward, he told Joseph
               "Lo, your father is ill." So he
               took with him his two sons, Manasseh
               and Ephraim.

"He" seems to be the same messenger who (cf. 47:29) had summoned Joseph to Jacob and will again call all the sons to the father's bedside (cf. 49:29). This time only Joseph is told that his father is ill. It was natural for Joseph to take his sons with him to see the ailing patriarch who might soon die and, perhaps, to receive his blessing (NaTsYB).

2   When he reported to Jacob, "Joseph
               your son is about to arrive," Israel
               summoned his strength and seated him-
               self on the bed.

As Judah (cf. 46:28a) had been instructed to announce Joseph's arrival, so was the messenger now. Thereupon Jacob, as "Israel," summons his strength and sits up on his bed. He wants to show his respect for Joseph's exalted position (RaShI) and/or to hide his illness (B. Jacob).

3   Jacob said to Joseph, *"El Shaddai*
               appeared to me at Luz in the land of
               Canaan, and He blessed me."

Joseph remembers the pilgrimage to Luz-Bethel (cf. *Background* 7). He was about fifteen years old when his father took his whole family to watch him fulfill the pledge he had made there, almost thirty years prior to this episode, (cf. *Appendix*

7d) during his flight from Esau (cf. 27:5). For *El Shaddai* see expos. on 43:14a.

4
　　　　"And He said to me, [1] 'I will make
　　　　you fertile and numerous, [2] and
　　　　establish you as *qehal 'ammim*,—a
　　　　sacred league of tribes; [3] and I
　　　　will give this land to your offspring
　　　　to come for an everlasting possession.' "

What God actually promised to Jacob, however, was:

　　　　"I am *El Shaddai*.
　　　　Be fertile and increase;
　　　　A nation, yea, an assembly of nations,
　　　　Shall descend from you.
　　　　Kings shall issue from your loins.
　　　　The land that I gave to Abraham and Isaac
　　　　I give to you;
　　　　And to your offspring to come
　　　　Will I give the land." (35:11ff.).

The deviations (1) and (2) in v. 4 coincide with the wording of Isaac's prayer for Jacob, about to leave for Haran:

　　　　". . . May *El Shaddai* bless you,
　　　　make you fertile and numerous,
　　　　so that you become a sacred league of tribes." (28:3).[1]

Deviation (3) coincides with God's promise to Abraham:

　　　　"I give the land to sojourn in to you
　　　　and your offspring to come, all the land of Canaan,
　　　　as an everlasting possession. I will be their God." (17:8).

Ad (1): This minor deviation is merely in style, caused by the different construction of the two sentences (B. Jacob).

Ad (2): Goy u-qehal goyim, rendered above as "a nation, yea an assembly of nations," a riddlesome phrase, may be the same as *"qehal 'ammim*—a sacred league of tribes." [2]

Ad (3): Jacob's purpose in adding God's words to Abraham, "as an everlasting possession," is to make Joseph impress upon his brothers that their land holdings in Egypt are but temporary and alienable, whereas their eternal homeland is the Land of

Promise (B. Jacob).[3] Turning his mind to its acquisition, he is about to allocate a double share of it to Joseph.

5   "Now then, your two sons, who were
    born in the land of Egypt before I came
    to you in Egypt, shall be mine; Ephraim
    and Manasseh shall be mine on a par with
    Reuben and Simeon."

We-'attah—now then—which always introduces a step in consequence of a situation just expounded,[4] implies that it was through Joseph that the fulfillment of Isaac's prayer about "a sacred league of tribes" became possible. By making him the father of two tribe-heads, as Jacob is the father of eleven, Joseph is now on a par with the patriarch himself, a fourth "Father" (B. Jacob). At the same time, the bestowal of a double portion of the father's inheritance (see Deut. 21:17) makes Joseph the *behor*—Firstborn—(cf. I Chron. 5:1). This aggrandizement, on the other hand, compensates him beforehand for Judah's unique destiny (see 49:8ff., not part of our exposition). Consequently, his progeny will be called "the House of Joseph" (cf. Josh. 18:5; Jud. 1:22, 35 etc). Ephraim and Manasseh will attain equal rights "on a par with Reuben and Simeon" to the "everlasting possession" as *shebet* (or *matteh*)—tribe—or as *mahaneh*—camp—of Ephraim and Manasseh (B. Jacob).[5] Already at this point Jacob gives precedence to Ephraim, as he does later when he blesses the two grandsons (*Pashte DeQra*).

6   "But progeny born to you after them shall
    be yours; in their inheritance they shall
    be called after the name of their brothers.

Such hypothetical younger sons of Joseph are nowhere mentioned. They would be included in the tribes of Ephraim and Manasseh and not receive territorial allotments as independent tribes (RaShI). This stipulation seems merely to assure Joseph's brothers that the adoption of Joseph's sons does not favor them over their sons, but signifies Joseph as *behor*. Jacob knows that since God Himself has so manifestly elevated Joseph, his brothers will no longer resent his decision. And Reuben resigns himself to having lost the *beḥorah.*

7   "And as for me, Rachel died to my sorrow
       in the land of Canaan when I was returning
       from Paddan. It was on the way still some
       distance from Ephrath. There, on the road
       to Ephrath (now it is Bethlehem) did I
       bury her.[6]

With "as for me" (see expos. on 43:14a) Jacob resumes his reminiscences (cf. vv. 3f.). This is the only time that the Torah shows Jacob express his grief over Rachel's death, perhaps because it was so inexpressibly deep and mentionable only now after he had honored her memory by making her the mother of three tribe-heads (Suzanne Lowenthal). "In the land of Canaan," seemingly superfluous, emphasizes that though he could not bury her in Hebron (RaShBaM), still, her grave is in the Holy Land (B. Jacob). Another reason for Jacob's mentioning Rachel here is that for "the House of Joseph" and the tribe of Benjamin her tomb will become as sacred as that at Hebron, where he will rest, will be for all tribes (B. Jacob). The Torah adds "now it is Bethlehem"; in Jer. 31:14 it is called "Ramah."

8   Glancing at Joseph's sons, Israel
       said, "Who are these?"

As some of Joseph's brothers had first stayed in the background before he presented them to Pharaoh (see expos. preceding 47:1), so Joseph's sons had respectfully remained at the back of the room (J. Pardo, cited by his teacher ShaDaL), as Jacob knows. Now he, as "Israel," wants them to approach. Therefore "Israel said," not "asked," "who are these?" Had Jacob thought them to be strangers, he would not have them witness his message, vv. 3-5 (B. Jacob).

9a   Joseph said to his father, "They are
       my sons with whom God has graced me here."

Joseph wants his father to know his gratitude for God's providential guidance and blessing in the foreign country. The grandfather mentioned "Ephraim and Manasseh" instead of naming the older one first. Joseph refrains from "correcting" him and merely says "my sons" (NaTsYB).

9b   "Please take them to me," he said,
           "that I will bless them." [7]

"Take them" indicates that Joseph should lead them by the hand as described in v. 13, so that they will know their father's intention to have the older at the patriarch's right hand.

10a   Now Israel's eyes were dim with age; he
          could not recognize [them]. So he brought
          them closer to him.

It seems that Jacob changed their position which puzzled Joseph. Then he assumed that because "Israel's eyes were dim with age, he could not recognize them," taking Ephraim, who perhaps was taller, to be Manasseh. That is why "he brought them closer to him" so that he could recognize them before blessing them.

10b   He then kissed them and embraced them.

Though he must have recognized them now, he still did not restore their correct position. The usual sequence of "embracing" before "kissing" (cf. 45:27f.; 46:30) is here reversed because he wants to keep them in his arms (B. Jacob).

11   And Jacob said to Joseph, "I had not
          expected to see your face again, and, lo,
          God has let me see even your progeny."

Anxious that the lads regain their right positions, Joseph intercepts the imminent blessing by first expressing his gratitude to his father for his intention to bless the lads after having raised them to tribe-heads.

12   Then Joseph removed them from his knees
          and bowed low, his face to the ground.

13   Now Joseph took the two of them, Ephraim
          on his right hand at Israel's left and
          Manasseh on his left at Israel's right,
          and brought them close to him.

The position of the elder was thus at Israel's right, so that in blessing the lads, his right hand would be on Manasseh's head.[8]

14   Yet as Israel stretched out his right
     hand he laid it on the head of Ephraim,
     the younger, and—crossing his hands—
     laid his left hand on Manasseh's head,
     although Manasseh was the firstborn.[9, 10]

As the exposition of vv. 17ff. shows, it is at this moment that Joseph at last protests. The Torah does not mention it yet here because it was of no avail.

15   And he blessed Joseph, saying,
     "O God, before Whom my fathers
      Abraham and Isaac walked;
     O God, Who has been my Shepherd
      from my birth to this day:

16a   "Charge the angel who has redeemed me
     from all harm to bless the lads."

The lads are not addressed. It is Joseph that is blessed in his sons. This is the meaning of "he blessed Joseph" (RaShBaM). The vocatives "O God" are suggested by TJ. Jacob invokes Him to charge the angel to bless the lads for the sake of his fathers (Sforno). Their merit was having "walked before God," "announcing His coming" (cf. 17:1; 24:40) as a herald walks and calls out before the approaching King (cf. I. Sam. 2:35).[11] For himself Jacob does not claim such merit. Instead, he appeals to God to charge His angel to protect and guide the lads as God has been his "Shepherd" (cf. Ps. 23:1; 28:9; 80:2; Isa. 40:11), an appropriate metaphor in the mouth of the ideal shepherd (A. Dillmann). Jacob recalls the crises in his life and recognizes that the "angels" in his dream (28:12) and those who "met him" (32:2) returning to Canaan after twenty years of exile, "redeemed me from all harm." He implies, as in v. 11, that his pessimism (cf. 37:35; 42:36,38; 43:14; 44:27ff.) turned out to be unwarranted (B. Jacob).

16b   In them be my name recalled,
     And the names of my fathers Abraham
      and Isaac,
     And may they become fish-like multitudes
      in the midst of the land."

Jacob concludes his blessing for Joseph by entreating God a) to aid the lads to become worthy of their paternal ancestors that their way of life exemplify the Fathers (see Sforno), b) to exceedingly multiply their offspring (the verb *weyidgu* seems to be denominative of *dag*—fish—the fertility of which is proverbial) "in the midst of the land," viz. while still in the land of Egypt.

17-19a   [17]When Joseph noticed that his father
         was about to lay his right hand on Ephraim's
         head, it displeased him. He grasped his
         father's hand to bring it away from Ephraim's
         head to Manasseh's [18] and said to his
         father, "Not so, father! For the other is the
         firstborn; lay your right hand on his head."
         [19a] But the father refused.

Yashit is future tense and should not be translated "laid (his hands)" but "was about to lay." [12] This indicates that vv. 17-19a are a parenthesis, relating what happened before Jacob pronounced his first blessing: To make sure that no error would again occur, Joseph had re-arranged the lads' position. As he noticed his father's obvious insistence to again give preference to the younger by "crossing his hands" (cf. v. 14) Joseph finally spoke up. As mentioned in the exposition on v. 14, the Torah postponed relating this incident because "the father refused" to heed Joseph's words. And his reason for not even replying to Joseph is that his first blessing would evenly apply to both lads.

19b   Then he said, "I know, my son, I know.
         He too shall become a people, and he
         too shall be great. But his younger
         brother will surpass him and his
         descendants shall attain the diversity
         of a whole nation." [13]

Only as he is about to give preference to the younger does Jacob reply, saying "my son" to express his affection for Joseph, irrespective of his seemingly presumptuous "not so, father!"

The words "great" and "surpass" do not connote quantity but importance and fame.[14]

20   So he blessed them on that day, saying
           "By you shall Israel invoke blessings,
           saying: God make you like Ephraim and
           Manasseh." Thus he put Ephraim before
           Manasseh.

"You" in "By you . . ." is singular, meaning "By each of you" (Speiser). In "God make you like Ephraim and Manasseh" the emphasis seems to be on the word "and," so that the Israelite father's prayer for his son will be that God may endow him with the fused virtues of Ephraim and Manasseh. "Putting Ephraim before Manasseh" reflects Ephraim's greater promise (cf. v. 19b) for which the prophetic spirit charges the patriarch to give his blessing. Neither Ephraim, however, nor Manesseh becomes the "Firstborn," for both are "on a par with Reuben and Simeon" (cf. v. 5). In Num. 26:28ff.; 34:23f. Manasseh is listed before Ephraim.

21   Then Israel said to Joseph, "Behold
           I die. But God will be with you and
           bring you back to the land of your
           fathers."

The words "you" are in the plural, referring to God's assurance to Jacob, before he left Canaan, concerning his descendants (cf. 46:3). As in v. 7, "As for me," heading the next verse, is a solemn declaration in reference to another event in Jacob's past.

22   "As for me, I bestow upon you *Sheḵem,*
           uniquely above your brothers, which I
           acquired from the hand of the Amorite
           with my sword and bow."

The attempt to ascertain the meaning of this sentence should be preceded by pondering why Jacob bought the field facing Shechem (cf. 33:18f.). Were not the patriarchs enjoined (cf. 17:8; 28:4, etc.) not to acquire land in Canaan but to remain "sojourners"? True, Abraham did buy the field at Hebron (cf. ch. 23), but that was needed[15] as a burial place, not for settlement. A reflection upon 33:20 may answer this question: "There he set up an altar, calling it *El-'elohe-Yisrael,* the Lord, God of Israel." The Hebrew verb form used here for "setting up" occurs nowhere else for erecting an altar, but it does occur in 35:20: "Jacob set up a pillar over her grave; it is the pillar at Rachel's grave to this day." That is why B. Jacob wonders whether Jacob may not have hallowed the altar-monument at Shechem as another sepulchre site, besides Machpelah, perhaps for Rachel, since only two more graves were available at Machpelah, and the last, next to his own, would belong to Leah, his first wife. B. Jacob adds that since Jacob had to leave Shechem (cf. ch. 34) he had to give up his original plan and now offers the site to Joseph for his interment. That Joseph accepted this field for his burial is clearly shown in 50:25b. Also Joshua understood it this way:

> And the remains of Joseph, which the Children of
> Israel brought up out of Egypt, buried they in
> Shechem, in a parcel of ground which Jacob bought . . .
> for 100 *qesitah;* and it became the inheritance of
> Joseph's descendants. (Josh. 24:32).

It may well be that Jacob intended the field not merely for Rachel's interment but also for himself and Leah. One ought to consider that Jacob became the patriarch "Israel" only after the tragedy of Dinah had purged him. Though 31:18 relates that when Jacob left Laban, he intended "to come to Isaac his father to the land of Canaan," it seems that after he had entered Canaan—and he had learned about his mother's death—he was not at all eager to be reunited with his father, for it must have taken ten years to reach his father after leaving Laban (cf. *Appendix* 7d). Since Jacob's return to Isaac was caused by the event reported in ch. 34, *he may originally not have wanted to leave Shechem at all but stay there for good.* The *Midrash* considers Jacob's naming the altar-monument on the field facing Shechem, *El-'elohe Yisrael* an impious arrogation since his name of honor was at that time merely predicted (cf. 32:29), not yet ratified, and sees God's punishment for him in what happened to Dinah.[16] The *Midrash* might have added that Jacob had moreover failed to fulfill his pledge (cf. 28:22) and to visit his father. Thus also Rachel's death, due to the strain of travelling during the family's flight from Shechem, might not have occurred, had Jacob not stayed on in Shechem. On the other hand, Dinah's misfortune and its ghastly consequences seem to have had a cathartic effect upon Jacob which made him ready to heed God's admonishment (cf. 35:1ff.). It was only then that he extracted the idols from his family before he took his household with him on his pilgrimage to Luz-Bethel. Only then and there did God consider him worthy of the name "Israel" and of His consummate blessing (cf. 35:9-12).

What remains enigmatic are the words following "I bestow upon you Shekem." The reason for spelling the last word Shekem and not Shechem is that it is followed by the words 'aḥad 'al aḥeka, lit.—one over your brothers—indicating that Shechem is punned with Shekem—shoulder—[17] perhaps implying that the bestowal of the field at Shechem would make Joseph tower "one shoulder above your brothers" (cf. I Sam. 9:2; 10:23). Riddlesome also is the sequence, "which I have acquired from the hands of the Amorite with my sword and bow." The Torah nowhere mentions Jacob's warfare with "the Amorite," wrestling Shechem from them.[18] [Most scholars identify "the Amorite" with the "Hivite" (34:2) who sold Jacob the field (cf. 33:19). In 15:16 "Amorite" stands for all peoples in Canaan.] Ibn Ezra seems to be the first to explain "which I acquired" as a "prophetic perfect," against which A. Dillmann objects that Jacob would not have singled out Shechem and would have used the plural "you" had he indeed beheld and spoken about the state of things after the conquest of that region. Abrabanel suggests that "with my sword and bow" is Jacob's sarcastic reference to those of his sons who committed the massacre at Shechem, whereas when he acquired the land at Shechem, his "sword and bow" were the ways of peace (cf. 33:18).

Jacob thus reminisced about God's blessing him at Luz-Bethel, his loss of Rachel, her funeral and his acquisition of the field at Shechem. With his elevating Joseph by making his sons tribe-heads, with blessing him in them, by blessing Ephraim and Manasseh thereafter and with bestowing the field at Shechem as a sepulchre site, the memorable meeting has come to its end and Joseph leaves his father with his sons.

GENESIS 49:28-31

1-27 These verses are omitted in this interpretation.

28a All these are the tribes of
Israel, twelve in number.

"Twelve" as the number of the Israelite tribes is mentioned throughout Scriptures. Whenever the tribes Ephraim and Manasseh are listed, either Levi is omitted (cf. Num. 1:6ff.; 13:6ff.; Ezek. 48:1ff.) or Simeon is unlisted (cf. Deut. 33:5-25). Both Levi and Simeon appear in Deut. 27:12; That is why in that verse "Joseph" occurs instead of Ephraim and Manasseh.[1]

28b And this is what their father had
spoken about them.

This sentence speaks of what preceded. *Lahem—about* them —refers to the sons as tribe-heads and must not be translated as *to* them, i.e., to the twelve sons as individuals (see B. Jacob; Speiser) to whom the next verse refers.

28c Then he blessed them. He blessed
each of them with a blessing as was
his blessing.

"As was his blessing" seems to refer to the blessing Joseph had received (cf. 48:15ff.). Now the other sons were blessed. "He blessed" is repeated, as "he interpreted" was (see expos. on 41:12). Just as there the repetition indicated an individual interpretation, so the repetition here connotes an individual blessing for each son.

29 Then he charged them and said to them,
"I am about to be gathered unto my
kin. Bury me unto my fathers unto
the cave which is in the field of
Ephron the Hittite."

In addition to the father's charge upon Joseph (cf. 47:29ff.)

all the sons are now enjoined to bring his remains to Canaan and bury him.

30   "In the cave which is in the field
of Machpelah, which faces Mamreh,
in the land of Canaan, which Abraham had bought with the field from
Ephron the Hittite for a burial site."

Chapter 23, particularly vv. 17 and 20, narrated how meticulously Abraham went about securing the title to the field with its cave. Now Jacob briefs all his sons about the location of the cave and states that it was bought by Abraham (to whom it was originally offered as a gift). Furthermore, Jacob emphasizes both here and in v. 32 that not only the cave but also the field was purchased to secure permanent free access to the grave (B. Jacob). This information is to assure the sons that both the cave and the field are their legally secured inheritance (Sechel Tob), in case of litigation by people who might have seized this property during their seventeen years' absence from Canaan (Abrabanel).

31   "Unto there they buried Abraham and his
wife Sarah. Unto there they buried Isaac
and his wife Rebekah, and unto there I
buried Leah."

This parenthesis underlines that the use of the cave confirmed its purpose (Abrabanel): "Unto there" Abraham had buried his wife Sarah (cf. 23:19) and there Ishmael with Isaac had buried Abraham (cf. 25:9). Jacob says "they buried" instead of naming those that did bury Sarah and Abraham, as well as Rebekah and Isaac, since he did not want to mention Ishmael, because he himself was not in Canaan when Rebekah died, and because he did not want to mention Esau with whom he buried Isaac (cf. 35:29; Sechel Tob; RaMBaN). Abraham is mentioned before Sarah and Isaac before Rebekah, though both women pre-deceased their respective husbands, to pay honor to the Fathers (Sechel Tob).[2]

32   "The field and the cave in it,
bought from the Hittites."

"The Hittites" (23:7) are the people of Ephron who witnessed the purchase. They had never disputed the rights of Abraham's family to the cave. Again (see expos. on v. 30) the field is also mentioned.

33   When Jacob finished charging his sons,
      he drew his feet unto the bed, expired,
      and was gathered unto his people.

"Finished charging" may have included other last testament utterances (Tseror Hamor) made while Jacob was still sitting up, retaining his mental and physical vigor, till his last word before "he drew his feet unto the bed" (RaShBaM).

In reporting the death of Abraham (cf. 25:8), of Ishmael (cf. 25:17) and of Isaac (cf. 35:29) the words "and he died" are added. From its omission here R. Johanan derives the homily to Jer. 30:10, "For lo, I will save you from afar, and your seed from the land of their captivity; and Jacob shall again be quiet and at ease, and none shall make him afraid": R. Johanan said, "Jacob is compared to his seed: As they are alive, so is he!" [3]

GENESIS 50

1   Then Joseph threw himself upon his
                 father, weeping and kissing his face.

This is the rendition of *NEB,* preferable to the literal translation, "Joseph flung himself upon his father's face and wept over him and kissed him." That Joseph closed the father's eyes[1] is implied (Pashteh deQra). It seems that such honor is reserved beforehand to the survivor acknowledged to have been closest to the departed. After Joseph had given the patriarch the parting kiss (cf. I Kings 19:20; Ruth 1:14) the other children, it seems, did the same (J. H. Hertz).

2   And Joseph ordered the physicians in
                 his service to embalm his father. So
                 the physicians embalmed Israel.

To avoid heathen cults, Joseph did not employ professional embalmers.[2] Instead of "and they did so," the Torah reports, "the physicians embalmed Israel," which seems to indicate that Joseph informed them and the public after his father's death that "Israel" was his God-given name of honor, though, from now on the father is no longer mentioned by either name (B. Jacob).

3   For him they added forty days, for
                 this is the full period of embalming.
                 Thus the Egyptians bewailed him for
                 seventy days.

The "seventy" days, mentioned by Herodotus (II 86-88) are obviously the above "forty" days, added to the minimal thirty days, mentioned by Diodorus Siculus (I 91). The mourning period for a Pharaoh lasted seventy-two days.[3] Thus Israel was bewailed almost as long as an Egyptian king (see Abrabanel).

4   When the wailing was over, Joseph
      had spoken to Pharaoh's entourage,
      "Do me this favor, and convey to
      Pharaoh this appeal":

"The Egyptians, who wear no hair at any other time, when they lose a relative, let their beards and the hair on the heads grow long" (Herodotus II 36), presumably prior to the funeral. That is why Joseph could not appear in person before Pharaoh and soon after his bereavement turned to members of the king's household (cf. 45:18) for them to submit his petition to Pharaoh. If it was granted, the cortege could leave right after the conclusion of the wailing period, all preparations previously completed.

5   "My father bound me by his oath, saying,
      'When I die, be sure to bury me in my
      grave that I made ready for myself in
      the land of Canaan.' May I, therefore,
      go up now, bury my father, and
      come back?"

In reality, Jacob did not swear as Abraham did, charging his bondman Eliezer (cf. 24:3) but made Joseph swear (cf. 47:31) which he could have refused to do. Having been bound, however, by Jacob's "oath," Joseph would have been given no choice. That is why Joseph used the above phrase (NaTsYB). Prudently he also paraphrases his father's words as "which I made ready for myself," [4] in keeping with Egyptian mores.[5] Pharaoh, fearing that Joseph may not return from his homeland, is put at ease by Joseph's assurance that he will "come back," (cf. Exod. 5:3ff.; 8:24; 10:8ff., 24; B. Jacob), presumably adding that Israel's sons would leave their little offspring, flocks and herds in Egypt, as v. 8 reports.

6   Pharoah replied, "Go and bury your
      father as his oath has bound you."

Though holding the funeral of a nobleman abroad would have been offensive to Egyptians, Pharaoh, perhaps in a per-

sonal note, permitted it in this unusual case (RaShI; see expos.
on v. 5).

7   Then Joseph left to bury his father;
    and with him went up all the officials
    of Pharaoh who were senior members of
    his court and all of Egypt's dignitaries,

Both words "all" should be understood hyperbolically[6] to
denote the reverence for the patriarch (Sechel Tob) and/or the
respect for his illustrious son (J. H. Hertz).

8   together with all of Joseph's household
    his brother, and his father's household;
    only their little ones, their flocks, and
    their herds were left in the region of Goshen.

"With all . . . his father's household" includes all servants of
his sons (NaTsYB). Joseph obviously provided for the protection of who and of what were left in Egypt.

9   He also brought up with him
    chariots and horsemen; it was
    a very imposing train.

Wa-ya'al in this verse, causative-singular with preposition
'im, is different from *wa-ya'alu 'itto*—they went up with him—
in v. 7. It means "he ordered to accompany him, going up,"
and should not be translated "they went up with him"
(RaShBaM). The chariots and horsemen were to protect the
train and to give battle if the burial should meet armed resist-
ance (*Genesis Rabbah* 100:5; cf. expos. on 49:30).

10   When they arrived at *Goren ha-Atad*
    —the Bramble Threshing Floor, which
    is beyond the Jordan, they held there
    a very great and solemn lamentation;
    and he ordered a mourning period of
    seven days for his father.

Whether "beyond the Jordan" is east or west of the river
depends on the standpoint of the speaker or narrator. In this
case it obviously means east of the Jordan, because v. 13a
reports that Jacob's sons "carried him (across the Jordan)[7]

to the land of Canaan," toward Hebron (B. Jacob).

11 When the Canaanites who lived there
saw the mourning at *Goren ha-Atad,*
they said, "This is a solemn mourning
by the Egyptians." This is why it
was named *Abehl-Mitsraim*—the
Egyptians' Mourning—which is in
Transjordan.[8]

The following verse indicates that the participation of the Egyptian outsiders in these impressive mourning rites was now concluded. Yet they waited for the bereaved ones to return home together with them. (NaTsYB).

12 Then his [Jacob's] sons did for
him as he had instructed them:

13 His sons carried him to Canaan,
and buried him in the cave of
the field of Machpelah, facing
on Mamreh, the field that
Abraham had bought from Ephron
the Hittite for a burial site.

The Egyptians remain in the background. All brothers, now on the same level with Joseph, carry the casket across the Jordan (B. Jacob).

14 After burying his father, Joseph
returned to Egypt, he and his
brothers and all who had gone up
with him to bury his father.

Wherever "father" appeared before the funeral it is in connection with Joseph as if to signify his greater intimacy with him. Otherwise the patriarch is referred to by pronoun. "His" father, instead of "their" is because of Joseph's reassurance to Pharaoh (cf. v. 5). Reversing the marching-order at the funeral procession (cf. vv. 7f.)—as is still Jewish custom—Jacob's house, upon their return, preceded the Egyptians (RaShI). There seems to have been no military activity (see expos. on 49:30; 50:3) because "All who had gone up with him" shows that none of the armed escort was killed.

15a	Then Joseph's brothers saw that their father was dead.
15b	And they said, "What if Joseph hates us? Then he will surely pay us for all the evil we did to him."
16	They sent a message to Joseph, saying, "Your father gave this command [just] before he died":
17a	"So shall you say to Joseph, 'Forgive, I urge you the transgression of your brothers and their sin although they did evil to you.' "
17b	" 'Now then, please forgive the transgession of the servants of the God of your father.' "
17c	While they spoke to him Joseph was in tears.

Prior to interpreting vv. 15-17 it is necessary to discuss the startling assumption by many ancient, later and modern Jewish exegetes that in what v. 17a reports, the tribal ancestors resorted to a prevarication to make peace between Joseph and themselves.[9] There are four reasons for this assumption, which is rejected by most modern exegetes:

1) Jacob's "command" is nowhere mentioned (*Genesis Rabbah* 100:8).
2) Jacob never suspected Joseph of harboring hate or thoughts of revenge against his brothers (RaShI).
3) Had the brothers ever confessed their guilt to their father, they would have implored him to command Joseph directly (RaMbaN).
4) That vv. 16f. are preceded by v. 15 proves that had the brothers not feared Joseph's revenge, they would not have conveyed the "message" to him, though it would have been imperative to do so. This shows that they prevaricated (B. Epstein).

Against this assumption B. Jacob argues that the father must certainly have been apprehensive about the relation of Joseph to the Ten once he was no longer alive. What B. Jacob over-looks is that the "assumption" is based on the premise that the father never learned the brothers' "transgression," though it seems that only RaMBaN and *Pesikta Rabbathi* are explicit about it: RaMBaN on 45:27 asserts that when at last Jacob believed his sons that Joseph was still alive, he simply assumed that Joseph had lost his way looking for his brothers at Shechem (cf. 37:15) where traders kidnapped and sold him to Egypt. Thus neither then nor before or after did the brothers ever tell their father about their transgression. On the other hand, *Pesikta Rabbathi* explicates that neither did Joseph ever tell the father about it. What the above exposition on 45:26f., however, arrives at is that though Jacob did not learn the truth from either the Ten or from Joseph, he fathomed it just the same: Had the brothers upon their second return from Egypt merely told Jacob that they found Joseph alive, the father might well have believed them. "His heart went numb, for he did not believe them" (45:26) because they added, omitting Joseph's own message, that "it is he who is the ruler over . . . Egypt." How could he have believed that it was his Joseph who had suspected them of espionage, had pumped them about Benjamin—who he insisted must be taken from his old father—and had kept Simeon as a hostage! When, however, the brothers precisely cited Joseph's own words, authenticating him as the author, and the father saw the crown carriages (permitted to go abroad only by royal permission). ". . . The spirit of their father surged up and Israel said, 'Enough! My son is still alive'!" He not only knew then that Joseph was indeed alive but the upsurging spirit of "Israel" intuited the answer to the riddle that made him first disbelieve his sons! He recognized that it was the Ten who had caused Joseph's enslavement and that because of this he, "the ruler over the land of Egypt," had first to "test" them before he could disclose himself to them. The word "enough!" implies that since the spirit had given him the answer, he would never ask any of his sons about it. Yet he wanted to help bring about a complete reconciliation and to give his charge the greatest impact, he made it "[just] before he died" (cf. v. 16).

Holding that the Ten truthfully reported Jacob's command,

the following is a rebuttal to the cited objections to this interpretation:

Ad 1): Even within the Narrative (see expos. on 37:21; 42:12,16,34b; 43:3,7), as elsewhere in the Bible, important information is given subsequently and indirectly.

Ad 2): Jacob surely knew Joseph's magnanimity, yet he also knew the Ten's obsessive pride. He wanted them to be able to live at peace with themselves after his protective presence no longer would be with them, by helping them to ask for Joseph's forgiveness.

Ad 3): The Ten may well have entreated their father to give Joseph his behest directly. If he refused, it was not only to avoid the impression that he had impelled Joseph (B. Jacob), but also to make them overcome their pride. One of the reasons for Joseph's tears (cf. v. 17c) is that he was so deeply moved not only by the father's anxiety but also by how he helped the Ten to express their guilt and plead for forgiveness by, as it were, doing it for them.

Ad 4): B. Epstein's is the only strong argument underlying the assumption of the brothers' "prevarication." It requires a longer refutation, implied in the first exposition on vv. 15a-17b:

Ad v. 15a: Though it was an agonizing shock for the Ten when they realized from the father's order that he knew about their "transgression" and "sin" (cf. v. 17a)—which, naturally, made them assume that it was Joseph who had told him about it—they did not yet fear Joseph because of the father's protective presence, recalling that Joseph had "kissed all his brothers, and wept over them" (45:15a) after he had told them, "Be not grieved and angry at yourselves . . . for . . . it was not really you but God Who sent me here" (45:5,8a). Nevertheless, they were ready to obey their father who wanted them to make up after his death for what they had left undone, to confess their guilt to Joseph and to ask for his forgiveness. They were convinced that this would add to Joseph's kindly feelings for them. Yet, that after the father's death "the brothers saw that their father was dead," indicates the traumatic effect of his death upon them. For whatever changes they imagined (cf.

RaShI on v. 15) having noticed in Joseph's attitude to them, they were one by one overcome with fear, as they found out when they felt the need to consult one another.

Ad v. 15b: They recall that after their own father had deprived his brother of his blessing, "Esau hated Jacob and said to himself, 'When the time of mourning for my father is at hand, I will kill my brother' " (cf. 27:41): Joseph may merely have pretended not to bear any grudge against them, to spare the father the anguish of seeing them punished. Though Joseph is no Esau—and would "if he hates us" not kill them—he still would "surely pay us for all the evil we did to him," by selling them as slaves as they had caused him to become a slave. Moreover, their fear is confirmed by what they only now recall: Hadn't Joseph refrained from declaring his forgiveness when he disclosed himself to them? Now their father's order appears to them in a new light: While before his death, its fulfillment would have run counter only to their pride, now they are eager to make use of it as a protection against Joseph's revenge.

Ad. v. 16: As Jacob did not dare to approach his brother directly but "sent messengers ahead to his brother Esau" (32:4ff.) to appease him before coming before him in person, so the Ten sent word to Joseph. But whereas Jacob sent gifts with his servants who conveyed his own words, the Ten have first the father's words sent instead.

Ad v. 17a: These are the father's words, not those of v. 17b (Abrabanel). Jacob appeals to his son to forgive the Ten, being his brothers.

Ad v. 17b: These are the Ten's own words, added to the father's, both conveyed, perhaps, by Benjamin, who by now naturally knew all about the matter, and Reuben of whom Joseph had learned (cf. 42:22) that he had opposed the plot. *They* do not use the father's words "your brothers," because they had acted so unbrotherly (S. R. Hirsch). Yet what they substitute for it, "the servants of the God of your father," gives their appeal even greater, nay, greatest power: All brothers are committed to their father's God Who expects each member of

His covenant not to bear any grudge against his kin. Besides, they omit the father's "did evil unto you."

Ad v. 17c: Upon these words, the brothers learn, Joseph said nothing, except that "while they spoke to him Joseph was in tears." The Ten assume that Joseph weeps because of his sorrow not to be able to fulfill his beloved father's behest since he feels that justice requires his brothers' punishment.

In reality Joseph cried for altogether different reasons: The first reason is that he heard words of his father from, as it were, his grave. He is deeply moved learning the father's anxiety about the Ten's future relation to him and the father's sagacity to express *for them,* as it were, their plea for forgiveness. He is distressed that the brothers must assume that *he* revealed their crime.[10] He is shocked that they fear his revenge and recognizes that, had they ever confessed to their father, they would not now suspect him of insincerity when he expressed his affection at his disclosure. What stirs him most is their declaration to have become "the servants of the God of your father," thereby having become "the Children of Israel" in the fullest sense, the germ cell of the "sacred league of tribes."

18   Then the brothers also went to him,
                flung themselves before him and said,
                "Oh, if we would but be your slaves!"

Though the brothers are convinced that Joseph will retaliate, his tears give them the nerve to approach him now directly. In their most contrite self-surrender they implore him to make them his own slaves, rather than sell them to cruel masters.[11]

Joseph's response opens up the profoundest *Torah* of the Narrative. Yet it is exceedingly condensed and requires the keenest scrutiny:

19a   But Joseph replied to them, "Have no fear!"

He recognizes that they misunderstood his reason for not having replied to his father's and their own plea, assuming that he will punish them now. That is why he first assures them that they need not fear his revenge.

19b   "For am I in the place of God?"

"For" introduces his real reason for having abstained from declaring his forgiveness. "Am I in the place of God?" are the same words his father once said to Rachel, reprimanding her for her folly (cf. 30:12). Yet Joseph uses for "I" a different pronoun, contrasting it with his father's words, as if to say, "Neither am *I* in the place of God," and giving his exclamation a much deeper meaning: "Neither I nor any human being may dare to arrogate what is exclusively God's" (Chaninah Maschler). Only God forgives the *ba-'al teshuvah* for the wrong he did to a person after having told him his sorrow and made good for it.[12] But human beings ought not ask one another for forgiveness, nor may they grant it. Though also in I Sam. 15:25; 25:28 a person pleads for another's forgiveness, the Bible of Judaism nowhere shows man forgiving man. On the other hand, cf. I Sam. 24:17ff.; Prov. 24:17; 25:21f.; Exod. 23:4f. Moreover, though Deut. 32:35 says of God, "Mine are vengeance and recompense," Lev. 19:17f. commands:

> You shall not hate your brother in your heart, [but] reprove, reprove your neighbor lest you incur guilt because of him. Neither take revenge nor bear grudge against your kinsfolk, but act lovingly to your neighbor as to yourself, I am YHWH.

This is precisely what Joseph's "Am I in the place of God" anticipates which, moreover, has been his constant fearful query, underlying the whole strategy in his dealings with his brothers since his first encounter with them in Egypt: He wanted to be God's instrument, never His substitute.

20   "Besides, you meant evil against me, but
       God meant it for good [—as it has turned
       out—] to save many people alive."

At his self-disclosure (cf. 45:1ff.) the brothers had said nothing about their guilt towards Joseph, though they had implicitly referred to their sin against God (cf. expos. on 44:16b). At that time, anyway, he wanted them to recognize that God is not only the Lord of Justice but also of Providence Whose design they had served (cf. expos. on 45:8). Now, however, after they had acknowledged their guilt towards him, Joseph has to add his view about it. He consents to their abstaining from endorsing the father's assertion that the Ten "did evil" (cf. expos. on v. 17b) by reducing their guilt to "evil intent." In the same breath, moreover, he discloses what he himself may then not yet have understood. It transcends ancient "wisdom," to wit, "A man's mind plans his way but YHWH directs his step" (Prov. 16:9), or "Man proposes, God disposes." The sublimity of his insight is expressed in the word "besides," preceding "you meant evil against me," and in the words which follow, "but God meant it for good. . . ." *This "besides," just a one-letter-particle in Hebrew, marks the fulcrum of the whole Narrative* (B. Jacob): Joseph teaches that at times, as here, God uses man's very transgression to serve His salvational purpose. Part of that purpose here was not merely—as he said to his brothers seventeen years before (cf. 45:7)—"to secure for you posterity on earth, and to save you alive for an extraordinary deliverance," but as he sees it now—twelve years after the lapse of the famine—"to save many people alive," not only the Jacob clan but all the many people alive," not only the Jacob clan but all Egyptians and many foreigners.

21a   "Now then, have no fear!"

In v. 19a "Have no fear!" preceded his reasoning why they need not fear him. "Now then, have no fear!" sums up v. 20: Because God's using their hatred, envy and evil intent[13] "for good" implies His forgiveness, they need neither fear God![14] At the same time "now then" introduces Joseph's "lifting his brothers' face," cf. note 12:

21b   "I will sustain you and your children."
             And he comforted them and spoke kindly to them.

He first assures them that everything will remain as it was while the father was alive (cf. 45:11; 47:12). Then "he comforted them," helping them no longer to reproach themselves for their past. "He spoke kindly to them," lit. "he spoke on their heart,"[15] means that he endeavored to win their affection. At his self-disclosure, before and after "he kissed all his brothers and wept over them" (cf. 45:15), he was not yet able to do so.

22a   Then Joseph, he and the household of his
             father lived [together] in Egypt.

Now he even draws them closer to him for the rest of his life than they had ever been before (Tseror Hamor). At the same time, marking the conclusion of the Narrative, "Joseph . . . lived in Egypt" relates to its prologue, "Jacob lived in Canaan." (cf. 37:1). It begins with "These are the *toledoth* —the History of—Jacob: Joseph was seventeen years old" (37:2ab). The ten *toladoth,* comprising *Genesis* (cf. expos. on 37:2a), give the Israelites an account of their origin. *Toledoth* Ya-'aqov, the last, begins when "Joseph was seventeen years old" and introduces the Book of Exodus. Guided by Providence, Joseph helped "the sons of Jacob" to enter Egypt as "the Children of Israel," united in love for their father and becoming "servants of his God."

22b   And Joseph lived one hundred and ten years.

These first words of the epilogue will also conclude it.

23   Joseph saw the third generation
            of Ephraim's line; also the
            children of Makir, Manasseh's
            son, were born on Joseph's knees.

It seems that Joseph lived to see all the grandchildren of *Ephraim,* whereas of *Manasseh's* grandchildren he saw only the children of Makir, Manasseh's firstborn (cf. Josh. 17:1). They and all these offspring "were born on Joseph's knees" (cf. 30:3), means that he formally and joyfully accepted them into the family.

24   And Joseph said to his brothers,
            "I am about to die, but God will
            surely remember you, and bring you
            up out from this land to the land
            which He promised on oath to Abraham,
            to Isaac, and to Jacob."

Chapter 48:4,21 relates that Jacob had told Joseph about this promise. Yet there should be no doubt that Joseph, knowing all of the Fathers' history, also remembers 22:16ff.; 24:7; 35:12. Above all he knows (see expos. on 45:5ff.) that God caused him to bring his father with his family to Egypt, initiating the fulfillment of His plan, revealed to Abraham. This prediction was "know well that your offspring shall be strangers in a land not theirs, and they shall be enslaved and oppressed . . . and in the end they shall go out . . . and return hither" (15:13). Joseph may have fathomed that God's main reason for making them suffer in the future is that with their redemption His entire people would experience God as a reality and His revelation before entering the Land of Promise. Joseph is the first to speak of "Abraham, Isaac and Jacob," the trio which with the beginning of the Book of Exodus will so often be included in the messages to Moses and to his people (B. Jacob).

25   Then Joseph bound the Children of Israel
    by his oath, saying, "God will surely
    remember you. Then you shall carry up
    my bones from here."

Joseph knows that his brothers will all die in Egypt. That is why he now binds "the Children of Israel," those born and to be born, to return his remains for burial, as Jacob's sons did for his burial, in his homeland, which will become theirs forever. Moses will not be among those privileged to enter it, but when "the Israelites went up . . . out of the land of Egypt, Moses took with him the bones of Joseph, who had bound on oath the Children of Israel, saying, 'God will surely remember you. Then you shall carry my bones from here with you' " (Exod. 33:19).

This passage is not to be understood to mean that nobody in Israel, except Moses, thought of taking care of Joseph's remains, but, on the contrary, all the Israelites, mindful of their duty toward Joseph, thought to honor him best by allowing their great leader Moses to take charge of the body of their dead leader. Similarly, when Israel subsequently entered the Holy Land, the descendants of Joseph did not think that the burial of their ancestor concerned only them, but saw to it that the entire nation participated in it" [16] (cf. Josh. 24:32).

26   Then Joseph died at the age of one
    hundred and ten years. He was
    embalmed and placed in the coffin
    in Egypt.

Throughout the epilogue (cf. vv. 23-26) Joseph is the only subject, but instead of being referred to by the personal pronoun, his name appears again and again. It indicates how much the Torah regrets to part from this noble and great man who in spite of all his honors and the splendor of the court remained the truest "son of Israel," faithful to his people and its legacy (B. Jacob). His lifespan, already given in v. 22, is, perhaps, repeated because "one hundred and ten years" was viewed by the Egyptians as the ideal lifetime of a man,[17] and/or because, though Joseph lived to see many offspring, his life was shorter than his brothers' for "Dominion buries him who exercises it." [18] In Hebrew the word for the "Ark" of the Covenant, the receptacle for the Tablets of the Decalogue, is the same word as used here, and nowhere else, for "coffin," Joseph's sarcophagus. Jewish Tradition gives the reason: "He who is enshrined in the one, fulfilled the commandments enshrined in the other."[19]

The definite article before "coffin" indicates that it was prepared by Joseph (Ibn Ezra) and/or it refers to "the" coffin as used in Egypt (A. Dillman). Significantly, the last Hebrew word of the epilogue and of Genesis reads "in Egypt." It prepares the mind for the new era that awaits the Israelites in Egypt, and for the great event of the Exodus (J. H. Hertz).

Appendix

The first six sections explicate chronological data from the Narrative itself. Part 7 attempts to approximate them through speculation.

¶1. Joseph was born at the lapse of Jacob's second septenary of service for Laban (cf. 30:22ff.). Since Jacob left Haran at the end of 20 years with Laban (cf. 31:41), Joseph was then six years old.

¶2. Reuben, Simeon, Levi and Judah, Jacob's first children, born by Leah (cf. 29:32-35), were then twelve, eleven, ten and nine years old, respectively.

¶3. After Judah's birth, Leah "stopped bearing," (30:9). Following the example of her seemingly barren sister (cf. 30:1-8), Leah gave Jacob her maidservant Zilpah as a concubine, adopting her sons Gad and Asher (cf. 30:10f.). Then, when Leah was again blessed with children, her fifth son, Issachar (cf. 30:11) must have been as old as Joseph and her sixth and seventh children, Zebulun and Dinah (cf. 30:19-21) less than one and two years younger than Joseph, respectively. Dinah was thus in her fifth year when her family left Laban's homestead.

¶4a. Joseph was abducted on his trip from Hebron when he was 17 (cf. 37:2 and 37:28ff.). It was 22 years later that his father was reunited with him in Egypt: Joseph was a slave till the age of 30 when Pharaoh elevated him (cf. 41:46). Jacob came to Egypt two years after the famine started, (cf. 45:11) nine years after Joseph's elevation, which was followed by the seven bountiful years (cf. 41:53).

¶4b. Joseph was thus 39 years old at the time of their reunion. Jacob was then 130 years old (cf. 47:9), and therefore

91 when Joseph was born, 108 when he disappeared. At that time Isaac was 168 since he was 60 years old when Jacob was born (cf. 23:26). Since he reached the age of 180 (cf. 35:28), Joseph was sold into Egypt 12 years before Isaac's funeral, which was one year before he left the Tower and was elevated.

¶4c. We know that Reuben and Judah were six and three years older, respectively, than Joseph (cf. *Appendix* 2). They were thus 45 and 42 when they came to Egypt with their families. For Benjamin's age then, cf. *Appendix* 7).

¶4d. Jacob died at the age of 147, having stayed with Joseph in Egypt for the last seventeen years of his life (cf. 47:28) just as Joseph had been with his father for the first seventeen years of his life.

¶5. The following events occurred in the years between Jacob's leaving Haran with his family and their arrival at his father's homestead in Hebron:

   a) The preparations for and the encounter with Esau (cf. 32:4-33:16).
   b) The journey to and stay at Succoth (cf. 33:17).
   c) The journey to and stay at Shechem (cf. 33:18-35:4).
   d) The pilgrimage to Luz-Bethel (35:5-15).
   e) Rachel's death on the way to Bethlehem, after she had given birth to Benjamin (cf. 35:16-20).
   f) The journey to and stay at Migdal-eder (cf. 35:21-22).
   g) The journey from Migdal-eder to Hebron (cf. 35:27).

¶6. Since Jacob was anxious to reach his father's homestead after his departure from Shechem, particularly after Benjamin's birth, and since Rachel could not possibly have conceived her second child after leaving Shechem, she must already have been pregnant. Thus the pilgrimage to Luz-Bethel, the journey toward Bethlehem, the mourning for Rachel and the journey to Hebron via Migdal-eder (cf. *Appendix* 5d-5g) took less than nine months. We know that Benjamin was already born before Joseph was abducted. But how much older was Joseph than Benjamin? How old was Benjamin when he came to Egypt with his family? The answer follows.

¶7a. An ancient tradition is that Rachel had to wait 12 years for the birth of her second son.[1] Another ancient source implies that Benjamin was 9 years younger than Joseph.[2] BT *Megillah* 17a implies that he was less than eight years younger.[3]

¶7b. Ibn Ezra remarks in his exposition on 33:20, "To my mind it stands to reason that Jacob tarried in Shechem for many years, for Dinah was not yet seven years old; also Simeon and Levi [who avenged their sister's violation by killing the male Shechemites] were little [when they arrived in Shechem]" (translation the author's). Ibn Ezra obviously implies that Dinah was in her fifth year when the family left Haran (cf. *Appendix* 3) and that before coming to Shechem Jacob stayed for two years in Succoth, for there he "built a house for himself and made stalls for his cattle." (cf. 33:17).[4] Dinah must have been at least 15 when Joseph was abducted at 17, nor could she have been younger than 14 when violated. The "many years" the family stayed in Shechem could thus not have been more than about seven. This *Appendix* accepts the assumption of F. J. Delitzsch[5] that Dinah "was in her fourteenth, Simeon in his twenty-first, and Levi in his twentieth year" at the time of the tragedy, so that Benjamin was born when Joseph was 15, thus 24 when he arrived in Egypt with his family.

¶7c. Hence Joseph was about 16 when the family arrived in Hebron.

¶7d. This was about 10 years after they had left Haran and about 30 years after Jacob had left his father and arrived in Haran.

¶7e. Thus they stayed in Hebron for about 23 years.

NOTES to Preface

1. Goethe, *Truth and Fiction* I, 4.

2. T. Mann, *Joseph and his Brothers*, 4 vols.

3. Joseph's entering Egypt prefigures the Israelites' enslavement there.

4a. G. von Rad, *Das Erste Buch Mose*, 31f.

4b. *Ibid., Genesis*, 11.

5. E. Simon, (ed.), *Franz Rosenzweig, Briefe*, 581ff.

6. N. N. Glatzer, *Franz Rosenzweig, His Life and Thought*, 158.

7. Note the intriguing "conclusion" of J. Vergote, *Joseph en Égypte*, 207-213. He holds that the Narrative is based on a tract from the hand of Moses:

> If we had to find in the early books of the Bible the national epic of the Jewish nation, it is to the Joseph Story that we would be inclined to attribute such a function. Would not he who created this people by liberating them from foreign bondage also have the desire to give them the character which made them aware of their unity, and assigned each of their members a place? (Cited by D. B. Redford, *A Study of the Biblical Story of Joseph*, 190).

Yet though Vergote's contribution to research on the famous Egyptological elements in the Narrative is indisputable, his dating them back to the Nineteenth Dynasty under Ramses II, "the Pharaoh of Oppression," has found few followers.

8. M. Himmelfarb, *Commentary*, XLII (1966), 72.

9. M. M. Kaplan, *Reconstructionist*, XXX, (May 15, 1964), 16b.

10. N. M. Sarna, *Understanding Genesis*, 1966, XXIV f.

11. Though the subject of my book is not the "genesis" of the Narrative, but its *content* as it has come down to us, mention should be briefly made of P. Volz and W. Rudolph, *Der Elohist als Erzaehler*. Their investigation led to the sensational denial of an Elohist source in Genesis. Rudolph deals with the Narrative. His findings are mainly based on B. Jacob, *Quellenscheidung und Exegese*, a keen analysis of the pivotal 37th chapter and other parts

of the Narrative. Bentzen, (*Introduction to the Old Testament*, II, 46f.) and others rejected Rudolph's rebellion against the traditional school of Julius Wellhausen. But Mowinkel, whom Bentzen calls "the unsurpassed master today," [vol. I, 103] writes, "I consider Rudolph's arguments and demonstrations of the Joseph Story's literary unity cogent. The whole narrative shows a clear and coherent progression (translation the author's). (See S. Mowinkel, *Erwaegungen zur Pentateuch Quellenfrage*, 61ff.).

Whybray regrets that Rudolph's thesis still "has too often been rejected without receiving the attention it deserves." (See R. N. Whybray, *VT*, XVII (1958) 528, n.1) Instead of explicitly discussing whatever Rudolph still considers a "gloss," dislocation," "insertion" (all summed up in his *Elohist*, 176) and two additional "erroneous glosses" seen by Mowinkel *Erwaegungen*, 62), my exposition will implicitly show them as nonexistent. For explicit discussion of Source-Criticism-items, see my expos. on 37:28, n. 29; 37:1, n. 2; 37:3a, n. 7; 41:46a, n. 30.

12. "Torah" will henceforth appear without italics, like Gospel, Koran, Bhagavad-gita, etc. See B. De Pinto, *JBL* 86, LXXXVI (1967), 154f. who refers to M. Buber, *Two Types of Faith*, 56f., and to A. J. Heschel, *God in Search of Man*, 325f.

13. E. A. Speiser, *Genesis*, 341.

14. Cf. R. C. Collingwood, *The Idea of History*, 231-249.

15. I have endeavored to refer each time to the first proponent of the respective explanation.

16. L. Ginzberg, *The Legends of the Jews*, 7 vols.

17. B. Jacob, *Das Erste Buch Der Torah, Genesis*.

NOTES to Background

1. The Torah mentions this as a reproach to Jacob. His father and grandfather lived in "tents," according to God's word that before their offspring should inherit Canaan, they were to live there as "sojourners" only (cf. 17:8; 23:4; 26:3; 28:4; B. Jacob).

2. For a masterly summary of the Torah's Abraham-tradition see M. Buber, *Judaism* V (1956), 291-305.

3. God's promise to Abraham to become a great nation and to inherit Canaan (cf. 12:2, 7; 13:14ff.; 15:5, 7, 18; 22:16ff.) was renewed to Isaac (cf. 26:2ff.) and to Jacob (cf. 28:13ff.). God will repeat it to Jacob after he has left Shechem (cf. 35:9ff.). Thus, it occurs ten times. About the "covenant," cf. 15:18; 17:2,4,7,11, 13,14,19.

4. Cf. I Chron. 5:1; L. Ginzberg, *Legends*, I, 415f.

NOTES to Gen. 37

1. Cf. *Preface* E.

2. Recent scholarly objections to MT's beginning of the Narrative with 37:1, claim that 37:1 and 2a still belong to ch. 36. Yet they overlook that the Torah *contrasts* 37:1 with 36:8,43 and 37:2a with 36:1,9. Only 35:23-26 are "parallel" with 36:1ff., 9ff.

3. Cf. B. Jacob, *Genesis* on 2:4a: *We-'eleh toledoth* merely introduces genealogies. They are a) Noah's sons (cf. 10:1-11:9); b) Terach's (cf. 11:27-25:11); c) Ishmael's (cf. 25:12-18); d) Isaac's (cf. 25:19-35:29); e) Esau's (cf. 36:1-43).

'Eleh toledoth, however, introduces the emergence of a) Heaven and Earth (cf. 2:4-4:26); b) of Adam (cf. 5:1-6:8, except that here the more explicit "This is the Book of Adam's *toledoth*" appears); c) of Noah (cf. 6:9-9:29); d) of Shem (cf. 11:10-26); e) of Jacob (see above).

Toledoth in 2:4 was aptly translated by LXX as "Genesis." From this word the first Torah Book got its name.

For another ancient attempt to explain the difference between the two Hebrew terms see *Genesis Rabba* 12:3, repeated in *Exodus Rabba* 1:2; 3:7; 9:2.

4. See D. Rosin in *Jubelschrift zum 90. Geburstag von L. Zunz,* 39ff.

5. Cf. P. Joüon, *Grammaire de l'hébreu biblique,* 121f.

6. Cf. 48:15; Hosea 4:16; Isaiah 40:11. See also *EBI,* vol. VI, Anthology, par. 22f.; Abrabanel; A. B. Ehrlich, *Randglossen zur Hebraischen Bibel I."*

7. Only *yeled zequnim* (44:20) is a late-born child. Already 30:10ff. should have cautioned that *ben zequnim* means something else, for only five of Jacob's children were older than Joseph (cf. *Appendix* 3). *Ben* is not only "the son of" but also introduces a word of quality, characteristic etc., cf. 15:2; Deut. 25:2; I Sam. 14:52; II Sam. 12:5; Isa. 5:1; 14:12; Ps. 89:23; Jonah 4:10. For nine other *ben*-idioms (in the plural) see *BDB* 121b, 8. Also *zaqen* is not only "an old man," but can connote "sage, elder, authority" (cf. 24:2; Isa. 9:14; BT *Qidushin* 32b).

Already TO, preceding RaDaQ and RaLBaG, had in mind that the idiom *ben zequnim* means something like "a mature person, a born leader."

8. Cf. Biberfeld, *Universal Jewish History,* II, 126. Cf. also Speiser, *Genesis,* 289f.

9. On the birthright, cf. Sarna, *Understanding,* 184ff.

10. The rendition "they could not speak in peace with him" would require *welo yaklu ledaber 'itto beshalom.* The above translation is according to ShaDaL. Also in Isa. 1:13 and Ps. 101:6 *y-k-l,* 'to be able to,' is used elliptically, "endure" to be supplied.

11. *Hinneh,* lit. "behold!", occurs thrice in this verse. It always introduces a surprising happening, rendered here as "imagine!", "lo" and "suddenly." Cf. E. L. Ehrlich, *Der Traum in Alten Testament* 76.

Gam, lit. 'also,' (or *wegam,* as here), rendered "yea,"—when placed between synonyms or (as here) seeming parallels—is one of the few Hebrew visual aids to express emphasis (B. Jacob).

12. Twice in this verse and again in v. 10, the indefinite absolute is added to the verbform. This expresses emphasis and is rendered here as "really," 'indeed," and "actually."

13. Cf. T. Mann, *Young Joseph* 140f.

14. "For his talk about his dreams" (Speiser, *Genesis;* NJPS) is lit. "for his dreams and for his words." RaShI asserts that "his words" refers to Joseph's reports (cf. v. 2e), brought to their knowledge. RaMBaN views "his words" as his effrontery in telling them his dreams. B. Jacob simply translates *"wegen seiner Träume und seiner Reden davon."*

15. BT *Berakoth* 55b, accepted by Abrabanel, actually avers that he who *interprets* a dream causes its realization. Von Rad in *Genesis,* however, asserts that it is *telling* of a dream that makes its inherent prophecy potent, according to Joseph's brothers (and others in the Bible).

16. While he merely said "another dream," the Torah, to contrast it with Pharaoh's "second" dream (cf. 41:5), emphasizes that Joseph's second dream was "different" (Chaninah Maschler; cf. 41:32, n. 15).

17. Under *'ehahw,* 'his brothers,' is an *etnah,* a cantillation mark to signify the end of a sentence. Over the Hebrew letters of *'et,* the particle to introduce a definitized noun—in this case "sheep"—there are two "diacritical" dots, used in MT to indicate the word underneath is spurious. *Aboth de Rabbi Nathan* I, 34, lists ten such words in the Torah: 16:5, 18:9; 19:33; 33:12, 37:12; Num. 3:39; 9:10;

21:30; 29:15; Deut. 29:28. The best known is in Num. 3.39, indicating that "and Aaron" be stricken.

18. Hebron, Jacob's homestead (cf. 35:27) was on the slope of a mountain (cf. Josh. 14:12, Num. 13:22). Cf. also 38:1, Judah "descending."

19. Cf. BT *Sotah* 11a.

20. Cf. *Genesis Rabbah* 84:13.

21. Cf. Ginzberg, *Legends,* II, 10; V, 328, n. 30.

22. Only in Ps. 105:25 does this same *Hithpa-'el* verbform appear: "He [the Pharaoh of Oppression] turned their [the Egyptians'] heart to hate His [God's] people, *lehitnakkel,* 'to act fiendishly,' against His servants [the Israelites]."

The *Pi–'el*-form of the same verb occurs in Num. 25:18, expressing the lewd seduction of the Israelites by the Midianites (suggested by Balaam) to cause their defeat.

The exposition of 42:7 will show an allusion to the above *Hithpa-'el* verbform.

23. Cf. J. Horovitz, *Die Josephserzaehlung,* 27ff. anticipated by RaMBaN.

24. Such passages are: 9:25f.; 15:2ff.; 16:9ff.; 19:9f.; 20:9f.; 30:27f.; 41:38f.,44; 47:3ff.; Num. 32:2ff.; II Sam. 16:10f.; 17:7f.; II Kings 6:27f. (A. Dillmann, B. Jacob).

25. For literature on these products see D. B. Redford, *A Study of the Biblical Story of Joseph,* 192, n. 7; 193, notes 1-10. For "myrrh" cf. Jer. 8:22; 46:11.

26. Cf. A. B. Ehrlich.

27. For slave trading in Ancient Egypt see Sarna, *Understanding,* 214 and literature cited, 229, notes 26ff.

28. B. Jacob deals at great length in his important *Quellenscheidung und Exegese,* 9ff (summed up in his *Genesis*) with RaShBaM's sensational, novel and elaborate explanation, accepted by many Jewish authorities and by W. Rudolph in *Elohist.*

29. V. 28 has also become the *shibolet* in the controversy about "Documentary Hypotheses" ever since the appearance of J. Wellhausen's *Die Komposition des Hexateuch und der historischen Buecher des Alten Testaments,* 54f. E.A. Speiser, *Genesis,* 291, still follows the "Master": "This single verse alone provides a good basis for a constructive documentary analysis of the Pentateuch. It goes a long way, moreover to demonstrate that E [the "Elohist"] was not just a supplement to J [the "Jahwist"], but an independent and often conflicting source." On p. 294 he writes, "A verse like 28 could hardly have been regarded as satisfactory by a conscientious redac-

tor. . . ." Thus Speiser allocates v. 28a to E, v. 28b to J and 28c again to E. The unbiased reader of the above exposition might become critical of "source-criticism" (cf. *Preface* C).

30. Cf. I. Mendelsohn, *Slavery in the Ancient Near East*, 117.

31. On *Sheol*, 'Netherworld,' cf. Walther Eichrodt, *Theology of the Old Testament*, II, 95, 210.

32. "Medanites" is simply a variant of Midianites as "Dothain," v. 17a, is of Dothan, v. 17b; II Kings 6:13 (Ibn Ezra).

33. "To Egypt" is a shipping term; the Midianites caused Joseph to be sold in Egypt (B. Jacob).

34. For "Potiphar" and "Pharaoh," see Sarna, *Understanding*, 215; lit. cited 229, n. 33.

35. For "courtier," cf. D. B. Redford, *Study*, 51 (39).

36. "Chief executioner" (TO; RaMBaN) seems more correct than other translations.

37. Cf. M. Samuel, in *Jewish Frontier Anthology*, 496f. For Samuel's own later evaluation of Joseph's character, see expos. on 45:26.

NOTES to Gen. 39

1. It was from the Ptolomaic Egyptian priest-historian Manetho (about 280 B.C.E.) that Flavius Josephus (c. 37-95 C.E.) adopted the tradition about the Hyksos. Even many modern historians have retained the assumption that there is a relation between these Hyksos and the Joseph Story. But though L. Ruppert, *Die Joseph-serzählung der Genesis,* München, 1965, 19, notes 22-29, presents an impressive list of scholars who share this view, he also cites J. M. A. Janssen, (*JEOL* XIV (1955/6, pp. 63-72): "The optimistic expectation that Egyptiology would be capable of giving here a definite solution has not been fulfilled."

2. This "Tetragammaton" seems to be a cipher, telescoping God's self-disclosing *ehyeh asher ehyeh,* 'I am that I am, I am that I shall be, I shall be Who I am,' etc. (cf. Exod. 3:14; 3:15; 6:3). It can, moreover, be the contraction of *yihyeh, hayah, howeh,* 'He will be, He was, He is.'

For a deeper understanding of the Exodus passages see B. Jacob, *MGWJ,* LXVI (n. F. 30, 1922), 11-33; 116-138; 180-200; F. Rosenzweig, *Kleinere Schriften,* 182-198; M. Buber, *Moses,* 39-55; and especially, A. Alt, *Essays on Old Testament History and Religion,* 5-100.

3. Later, Joseph will speak of *'elohim* to the two courtiers who were with him in custody (cf. 40:8) and to Pharaoh (cf. 41:16,25, 28,32). Also, Joseph's own steward learned about Him (cf. 43: 23), and even in Joseph's appeal to Potiphar's wife, he speaks of God (cf. 39:9).

4. Cf. 26:28 where the Philistine king, his councilor and the chief of his troops say to Isaac, "We now see plainly that YHWH has been with you. . . ."

5. Cf. 30:27, where Laban says to Jacob, "YHWH has blessed me on account of you." See also Deut. 15:10,14,18; 28:3ff. (B. Jacob).

6. See Ginzberg, *Legends,* II, 43; V, 338, n. 103 A. B. Ehrlich, moreover, refers to such an allusion (about "drinking") in BT

Nedarim 20b, also to Prov. 30:20. Note also the following interpretations:

(1) Joseph was in charge of everything except food, which he must not handle, since the Egyptians would regard it as abominated (cf. 43:32), if touched by a Hebrew (Ibn Ezra).

(2) "With him [Joseph], he [Potiphar] did not know anything [that Joseph would appropriate for himself] except the bread he [Joseph] ate." Other servants had always schemed to enrich themselves at Potiphar's expense (RaMBaN).

(3) Having Joseph around, Potiphar had no concern for anything except for his own meals (RaShBaM).

7. Ginzberg, *Legends* II, 137; V, 365, n. 370.

8. Ginzberg, *Legends* II, 44; V, 338, n. 106.

9. This phrase (cf. Ps. 123:1, 2; Jer. 3:2; Ezek. 33:25) indicates looking entreatingly at a superior being. Abrabanel puts these words into her mouth: "After you have become the ruler of all around here, rule me also." A. B. Ehrlich writes, "The woman, madly in love with her handsome, but chaste slave, knelt before him and, humbly and entreatingly looking up to him, implored him to return her love" (translation the author's).

10. *"Wayema'en"* is derived from *'en*, 'No!' (B. Jacob).

11. Cf. Deut. 22:23ff. Cf. also Exod. 20:15; Lev. 18:20; Deut. 22:14ff. In 38:24, Judah could not know who the "harlot" was; what both did was not considered "sin."

12. Cf. *ANET*, 171c (129); 181b/c (14-16); 196d (198), respectively. See also M. Greenberg, "Postulates of Biblical Criminal Law," *YKJV*, 11ff.; W. Kornfeld, *RB*, LVII (1950), 92ff.

13. Cf. 20:11; 22:12; 42:18; Exod. 1:17,21, etc. See also W. Eichrodt, *Theology* II, 268-277, 322-325.

14. For "as usual"—lit. "as on this day"—see A. M. Honeyman, *VT* II (1952), 85ff. "To the interior (chambers) of the house"— lit. "to the house" (B. Jacob).

15. *Genesis Rabbah*, 87:7.

16. The verb of *vatitpeshehu*, "she seized him," connotes attempted rape (cf. Deut. 22:28: B. Jacob).

17. The Hebrew word used here and in v. 17 for "sporting, making love," is used with a preposition different from the one used in 26:8 where it means actual intercourse (A. B. Ehrlich).

18. See A. Dillmann, *Genesis Critically and Exegetically Expounded*, II.

19. Cf. J. Milgrom, *Conservative Judaism*, XX (1966), 73-79, 76f. For more, see expos. on 42:38, n. 19.

20. H. Gunkel, *Genesis,* lists seventeen similar episodes in ancient texts. Most cited in this context is "The story of the two brothers," fully translated in Erman, *Literatur,* 197-209. J. Horovitz *Josephserzählung,* 98, convincingly refutes its influence on the Narrative.

21. Cf. 2:15; 40:11; Exod. 40:20; Num. 4:12; 5:17; Jer. 32:14.

22. Cf. Vergote, *Joseph,* 25ff.

23. The usual translation of 1) as "he extended kindness to him" would make 2) redundant. Though "caused affection" seems to require the *Hif-il* verbform *wa-yat* (instead of *wa-yet,* used here in *Qal*), the latter sometimes expresses a causative meaning. Why then could not the reverse occur? It thus seems unnecessary to amend MT, with *KBL,* p. 318a.

24. Lit. "He gave his grace in the eyes of the chief jailor," i.e., "He caused the chief jailor to become aware of his grace" (cf. Exod. 3:21; 11:3; 12:36; B. Jacob).

NOTES to Gen. 40

1. Following Sehel Tob and Abrabanel, Sforno asserts that "the cupbearer and the baker" in v. 1 were servants of the "two courtiers . . . the chief cupbearer and the chief baker," mentioned in v. 2. The reason for this assumption, NaTsYB explains, is that otherwise "to their lord"—which can also be read as "their lord*s*"—in v. 1 is superfluous. According to this interpretation, Pharaoh held his courtiers responsible for their servants' offense. (For speculations on this offense, cf. Ginzberg, *Legends,* II, 60; V 342, n. 143). About "A trial for Conspiracy," see *ANET,* 214a-216a. NaTsYB adds that the courtiers themselves would serve the king on the day of their appointment and on other important occasions such as his birthday (cf. 40:20).

2. In a document from the time of Rameses III (12th century), we find butlers sitting as judges. The office of "chief baker" is interesting in the light of what is known as Egyptian gastronomy. No less than fifty-seven varieties of bread and thirty-eight different types of cake are attested in the texts (see Sarna, *Understanding,* 218). For the royal titles "Pharaoh," "Abimelek," "Hiram," and "Agag," see RaShBaM and Ibn Ezra on 41:10.

3. For "custody," cf. 42:17; Lev. 24:12; Num. 15:34.

4. *Yamim,* though literally "days," has the same meaning here as in Exod. 13:10; Lev. 25:29f.: "a year" (cf. RaShBaM and BT *Arakin* 31a). It seems that they were put in custody on Pharaoh's last birthday, which is a day of judgment (see v. 20).

5. My rendition is derived from RaShBaM's interpretation. NJPS translates, ". . . each his own dream and each dream with its own meaning." Speiser translates, ". . . had dreams the same night, each dream having its own meaning." *NEB* has, ". . . each needing its own interpretation." Cf. E. L. Ehrlich, *Der Traum in Alten Testament,* 66f.; A. L. Oppenheim, *The Interpretation of Dreams in the Ancient Near East.*

6. For "distraught," cf. L. Knopf, "Arabische Etymologien zum Bibelwoerterbuch," *VT* IX (1959), 254.

7. Cf. Y. Kaufmann, *The Religion of Israel, from its Beginning to the Babylonian Exile,* 93 (see expos. on 41:8). Cf. also lit. cited by Sarna, *Understanding,* 229, n. 48.

8. *Nitsah* 'its blossom,' means the same as the expected *nitstah,* analogous to *pinnah* for *pintah* (cf. Prov. 7:8) and *middah* for *midetah* (cf. Job 11:9; ShaDaL).

9. "Pardon you," lit. "lift your head" (cf. II Kings 25:27; Jer. 52:31). The petitioner stands or kneels with bowed head while the one on the throne takes him under the chin and raises his head (von Rad). See also lit. cited by E. L. Ehrlich, *Traum,* 69, n. 2.

10. *Salle ḥori,* 'wicker baskets,' (RaShI) (cf. Is. 19:9; Job 30:6). A. S. Yahudah, *Die Sprache* . . . 91ff. assumes that the baskets were named according to the Horites (cf. 14:6; 36:20ff.; Deut. 2:12, 22, etc.). One reason for A. B. Ehrlich's rejection of the customary translation "baskets of white bread" (cf. Esther 1:6; 8:15) is that the *next* verse speaks of the baskets' contents.

11. Cf. E. L. Ehrlich, *Der Traum,* 70f., n. 2 (on aggressive birds); also 72ff. on Midrash, on Josephus, and on the Koran to this text.

12. Cf. lit. cited in A. Dillmann, *Genesis,* 365, n. 4.

13. Cf. Exod. 30:12; Num. 1:2; 4:2,22. See also Yahudah, *Sprache,* I, 59ff.; E. L. Ehrlich, *Traum,* 69, n. 2.

Notes to Gen. 41

1. *Miqets* does not mean "after the lapse of," but "at the end of" (cf. 8:6; Deut. 15:1; Jer. 34:14); (TO; RaShI; B. Jacob).

2. *Shenata-yim yamim*, lit. 'two years of days' (cf. II Sam. 13:23; 14:28; Jer. 28:3,11) means "two full years," analogous to "a month of days" (cf. 29:14). Cf. expos. on 40:4b.

3. The inverted order, *u-phar-'oh holem* instead of *wa-yahalom par-'oh* puts the emphasis on "Pharaoh" (MaLBYM).

4. The text has *'al ha-ye'or*, lit. 'on the Nile,' not "at the bank of the Nile" (cf. v. 17). "On the Nile" is to be understood perspectively: Pharaoh sees himself "above" the Nile, standing on its other side and watching the scene taking place in the foreground, on this side of the Nile. The text has *ye'or*, 'river,' for Nile. Cf., lit. cited in Sarna, *Understanding* 229, n. 45.

5. On an Egyptian relief, seven cows are feeding in a meadow under trees. Cf. A. S. Yahudah, *The Accuracy of the Bible*, 8.

6. For *'ahu*, 'reed grass,' an Egyptian loan word, also for the seven cows motif in Egypt, see lit. cited in Sarna, *Understanding*, 229, notes 46f.

7. For the significance of "seven" in Ancient Egypt, see E. L. Ehrlich, *Der Traum*, 80, notes 1f.

8. "Sturdy," lit. "healthy (robust of flesh)" (E. A. Speiser).

9. "Healthy" translates the same word which in v. 2 was rendered as "sturdy."

10. *Genesis Rabbah*, 89:5; BT *Berakoth* 55b take "in the morning" as the last words of v. 7. For their views concerning "morning dreams" and similar views held by Mohammed, the Hindus, Dante etc., see E. L. Ehrlich, *Der Traum*, 74f., n. 2.

11. For their "interpretations," cf. L. Ginzberg, *Legends* II, 65f.; V, 343, n. 162; E. L. Ehrlich, *Der Traum*, 77, notes 2f. (Note 3 gives information about the Egyptians' "House of Life," an Academy for dream interpretation).

12. The unusual *wa-nahalmah*, 'we dreamt,' referring to 40:5 is (like *wa-na-'ufah*, Ps. 90:10) "historical tempus," cf. E. Kautzsch and A. E. Cowley, *Gesenius' Hebrew Grammar*, par. 49(e).

13. Other occurrences of "listening" as "understanding" are 11:7; 42:23; I Kings 3:9; II Kings 18:26.

14. E. L. Ehrlich, *Der Traum*, 81f., n. 1, lists texts in Talmud, Philo, Sophocles, Plato, etc. which also assert that such double-dreams forecast the imminence of irrevocable events to come. For duplications in general see U. Cassuto, *Genesis*, II, 306ff., 340. Joseph's own dreams forecast distant and separate events because they happened on different nights (RaShBaM; see expos. on 42:9a). 42:9a).

15. If, as most exegetes assume, Pharaoh himself is to appoint the overseers, the task of the "discerning and wise man" remains strangely undefined. Sforno's bracket in v. 34 is supported by D. Rosin (*Jubelschrift*, 42), regarding *ya-'asseh* causative with *we-yafqid;* NaTsYB, moreover, refers to *'oseh* (cf. 39:22) as analogous.

16. RaShBaM seems to be the first to see *himmesh* as a verbalization of *hamesh*, 'five.' "To fifth" thus means the imposition of a 20% grain tax (see expos. on 47:24). This grain, it seems, was to be stored up in the metropolitan crown granaries (see expos. on v. 49).

17. Von Rad refers to Isa. 22:20ff. and II Kings 18:18,37. It seems that this appointment gives Joseph control over the king's personal estates. For comprehensive information about *all* of Joseph's titles according to Ancient Egyptian titularies, for his functions and for Egyptian bureaucracy, see W. A. Ward, *JSS*, V, (1960), 144-50. See also other sources listed by Sarna, *Understanding* 230, notes 56, 59, 60, 62.

18. This translation is according to RaShI (preceded by TO and TJ), referring to 15:2. B. Jacob discusses other attempts to interpret the problematic Hebrew idiom, but supports RaShI by referring also to 15:3; 24:2, the latter implying "authority." For other interpretations, see D. B. Redford, *Study*, 166, n. 4.

19. "I herewith install you," lit. "I have given you" (cf. I Kings 16:2).

20. W. A. Ward, *op. cit.*, refrains from calling him "Grand Vizier."

21. Cf. A. Erman and H. Ranke, *Aegypten und aegyptisches Leben im Altertum*, 174; Sarna, *Understanding* 230, n. 73, cites other relevant literature.

22. For this ritual, cf. B. Jacob and the literature he lists; Sarna, *Understanding* 230, notes 59f.; D. B. Redford, *Study*, 208, notes 5, 6.

23. Ibn Ezra and most other exegetes understand *mirkevet-hamishneh* as "the chariot of the second-in-command," referring to I Sam. 23:17; Esther 10:3; II Chron. 28:7. Yet, the above rendition by B. Jacob (cf. I Kings 20:33; II Kings 10:15) seems preferable. Joseph may have been riding at the side of Pharaoh.

24. About the enigmatic *"Abrek!"*—perhaps Eg. "Attention!"—see lit. cited by B. Jacob; Speiser, *Genesis;* L. Ruppert, *Die Josephserzählung,* 80 n. 33.

25. This means to carry on any activity whatsoever, cf. S. Morenz, *"Joseph in Aegypten," TLZ,* LXXXIV (1959), 408.

26. This is analogous to "I am YHWH" (Exod. 6:2, 6,8, etc.; B. Jacob).

27. For the bestowal of a new name to signify acquired dignity, cf. 17:5; 32:29; 35:10; Num. 13:16; II Kings 23:34; 24:17; Isa. 62:2; 65:15; Jer. 11:16; Zech. 6:12; Dan. 1:7 (B. Jacob). Joseph's new name, according to NJPS, is "Egyptian for 'God speaks; he lives,' or 'creator of life.' " J. Vergote, *Joseph,* 141-146, arrives at *"l'homme qui sait les choses,"* which is strikingly similar to TO, "he for whom the hidden is disclosed." For other literature, see B. Jacob; Sarna, *Understanding,* 230, n. 67; Redford, *Study,* 230, n. 2.

28. "Shone forth" is B. Jacob's rendition for lit. "went out," referring to 19:23 and ancient Near Eastern texts. "Shone forth" would allude to Joseph's having been extolled as "the Sun of Egypt." Ibn Ezra simply reads "Joseph('s name) went out," became famous. E. A. Speiser translates similarly, "became known." (In his note, "Ps. LXXXVI 6" should be corrected to "Ps. LXXXI:6). NJPS has "emerged in charge of."

29. Cf. I Kings 17:1; 18:15; II Kings 3:14; 5:16 (B. Jacob).

30. Cf. 37:2a, which, like 16:16; 17:24f.; 25:26b; Exod. 7:7, is considered by Biblical scholars "a gloss of 'P.' " See also U. Cassuto, *Genesis* II, 306ff.; 316.

31. H. E. Ryle, *The Book of Genesis,* 380b, shows a picture of "Egyptians measuring the wheat and depositing it in the granaries."

32. The verb pattern of *nashani,* presumably, is causative *Pi'el* of the stem *n-sh-h.* Instead of the expected *nishani, nashani* seems to be in consonance with *Menasheh,* 'Manasseh' (B. Jacob).

33. S. R. Hirsch objects that if *n-sh-h,* 'to forget,' underlies this naming, Joseph would have forgotten his beloved father, which Hirsch considers impossible. (Actually, "God has caused me to forget . . ." cannot mean "not remember," since he does mention what he "forgot.") Asserting, instead, that *n-sh-h* here is the

same homonym as in Deut. 15:2; 24:10—where it means becoming a creditor—Hirsch arrives at the original rendition, "God has caused all my trouble and my paternal home to become my creditors," meaning that he is indebted to God that his misfortune turned out to cause his good fortune.

34. Cf. *Genesis Rabbah* 90:6.

35. The above MT-translation requires the bracketed "granaries" and "grain." Yet, they seem too essential to have been omitted. Therefore, MT was changed even in ancient renditions (cf. E. A. Speiser). A. B. Ehrlich merely changes *bahem*, 'in which,' to *baham*, 'he looked up.' He thus arrives at the rendition "he opened all that he had locked up." Though such a verb *b-h-m*, 'to lock up,' nowhere appears in Scriptures, it does occur in Arabic. I add that the Hebrew *behemah*, 'cattle,' is derived, according to *GB*, from such a hypothetical Hebrew stem *b-h-m*, 'to be mute ("locked up").' It may well be that the masoretes changed the original *baham* to *bahem* because *baham* made no sense to them.

36 RaShI follows *Genesis Rabbah* 91:5. Their interpretation accounts for the unusual *'al kol pene ha-'arets*, 'over all of the land,' instead of the expected *'al pene kol ha-'arets*, 'over the whole land.'

37. *Wayishbor*, 'he rationed,' is derived from *sh-b-r*, lit. 'to break.' RaDaQ explains that victuals "break" the hunger (cf. "break-fast" in English). B. Jacob reminds us that in Ps. 104:11 also thirst is "broken" by water. *Sh-b-r* also connotes "to purchase victuals" (cf. v. 57; 42:2, etc.). *Sh-b-r* also occurs in the noun *Sheber*, 'provision' (cf. 42:1, etc.). Another noun derived from this stem is *mashbir*, 'provider' (cf. 42:6).

NOTES to Gen. 42

1. The thirteen years of Joseph's enslavement (cf. 37:2 with 41:46) were followed by eight years (cf. 41:47f. with 41:53ff.)

2. Cf. lit. on *Shallit* in D. B. Redford, *Study* 61, n. 4.

3. For this cf. A. Erman, *Aegypten*, 999ff.

4. The Hebrew letter for *r*, the last in *wayitnakker*, and the Hebrew letter for *l*, the penultimate letter in *wayitnaklu*, interchange occasionally. It is remarkable that TO almost translates *wayitnakker* as if it meant "he conspired a plot!"

5. RaMBaN wrongly assumes that since only ten of Joseph's brothers bow before him, the first dream was not yet fulfilled, overlooking not only that it is the second dream which explicitly mentions "eleven" (stars), but also that Benjamin was much too young, to "bind sheaves" (see *Appendix 7*).

6. A. Dillmann, *Genesis*, 383, notes 2ff., lists such expressions in the Koran, the *Iliad*, and in Caesar's *Bell. gall.*

7. L. Ginzberg, *Legends* II, 83; V, 347, n. 208.

8. About "the fear of God" see W. Eichrodt, *Theology*, II, 269-277.

9. J. Z. Meklenburg translates *'aval 'ashemin 'anaḥnu*, 'Alas, we are being punished' more literally as "but we are guilty," assuming that what preceded it was "Of what the regent suspects us, we certainly are innocent."

10. For "accounting" cf. J. L. Palache, *Semantic Notes on the Hebrew Lexicon*, 22.

11. When he is about to hear Benjamin's voice (cf. 43:30), he is still able to hide his tears. No longer, however, can he control himself after Judah's appeal (cf. 45:1ff.); and from then on, he weeps freely: When he embraced Benjamin (cf. 45:14), kissed his brothers (cf. 45:15), met his father (cf. 46:29), after Jacob's death (50:1), and when realizing his brothers' fear of his taking revenge (cf. 50:17). Of Jacob, supposedly more emotional than Joseph, the Torah mentions his tears only four times, (cf. 29:11; 33:4; 37:35; 46:29). And of Abraham's weeping, the Torah speaks only after his wife's death (cf. 23:2).

12. Maimonides, *Mishneh Torah, Hilkoth Teshuvah* II, 1, based on BT *Yomah* 86b.

13. For this scene cf. W. Baumgartner, *TLZ*, III (1947), 474.

14. For "exchanged . . . other," cf. G. R. Driver, *VT* Suppl. 16 (1967), 54ff.

15. *Tis-ḥaru*, usually translated as "you may trade" was already recognized by RaShI as "you shall be free to move around" (NJPS). See also Speiser on 34:10.

16. Cf. L. Ginzberg, *Legends* II, 88; V, 349, n. 222.

17. "In my care" is S. Dubno's rendition for lit. "upon my hand." ShaDaL refers to I Sam. 17:22; II Kings 10:24; 12:12; 22:5, 9.

18. For ". . . white head . . . in grief," both here and in 44:31 see Speiser, *Genesis,* 323, n. 38.

19. Cf. n. 19 to expos. on 37:38; L. Ginzberg, *Legends* VII (Index s.v. "measure for measure"). See also B. Jacob, *Auge um Auge,* U. Cassuto, *EBH,* III, Col. 718 f. and his Commentaries, Indexes, s.v. "Measure for Measure." BT *Sanhedrin* 90a states dogmatically this principle is divine.

20. See Abrabanel, *Perush ha-Torah,* 20.

NOTES to Gen. 43

1. "Come before me" (cf. 43:5; 44:23,26), lit. "see my countenance," means obtaining an audience with a superior. Cf. W. Eichrodt, *Theology,* II, 36.

2. Cf. Exodus 19:21,23; etc.; also I Kings 2:42. Such forwarning is an essential element in Jewish law and is called *hatra-'ah* (B. Jacob).

3. NJPS changes the sequence of "we and you" to "you and we" because the former seems disrespectful of the father. Judah's reason, however, is that what follows is ". . . and not die"; besides, "we" includes Benjamin, the father's utmost concern, and Simeon.

4. The *Midrash* attributes to Judah also, "If Benjamin goes with us, he *may* die, but if he will not, he *will* die with all of us. You better concern yourself with what is certain than doubtful." (Ginzberg, *Legends,* II, 89; V, 349, n. 229.)

5. For "surety" by compulsion, i.e. "hostage(s)," cf. 42:16,19. Hezekiah (cf. Isa. 38:14), the Psalmist (cf. 119:122) and Job (17:3) petition God to be their "surety." Judah's pledge prefigures the classic Jewish dictum *Kol Yisra-el 'arevim zeh bazeh,* 'All of Israel are sureties one for another,' BT *Shevuoth* 39a.

6. There was no need to bring *bee*-honey to Egypt. *Devash,* here, is the Arabic *dibs,* grape-must, concentrated to one third, used with water (ShaDaL). F. J. Delitzsch translates, "take . . . of the cutting (crop) of our land," deriving *zimrah* from *z-m-r* 'to trim.'

7. Cf. *Genesis Rabbah* 91:11.

8. Cf. B. Jacob, MGWJ LXVI (N.F. 30, 1922), 11-33; 116-138; 180-200, and his *Genesis,* 315ff.

9. *Habaytah* (cf. 39:11; 43:26; I Kings 13:7) means "to the parlor, reception room, home." "To, toward, into the house" is expressed by *betah* (cf. 28:2; 43:17, 24; 44:14; 47:14; B. Jacob).

10. "Set your mind at rest" is lit. "Peace be to you" (Cf. Jud. 6:23; I Sam. 20:21; B. Jacob).

11. *Qatan* or, as here, *qaton* means either "young, youngest" or "small, little." Originally (cf. 42:13) the brothers referred to him as "the youngest." Yet when they implored the regent to desist from

his demand to have him come before him (cf. 42:16) as cited subsequently (44:20), they called him "little, the son of his old age" to move him to pity.

12. *Genesis Rabbah*, 74:10; 92:5, correlates Joseph's prayerful words with 33:5, when Jacob, before Benjamin's birth, informs his brother Esau after the reconciliation that his sons are "the children with whom God has graced your servant." Now *Joseph* implores God to include *Benjamin!*

13. *Raḥamaw*, 'his emotion,' is derived from *reḥem*, 'womb, bowels.' The plural, as used here, connotes the innermost feeling of compassion, love or pity (cf. Hos. 11:8). In I Kings 3:26 the same plural occurs also in conjunction with "seething" (B. Jacob).

14: Cf. 31:35; Deut. 12:17; 14:3; 16:5; 17:15; 21:16; 22:3,19, 29. Compare also Num. 9:6. For "detestable" cf. 46:34; Exod. 8:22; Herodotus 2:41.

15. *Lefanaw*, lit., 'before him,' means here "by his direction." This view of RaShBaM and A. B. Ehrlich is supported by Speiser, *Genesis*, LXVIII; 329 n. 33.

16. Cf. T. Mann, *Joseph the Provider*, 421ff.

17. L. Ginzberg, *Legends* II, 98; V, 351 f., n. 252.

18. For "portions" cf. II Sam. 11:8.

19. Five "times," lit. five "hands" (cf. 47:25; II Kings 11:7). The Egyptians considered the number "five" of special significance (cf. 41:34; 45:22; 47:2,24; Isa. 19:18). *ANET* 28a reports Ta-net-Amon's several five-fold gifts.

NOTES to Gen. 44

1. J. Z. Meklenburg, who accepts the comment of *Sefer Haya-shar,* (see expos. on 43:33), makes "as he had spoken" refer to what Joseph had disclosed to Benjamin.

2. See B. Jacob's painstaking investigation. He is guided—as are ShaDaL, RaDaQ, Hizkuni and Abrabanel—by BT *Sanhedrin* 65b, 66a and BT *Hullin* 95b, dealing with "portents." These exegetes also refer to 24:14f.; 30:27; I Sam. 14:8f.; I Kings 20:33. My rendition translates *bo* as "in it," i.e. "in its theft."

3. This is RaMBaN's rendition. TO preceded him, translating *be* as "concerning, about, for" as in 29:20; Deut. 24:16, etc. J. Z. Meklenburg explicates TO and anticipated A. Van Hoonaker, in *Isidoor Teirlinck Album,* 239-243. About magic divination cf. 30:27; Lev. 19:26; Num. 24:1; Deut. 18:10; II Kings 17:17; 21:6; II Chron. 33:6.

4. This is the translation of LXX, accepted by most modern scholars. They interpret *be* as "instrumental," cf. Amos 6:6. For lit., cf. Sarna, *Understanding,* 231, notes 80-82.

5. Cf. D. Daube, *Studies in Biblical Law,* 235-257.

6. Derived from *Genesis Rabbah* 92:8, RaShI interprets, "What you propose is indeed the law; a whole group is responsible for the crime of one of its members. But I will be merciful and punish only the actual thief." Most interpreters follow RaShI and render the steward's words as "Even though what you propose is just, only he who is found to have it shall become my slave, and the rest of you be exonerated." (Speiser.) According to Saadiah b. Joseph, the steward yields to the brothers' argument (cf. v. 8) that they cannot all be thieves and therefore only he should be punished with whom the object is found. The above rendition, the steward's reference to the brothers' own words (cf. v. 9), is in part derived from B. Jacob.

7. *Genesis Rabbah* 92:8, however, makes the brothers reproach Benjamin with the following words: "What! you are a thief and the son of a thief!" They refer to Rachel's theft of her father's *teraphim*—idols (cf. 31:34).

8. Cf. *Genesis Rabbah* 92:5.

9. Cf. *Genesis Rabbah* 85:2; 92:2; H. E. Ryle; *Book of Genesis* refers to "Your sin will overtake you" (Num. 32:23).

10. *Genesis Rabbah* 93:9 makes them cry out, "How can we think of peace in our father's house, returning without Benjamin?"

11. *Davar,* 'word' means also "request" (cf. II Sam. 14:15, 22).

12. Cf. 20:8; 23:10,13,16; 50:4, where it connotes "speaking directly" without mediator, or, as here, interpreter (F. J. Delitzsch). Judah must meanwhile have learned to speak Egyptian.

13. They had to emphasize that the father was old because his oldest son Reuben was then only forty-five years old. Ibn Ezra arrives at this age because Joseph, six years younger than Reuben (cf. *Appendix* 3), was then thirty-nine.

14. This certainly would have been a better solution than RaShI's "Judah uttered this untruth out of fear thinking that if he would tell him that he is alive, the regent may say, 'Bring him to me.' "

15. RaMBaN supports with linguistic reasons RaShI's view that "he" in "he would die" refers to Benjamin. B. Jacob adds that when the brothers made this declaration (see expos. on 42:16) they shared the father's fear that Benjamin might suffer a fatal accident, just as his mother had died "on the way" (see expos. on 42:4). Bechor Shor, RaShBaM and all modern exegetes assume that "he" refers to "his father." Still, it is strange that most Bible translations actually substitute "his father" for "he" without any footnote.

16. Though the Torah nowhere mentions what Judah cites in vv. 27f., it leaves no doubt that Jacob, indeed, spoke so exclusively of Rachel. Otherwise he would not have omitted "my wife," speaking of Leah (see expos. on 49:31). The Torah itself confirms his singular relation to Rachel, for in Jacob's genealogy only of Joseph and Benjamin is it stated that they were the sons of Jacob's wife (cf. 46:19; RaShI, Sforno). Not only Zilpah and Bilhah but also Leah are merely called *their respective sons' mothers,* not Jacob's "wives" (cf. 46:15, 18,25). For Jacob's special relation to Rachel, cf. also 29:11, 18, 30; 31:4, 14; 33:2,7 and Ruth 4:11, where Rachel precedes Leah (RaMBaN). Rachel precedes Leah also at the parental blessing of daughters in Jewish observance.

17. Cf. J. Strahan, *Hebrew Ideals,* 321f.

NOTES to Gen. 45

1. In reality it was the Midianites not the brothers, that "sold [Joseph] into Egypt," (see expos. on 37:28). Yet in Hebrew (cf. 42:38; Num. 17:6; Jer. 38:23) deeds can also be attributed to indirect perpetrators (ShaDaL). Anyway, was it not more tactful and simpler for Joseph to say what he said than to recapitulate the tangled episode by starting "when you flung me into a cistern to die therein"?

2. For "instrument of survival" cf. E. W. Heaton, *ET* LIX (1947-8), 134.

3. "No yield from tilling," lit. "neither ploughing nor harvest," is an instance of hendiadys (NJPS and E. A. Speiser, following A. B. Ehrlich). In spite of the famine there remained in Egypt enough pasture for the flocks and herds (cf. 47:4,16), not in Canaan (cf. 47:4).

4. For "to secure ... posterity," cf. Heaton, *op. cit.*, 134, n. 11.

5. See N. Leibowitz, *Iyunim*, 275; 338, n. 2; 353.

6. In Jud. 17:10; 18:19 the *priest* is revered as the "father" because of his wisdom, authority and closeness to God. In II Kings 5:13; 6:21; Isa. 22:21 the *prophet* is called "Father." For the Egyptian usage of this word cf. Vergote, *Joseph,* 114f.

7. For the capital Avaris, also called Tanis (or Zoan in Hebrew) and other related items, see Sarna, *Understanding,* 234f. and sources, p. 231, notes 67, 89, 92, 93, 95, 96.

8. Seventeen years later, after the father's death, he will recognize with tears that the brothers still fear his revenge (cf. expos. on 50:17c).

9. Though the patriarchs and Jacob's family have also been farmers, their main occupation has been sheep-rearing, cf. Sarna, *Understanding,* 106.

10. RaShBaM's reference to the *Pi'el* verb-pattern of the Hebrew word for "he sent off" does not prove it.

11. What it was that happened to Jacob because "he did not believe them" is either that his heart "fainted," (JPS), "went numb" (NJPS), "remained unmoved," (RaShI), or that "he was stunned,"

(*NEB*). See the many interpretations cited by B. Jacob and in *EBI*; also E. ben Yehuda, *Thesaurus*, 4843a-4846a.

12. This is the only acceptable but important contribution of Samuel's essay on Joseph, in *Certain People of the Book*, p. 326.

13. RaShI understands "enough" as merely implying, "I require nothing more"; RaShBaM and Ibn Ezra as implying, "even if he were not the ruler," to which B. Jacob adds "and I will not deign to look at his gifts."

14. L. Ginzberg, *Legends*, II, 137; V, 365, n. 370.

15. RaLBaG, Abrabanel, MaLBYM and NaTsYB, also *Sefer Hayashar*, assume that he did not even intend to remain in Egypt for the duration of the famine.

NOTES to Gen. 46

1. Beer-sheba was founded by Abraham (cf. 21:31) who "planted a tamarisk at Beer-sheba and invoked there the name of the Lord, the everlasting God" (cf. 21:33). There Isaac was born (cf. 21:14) and Abraham was told to sacrifice him (cf. 22:2); and thereto both returned after the awesome test (cf. 22:19). But also for Jacob, Beer-sheba was a place of most precious and solemn memories, for there he too was born and spent most of his life before fleeing to Haran (cf. 28:10).

2. To Abraham, 15:1; to Isaac, 26:24; to Jacob, 31:11ff.

3. Cf. "Abraham, Abraham" (cf. 22:11); "Moses, Moses" (cf. Exod. 3:4); "Samuel, Samuel" (cf. I Sam. 3:10). Cf. Ginzberg, *Legends,* II, 118; V. 357, n. 303.

4. It is in retrospect to this retention of identity that Moses will say to his generation that God has taken "for Himself one nation [Israel] from the midst of another nation," the Egyptian (Deut. 4:34).

5. B. Jacob points out that this explanation of Ibn Ezra was preceded by R. Saadiah, but he shares the view of RaShBaM, Bechor Shor, Hizkuni, and Sforno that the phrase connotes God's assurance to Jacob that for the rest of his life he would not have to "look after things" because Joseph will provide for his needs.

6. According to *Genesis Rabbah* 80:11, "the Canaanite woman" is Dinah who conceived a son from the "Canaanite" Shechem (cf. 34:2), killed by Simeon who adopted this son and called him Shaul. Ohad (10) is missing in Num. 26:12 and I Chron. 4:24 where Yemuel (8) is called Nemuel. Yachin (11) is listed as Yarib in I Chron. 4:24. Tsohar (12)—perhaps to distinguish him from the *Hittite* Tsohar (23:8; 25:9)—is listed as Zerah in Num. 26:20; I Chron. 4:24. Both names mean almost the same.

7. Gershon (15) is Gershom in I Chron. 6:1,5,28,56; 15:7. Yet other passages in I Chron. and elsewhere do list him as Gershon.

8. Puvvah (26) is listed as Pu-ah in Judg. 10:1; I Chron. 7:1. In

the latter and in Num. 26:24 Yob (27) appears as Yashuv.

9. a) Leah had twice the number of children of her maidservant Zilpah (cf. v. 17; A. Dillmann).

   b) Rachel had twice the number of children of her maidservant Bilhah (cf. v. 22 with v. 25; B. Jacob).

   c) Because Leah had 32 children (cf. v. 14), Zilpah had 16 (cf. v. 18), Rachel had 14 (cf. v. 22), and Bilhah had 7 (cf. v. 24), they are listed in this order. (B. Jacob).

   d) Leah's 32 children, added to Rachel's 14 = 46—if crosswise counted, i.e. four plus six—are double the total of the concubines', 16 + 7 = 23, = two plus three (cf. H. Eising, *Formgeschichtliche Untersuchung zur Jakobserzaehlung der Genesis,* 340ff.

10. Tsiphion (2) and Etsbon (5) are Tsephon and Ozni in Num. 26:15f. where Arodi (7) is Arod. In I Chron. 5:11-17, Gad's offspring are quite different.

11. For the fascinating stories about Serah (14) the only listed granddaughter of Jacob, see L. Ginzberg, *Legends,* VII, Index under "Serah."

12. The *four* sons (10), (11), (12), and (13) are listed as only *three* in Num. 26:38f. under the names of Ahiram, Shephupham and Hupham. It seems that the letters in the name Rosh (11) were added to (10) and (12). It was perhaps to preserve the names of (9) and (14), also extinct in Num., that these names are given there and in I. Chron. 8:3f. to Benjamin's son and as the *grandsons* from (5). (8) is not listed in Num. In I. Chron. 8:3 he is the son of (5), but he appears in Judg. 3:15 as Benjamin's son and as the father of Ehud, the Judge. In II Sam. 19:17, 19 and I Kings 2:8 he is Shim-i's father. In I Chron. 8:3 he is the son of (5). While (6) is not listed in Num. 26:38f. as Benjamin's son, it seems that Ephraim called his son, v. 35, after him.

13. Also 36:25; Num. 26:8, I Chron. 2:8 list only one son, yet use the plural, "sons" (just as v. 15 seems to call Dinah "daughters"). *Genesis Rabbah* 94:9 reports that "the Torah scroll of R. Meir read 'The *son* of Dan: Hushim.' "

14. Part of this assumption has been dealt with by F. J. Delitzsch in his *Genesis.*

15. Not only v. 27 but also Exod. 1:5 and Deut. 10:22 speak of these "seventy." The importance of this number is evidenced by the impressively long list in the Index of L. Ginzberg, *Legends,* VII s.v. "Seventy." Among them is "Seventy Elders" (Exod. 24:1,9; Num. 11:16), the representatives of the Tribes and principal kinships

from the time of Moses and onwards to the time of the Sanhedrin.

16. See B. Jacob, *Genesis,* 272-286, also p. 295. He lists fourteen from Japhet, thirty-one from Ham, and twenty-five from Shem.

17. The same Hebrew word as used here for "now" occurs also in 2:23; 29:34; 30:20 at the long-delayed fulfillment of a passionate desire (F. J. Delitzsch).

18. It is hard to understand why von Rad, *Genesis* 399, writes, "If one reads vv. 31-34 impartially, one gets the impression that the Pharaoh is here (in contrast to ch. 45:16ff.) to be informed for the first time about the coming of Joseph's relatives," and why Speiser, *Genesis,* 340, following von Rad, writes, "The news of Jacob's arrival comes as a surprise to Pharaoh." There is no puzzle at all: Pharaoh had told Joseph (cf. 45:17ff.) to invite his father's households, etc., and Joseph simply plans now to inform the king that they have *arrived!*

19. For Abraham's, Isaac's and Jacob's herdsmen cf. 13:7,8; 26:16; 32:17ff., respectively.

NOTES to Gen. 47

1. For "five," a number significant for Egyptians, see expos. on 43:34; 45:22; cf. also 41:34; 47:24.

2. They find themselves in the same situation as depicted in Num. 32:2,5 (B. Jacob). For other passages of repeated "they (or he) said," see exposition on 37:22.

3. Cf. J. Skinner, *Genesis*, 488.

4. With this explanation, in part derived from remarks of A. B. Ehrlich and von Rad, the above mentioned "corrected" but awkwardly repetitive LXX version, cited and accepted by A. Dillmann, *Genesis*, should be discarded.

5. Cf. II Sam. 16:16; I Kings 1:31 (8:66); Dan. 2:4; 5:10; 6:7; also Egyptian and Babylonian texts (B. Jacob).

6. Cf. U. Cassuto, *EBH*, III, col. 718f. and Sarna, *Understanding*, 183f., both condensing the Torah's data on Jacob's adversities.

7. According to Ibn Ezra on v. 1, this *district* Ra'-meses (mentioned also in Exod. 12:37; Num. 33:3,5) is different from the *city* Raamses (Exod. 1:11), one of the two storage or garrison-cities which "the Pharaoh of the Oppression," perhaps Rameses II, will force the enslaved Israelites to build.

8. *Lamah*, the first Hebrew word in v. 19, lit. "why," seems to mean here "lest" (cf. S. R. Driver, *Notes on the Hebrew text . . . of the Books of Samuel*, 158; G. R. Driver, *Aramaic Documents of the Fifth Century B.C.*, 83). Cf. also BDB 554a, last *loci* under 4d. NJPS translates, "Let us not . . . ."

9. Because the above cited MT words were considered to mean "he moved it to the cities," they were "corrected" into *he'evid 'oto le'avadim*, 'he enslaved them to slaves' by LXX, Samaritan and Vulgate who may have wondered who would till the fields once all the people were removed to the cities. The translators of LXX, moreover, may have been embarrassed to have their fellow Jew, Joseph, appear guilty of "deporting" the population rather than enslaving them as they themselves had offered. This "correction," however, has to be rejected because, as vv. 23f. clearly show, Joseph *refused* to make them slaves! Moreover, "enslaved them to slaves" is not only intolerably tautological but also is unacceptable for

other linguistic reasons (cf. B. Jacob). The traditional adherents to MT interpreted the phrase to mean "city by city" and explained it according to a forced explanation of R. Simeon b. Lakish (BT *Hullin* 60b). Our rendition of *le'arim* as "city-wise" is based on R.M. Ehrenreich's suggestion (cited by his teacher ShaDaL) that the particle *le* in the "distributive" sense occurs also in "by their group" (Num. 1:3), "by their clans" (Num. 26:12), "by your tribes . . . families . . . houses . . . men" (Josh. 7:14). Instead of these passages, GB 372a, 8d, lists many others, suggesting that *le* in them be taken adverbially. The same verb *he'evir*, which precedes *le'arim*, is analogously used as "transferring" in Num. 27:7f., except that there is does not mean the landowners' transference to a distant spot but the transference of a land-title to a distantly located person. (B. Jacob). The literal translation of the last words in v. 21 is not "from one end of Egypt's border to the other," for that would require the preposition *'el*, instead of *'ad*, used here (S. Dubno).

10. Cf. Josephus, *Antiquities* II 7:7, RaShBaM and others assume that the reason was to secure the expropriation against future attempts of contest. Others see it "to break up illegal associations, nests of sedition as well as sectional enmities that used to endanger law and order," cf. Marcus Dods, *Genesis*, referring to H. K. Brugsch, *History of Egypt*, I, 16.

11. F. J. Delitzsch, *Genesis*, II, 352.

12. A. Erman, *Life in Ancient Egypt*, 129, cites an inscription from which it appears that 185,000 sacks of corn were annually given by Rameses III (1202-1171 B.C.E.) to the Egyptian temples. See also Diodorus, I, 73; Herodotus, II, 168; J. Vergote, *Joseph*, 191.

13. Cf. N. Leibowitz, *Iyunim*, 378f.

14. On the legal background of this act, see R. Yaron, *RIDA*, VI (1959), 155ff.

15. Martin Luther's commentary contrasts it with the rate of one-third to one-half in the Germany of his time. A. Dillmann, *Genesis*, 1897, 429f., cites nine sources, beginning with I Macc. 10:30, according to which up to three-fourths of the harvest was paid to the government by the tenant. For Egyptian taxes and other information relevant to this passage see lit. cited in D. B. Redford, *Study*, 236 n. 2; 237, notes 1-6.

16. The literal translation of v. 25b is "Let us find grace in the eyes of my lord, and we will be Pharaoh's slaves." This sentence clearly shows that they did *not* become slaves and speaks against the "correction," viz. "he enslaved it (the population) to slaves" (cf.

note 9 in expos. on v. 21). Yet only Speiser seems to have realized this and, to reconcile it with the "correction," he "translates" v. 25b, "We are thankful to my lord that we can be serfs to Pharaoh." Even though the word "tenant" is omitted in the text, it nowhere shows that Joseph made them "serfs." And what kind of "serfdom" is it that grants four-fifths of the produce to the "serf?"

17. In spite of the people's ovation and in spite of Joseph's refusal to enslave them, Joseph's policy has often been made "the showpiece in the arsenal of anti-Semitic polemic against the Old Testament" (G. von Rad, *Genesis*, 405). Thus even F. J. Delitzsch, *Genesis* 352, accepts the judgment that "the history of Joseph is a dangerous model for crafty ministers . . . In Joseph's financial speculation . . . one of the unamiable sides of Semitic (Jewish) hereditary peculiarity comes to light. . . ." Yet two sentences before he writes "Joseph undoubtedly had in view no less the good of the country than that of the king." Delitzsch should have been cautioned in his defamation of Joseph by the praise of the Torah, "he brought them through," (see expos. on v. 17). B. Jacob deals thoroughly with this controversial issue, 856-858. See also Speiser, 353. But none of these or other scholars has given as keen and fair a moral evaluation of Joseph's agrarian measures as T. Mann, *Joseph the Provider*, 247ff; 536ff.

18. "Seventeen" are also the *crosswise* counted years of Abraham, Isaac and Jacob, 175, 180, 147 years—respectively—if expressed as $5\times5\times7$, $6\times6\times5$ and $7\times7\times3$ i.e. $5+5+7$; $6+6+5$; $7+7+3$. For literature on this see L. Ruppert, *Die Josephserzaehlung,* 178f., n. 40. For other such "number harmony," "paradigmatic historiosophy," cf. Sarna, *Understanding* 83f., 100.

19. Instead of articulating the oath to the conjuring person, a hallowed object of his is being touched. In this case it is the mark of the Covenant (cf. 17:11). In 24:9 Abraham's servant *enacts* this ritual confirming his master's summons (cf. 24:3-8). For "steadfast loyalty," see Speiser on 24:7.

NOTES to Gen. 48

1. Though what Jacob had hence to go through must be viewed as "ten chastisements" (cf. U. Cassuto, *EBH* III, 719), to purge him from his sin of fraud, it should be noted that Isaac, knowing about it (cf. 27:35), would not have blessed him, had he considered his son's deception a "monstrous crime" as von Rad (*Genesis*, 273) does.

2. *Am*, the singular of *'ammim*, 'peoples,' is sometimes used for smaller units (cf. 19:4; 48:19; I Sam. 9:12f.; Jer. 29:16, 25; II Chron. 31:4) and *'ammim* connotes in the poetic language of Deut. 33:2, "tribes" (RaShI, ShaDaL, B. Jacob). Also, Isaac must have meant "tribes." *Qahal* in Deut. 5:19; 9:10; 10:4 connotes a sacred league, *Qehal 'ammim* in Isaac's prayer thus means "a sacred league of tribes."

3. *God's* reason to add (cf. 35:12b) to His blessing for Abraham in His blessing for *Jacob* the words "will I give the land" may be that most of Abraham's and Isaac's offspring were excluded from the inheritance of Canaan, whereas *all* of Jacob's offspring will have their share in it.

4. See expos. on 37:20; 41:33; 44:30,33; 45:5,8; 47:4 and 50:5,17,21.

5. Cf. Num. 2:18; Josh. 14:4. The other eleven *tribes* are also listed in Num. 2. Each tribe has a relatively autonomous home-rule under a "prince" and has its special banner. The generations sired by Jacob's and Joseph's sons are called "families" (cf. Num. 26; B. Jacob). The option to a portion of Canaan, allocated by Joshua, was inherited by those who entered Canaan from those who left Egypt. They, in turn, had acquired it from those who "entered Egypt" (see expos. on 46:7, 27), including Manasseh and Ephraim. (BT *Baba Bathra* 117ab; B. Jacob). Though there are thus thirteen "tribes," the tribe of Levi did not receive a share in the land: "YHWH is their inheritance," (Deut. 18:1f.) BT *Horayoth* 6b elaborates on this matter.

6. "Died to my sorrow," lit. "died upon me," takes the Hebrew for "upon" in its adversative sense (cf. 33:13, Speiser; cf. 42:36, B. Jacob; cf.) Num. 6:9, (RaShI).

7. Though Otto Proksch seems right in saying that the Hebrew for "that I may bless them" could also mean "that I may take them on my knee," *NEB*, nevertheless, should not have thus translated it here, for these lads were older than nineteen years! They were born before the famine years set in, so that seventeen years before this scene they were already more than two years old (cf. 41:50 with 45:6; 47:28).

8. The laying on of hands conveys the blessing. The right hand symbolizes the preference (cf. 35:18; I Kings 2:19; Ps. 45:10; 110:1), due to the elder (cf. Deut. 21:17; B. Jacob).

9. "Crossing his hands" is the rendition of TJ and other ancient translations, accepted by modern scholars who see in the verb a cognate to Arab for "plaiting." *BDB* 968b, however, anticipated by TO, Saadia, RaShI and others, derives the verb from *s-k-l* 'to be prudent, aware.' B. Jacob accepts this view that Jacob "guided his hands wittingly."

10. *Ki,*—although—is listed by *BDB*, 473b (sub c); yet neither this passage nor Exod. 34:9 is mentioned there, also viewed as *although* by Ibn Ezra, accepted by Speiser and NJPS.

11. Cf. Martin Buber, *The Prophetic Faith*, 38; *Judaism,* V (1956), 299, a view anticipated by R. Simeon b. Lakish, *Genesis Rabbah* 97:2.

12. Cf. TJ; S. Dubno; B. Jacob.

13. The last words of the verse are lit. "the fullness of the nations." NJPS renders them "plentiful enough for nations"; *NEB,* "a whole nation in themselves." F. J. Delitzsch translates "a fullness of nations." What seems to be meant is self-sufficiency through diversity, typifying "nationhood" (B. Jacob).

14. A comparison of both tribes' censuses in Num. 1:33, 35, shows Ephraim to exceed Manasseh by 8,300, yet in Num. 26:34, 37 Manasseh was 20,200 above Ephraim. Since the time of the Judges, however, Ephraim became the greatest of all tribes in power and extent. Subsequently it assumed the name "Israel" which it gave to the whole northern kingdom of ten tribes. Most of the later renowned places and centers of worship (Bethel, Shechem, Ramah, Shiloh) as well as Mounts Ebal and Gerizim were located in its domain.

15. Cf. A. B. Ehrlich's important note on 23:20 in *Mikra Ki-feshutoh.*

16. Cf. L. Ginzberg, *Legends*, I, 395; V, 313, n. 382.

17. Most modern scholars take *Shekem* to signify "a shoulder ridge," punning with Shechem, the town on this "ridge" of land. Yet

A. B. Ehrlich objects that only *Kateph* can be used for such "ridge," not *sheḳem*. Besides, how can Jacob allocate Shechem, which he does not own? (B. Jacob).

18. The *Midrash* "solves" the problem by spinning fascinating tales about such happenings (cf. Ginzberg, *Legends,* I, 400-411; II, 138f.; V, 314, notes 289-292; 366, n. 377).

NOTES to Gen. 49:28-31

1. These twelve tribes are symbolized also in the twelve jewels on the High Priest's Breastplate (cf. Exod. 28:9f.,30), in the "stones" on which Moses wrote (cf. Exod. 24:4), and those which Joshua had the Israelites take out from the Jordan and erected at Gilgal (cf. Josh. 4:3-9,20). Also Elijah built the altar from twelve stones (cf. I Kings 18:31.).

2. Neither Leah's nor Rebekah's death and interment have been mentioned in the Torah before. About Esau's death no word is said. The Midrash, however, has it that he died when he and his sons fought with Jacob's sons at the cave, alleging that with Leah's interment therein Jacob had forfeited his claim to what he, Esau, was entitled to. (Ginzberg, *Legends,* II, 153ff.; V, 371ff., notes 422-426).

3. Cf. BT *Ta-anith* 5b.

NOTES to Gen. 50

1. Cf. expos. on 46:4, n. 3.

2. Cf. J. Vergote, *Joseph,* 199.

3. Cf. Diodorus, I, 72; Vergote, 197ff.

4. This is TO's translation of the literal "which I dug for myself," connoting his having excavated an additional grave, adjacent to the others, in the rocky cave; see Mishnah *Baba Bathra* VI:8 (B. Jacob).

5. Cf. A. Erman, *Aegyptisches Leben im Altertum,* 429ff.

6. Cf. Pashteh deQra who compares "all" here with "all" in "the hail smote all trees of the field" (Exod. 9:25), followed by the next plague: ". . . They shall devour the surviving remnant that was left to you after the hail" (Exod. 10:5).

7. Most scholars consider it impossible that the cortege could have taken this circuitous route around the Dead Sea. Yet taking an indirect route for a funeral procession is in accord with Jewish tradition, signifying regret at having to bury an honored person (NaTsYB). Moreover, the Israelites after the Exodus took the same route (Meyuhas). "What happened to the Fathers forecasts what happens to their offspring" is a famed axiom in Jewish tradition.

The seven-day mourning period at *Goren ha-Atad,* held *before* interment (Bahyah, *EBI*) is not the *shiv'ah,* (the traditional Jewish) 'seven' (day mourning period). For details about mourning rites in Biblical times, see B. Jacob.

8. *Abehl,* presumably 'watercourse, conduit,' (cf. Num. 33:49; Jud. 7:22; 11:33; II Sam. 20:15; I Kings 4:12; 15:20) is punned upon here with *'ebel,* 'mourning'; cf. W. F. Albright *BASOR* LXXXIX (1943), 15, n. 44 (cited by Speiser).

9. Cf. BT *Yebamoth* 65b; Ginzberg, *Legends,* II, 167; V, 373, n. 427 among many others.

10. The exposition on 42:28a explained how the father attained his knowledge without being told by either the Ten or Joseph.

11. The translations "Behold, we are your slaves," or "We are

prepared to be your slaves" would have required *"hinenu 'avadeḳa."* But they say *"hinenu leḳa la'avadim,* placing the emphasis upon "your" (see NaTsYB).

12. Thereupon the wronged person is expected to "lift the other's face," (cf. 32:21; I Sam. 25:35), by showing him his favor and *reconciliation,* not "forgiveness."

13. "You meant [but did not do] evil" is an additional proof (see expos. on 37:28) that the brothers did not sell Joseph (J. Z. Meklenburg).

14. RaShBaM and Abrabanel hold that since the Ten unwittingly carried out the design of Providence, they did not even sin in the first place. NaTsYB goes further: God actually blinded their judgment about Joseph's dreams, causing them to fear that *he* "had meant evil" against *them,* wherefore they could not help plotting against him.

15. See A. B. Ehrlich (cf. 34:3; Jud. 19:3; II Sam. 19:8; Hos. 2:16; II Chron. 30:22; 32:6).

16. Cf. L. Ginzberg, *op. cit.,* V, 375f., n. 437.

17. Cf. the sources listed by A. Dillmann, *Genesis* on 50:22.

18. Cf. Ginzberg, *op. cit.,* II, 169; V, 373f. n. 429.

19. *Ibid.,* II., 183; V, 376, n. 442.

NOTES to Appendix

1. Cf. L. Ginzberg, *Legends*, I, 415; II, 220.

2. Cf. *Numbers Rabbah* 14:8, stating, "Benjamin was born when Jacob was 100 years old." Jacob was 91 when Joseph was born (cf. *Appendix* 4b).

3. This Talmud passage states that Jacob returned to his father 22 years after his arrival in Haran. Since Joseph was six years old when the family left Haran, 20 years after Jacob's arrival there (cf. 30:22ff. with 31:41) and since Benjamin was born shortly before Jacob's return to his father, BT *Megillah* 17a thus implies that even less than two years had passed between Joseph's reaching the age of six and Benjamin's birth.

Behind this assertion is the intent to arrive at another Divine "measure-for-measure" dispensation. As the Torah indeed reports that just as Joseph stayed for the first 17 years of his life with his father, and Jacob enjoyed his last 17 years living in Egypt with his son (cf. *Appendix* 4d), so the above BT passage wants to see their 22 years of separation as God's punishment for Jacob's having spent 20 years in Haran and two years in Canaan before returning to his father. It is amazing how with this assertion, that Jacob spent only two years in Canaan before he returned to his father in Hebron, all the seven phases (cf. *Appendix* 5) are compressed to less than two years, notwithstanding the implication that Dinah would have been in her seventh year when she was violated and her two avenging brothers little boys when taking up the sword.

4. BT *Megillah* 17a also states that Jacob stayed in Succoth for 18 months. *Genesis Rabbah* 78:16 holds this same view, derived from the wording of 33:17. RaShI accepted it.

5. Cf. F. J. Delitzsch, *Genesis*, II, 219, 234, 339.

ABBREVIATIONS

Acta Or.	*Acta Orientalia*
AJSL	*American Journal of Semitic Languages and Literatures*
ANET	Pritchard, J., ed. *Ancient Near Eastern Texts Relating to the Old Testament*
ASAE	*Annales du service des antiquités de l'Egypte*
BASOR	*Bulletin of the American Schools of Oriental Research*
BAT	*Die Botschaft des A.T.*, Calver Verlag, Stuttgart
BDB	F. Brown, S. R. Driver, A. Briggs, *A Hebrew and English Lexicon of the Old Testament*, Oxford, 1907
Bib. Or.	*Biblioteca Orientalis*
BSFE	*Bulletin de la société française d'égyptologie*
BT	Babylonian Talmud
BZ	*Biblische Zeitschrift*
BZAW	*Beihefte zur ZAW*
CBQ	*Catholic Biblical Quarterly*
EB	*Encyclopaedia Biblica*
EBH	*Encyclopaedia Biblica* [Hebrew]
EBI	*Encyclopaedia of Biblical Interpretations*
EJ	*Encyclopaedia Judaica*
ET	*The Expository Times*
GB	Gesenius, W. and Buhl, F.; *O.T. Dictionary*, Leipzig 1915
JA	*Journal Asiatique*
JAOS	*Journal of the American Oriental Society*
JBL	*Journal of Biblical Literature*
JEA	*Journal of Egyptian Archaeology*
JEOL	*Jaarbericht Ex Oriente Lux*
JNES	*Journal of Near Eastern Studies*
JPS	Jewish Publication Society, Philadelphia
JQR	*Jewish Quarterly Review*
JSS	*Journal of Semitic Studies*
JTS	*Journal of Theological Studies*
KBL	Koehler, L. and Baumgartner, W., *Lexicon in Veteris Testamenti libros*
LCL	Loeb Classical Library

LXX	Septuagint
MGWJ	*Monatsschrift fuer Geschichte und Wissenschaft des Judentums*
MT	Masoretic Text
MVAG	*Mitteilungen der vorderasiatischen Gesellschaft*
NEB	*New English Bible*
NJPS	*The Torah,* New Translation, JPS
OLD	*Oz LeDavid*
OLZ	*Orientalistische Literaturzeitung*
OMRO	*Oudheidkundige Mededeelingen uit het Rijksmuseum van Oudheden te Leiden*
OT	Old Testament
PEFQ	*Palestine Exploration Fund Quarterly*
RB	*Revue biblique*
RIDA	*Revue internationale des droits de l'Antitiquité*
TJ	Targum Jonathan
TO	Targum Onkelos
TLZ	*Theologische Literaturzeitung*
VT	*Vetus Testamentum*
YKJV	Haran, M., ed., *Yehezkel Kaufmann Jubilee Volume*
ZÄS	*Zeitschrift fuer aegyptische Sprache*
ZAW	*Zeitschrift fuer die alttestamentlichen Wissenschaften*
ZDMG	*Zeitschrift der Deutschen Morgenlaendischen Gesellschaft*

BIBLIOGRAPHY

Abot De Rabbi Nathan, tr. by Judah Goldin, New Haven, 1955.

Abrabanel, Isaac, *Perush haTorah*, Warsaw, 1861.

Adar, Z., *"Sippur Joseph we-hora'ato," Iyunim* III, (1965).

Alt, A., "The God of the Fathers," *Essays on Old Testament History and Religion*, New York, 1968, 5-100.

Aqedath Yitshaq, homiletics and commentary on Bible, by R. Isaac Arama b. Moses, Warsaw, 5643.

Baal Haturim, Torah commentary by R. Jacob b. Asher, ed. M. Rosenthal, Hannover, 1838.

Babylonian Talmud: *Arakhin, Baba Bathra, Berakhot, Horayoth, Hullin, Makkot, Megillah, Nedarim, Qiddushin, Sanhedrin, Shevuoth, Sotah, Taanith, Yomah*.

Bahya: Bible commentary by R. Bahya b. Asher *(EBI)*.

Baumgartner, W., "Nicht Quellen, sondern Syntax," *TLZ* III (1947), 473f.

Bechor Shor, Bible commentary by R. Joseph Bechor Shor, ed. Jellinek, Leipzig, 1856.

Bentzen, Aage, *Introduction to the Old Testament* II, Copenhagen, 1948.

Ben Yehuda, Eliezer, *Thesaurus Totius Hebraitatis* [Hebrew], New York, 1959.

Biberfeld, Philip, *Universal Jewish History* II, New York, 1962.

Brown F., Driver, S. R., and Briggs, C. A., *A Hebrew and English Lexicon of the Old Testament*, Oxford, 1966 edition.

Buber, Martin, "The Burning Bush," *Moses*, Oxford, 1946, 39-55.

———, *The Prophetic Faith*, New York, 1949.

———, *Two Types of Faith*, London, 1951.

———, "Abraham the Seer," *Judaism* V. (1956) 291-305.

Cassuto, Umberto, *Genesis* II, Jerusalem, 1964.

———, "Jacob," *EBH*, III, col. 715-722.

———, "Joseph," *EBH*, III, col. 614-616.

———, *The Documentary Hypothesis and the Composition of the Pentateuch*, Jerusalem, 1961.

Collingwood, R. G., *The Idea of History*, Oxford, 1965.

Daube, David, *Studies in Biblical Law*, Cambridge, 1947.

———, "Rechtsgedanken in den Erzählungen des Pentateuchs," (*BZAW*), Berlin, 1958, 32ff.

Delitzsch, Franz J., *A New Commentary on Genesis* II, Edinburgh, tr. from German, 1888.

Dillmann, A., *Genesis Critically and Exegetically Expounded*, II, New York, 1889. tr. from German, Edinburgh, 1897.

Diodorus Siculus, *The Library of History*, I, *LCL*, London, Cambridge, Mass. 1921.

Dods, Marcus, *Genesis, The Expositor's Bible*, Grand Rapids, Mich. 1943.

Driver, G. R., "Hebrew Homonyms," *VT Suppl.* XVI (1967), 50ff.

———, *Aramaic Documents of the Fifth Century B.C.*, Oxford, 1957.

Driver, S. R., *Notes on the Hebrew Text of the Books of Samuel*, Oxford, 1913.

Dubno, S., *Commentary on Genesis*, Krotoschin, 1839.

Ehrlich, A. B., *Mikra Ki-Feshuto* I, (Pentateuch), Berlin, 1899.

———, *Randglossen Zur Hebraeischen Bibel* I, (*Genesis und Exodus*), Leipzig, 1908.

Ehrlich, E. L., *Der Traum im Alten Testament*, (*BZAW* 73) Berlin, 1953.

Eichrodt, Walter, *Theology of the Old Testament* II, London, 1961.

Encyclopedia of Biblical Interpretation by M. M. Kasher (*Torah Shelemah*, tr. and ed. by H. Freedman) vols. I-V, New York, 1953-1965.

Encyclopedia Judaica, Jerusalem, 1971.

En Shelomoh Astruc, ed. S. Eppenstein, Berlin, 1899: by R. Anselme of Barcelona, 14th c.

Epstein, B., *Torah Temimah*, Vilna, 1904.

Erman, A., *Die Literatur der Ägypter*, Leipzig, 1925.

Erman, A. and Ranke, H., *Ägypten and ägyptisches Leben im Altertum*, Tübingen, 1925.

Genesis Rabbah, tr. and ed. H. Freedman and M. Simon, London, 1939.

Gesenius, W., and Buhl, F., *Hebraeisches und Aramaeisches Handwoerterbuch ueber das Alte Testament*, Leipzig, 1915.

Ginsberg, C. D., *Introduction to the Massoretic-Critical Edition of the Hebrew Bible*, London, 1897.

Ginzberg, L., *Legends of the Jews*, 7 vols. Philadelphia, 1909-1938.

Glatzer, N. N., *Franz Rosenzweig, His Life and Thought*, Philadelphia, 1953.

Goldman, Solomon, *The Book of Human Destiny*, 2 vols. Philadelphia, 1948-9.

Greenberg, Moshe, "Postulates on Biblical Criminal Law," *YKJV*, 11ff.

———, see Kaufmann, Y.

Gressman, H., "Ursprung und Entwicklung der Joseph-Saga," *Eucharisterion für Gunkel* (1923), 1 ff.

Gunkel, H., "Die Komposition der Josephgeschichte," *ZDMG NF* 1 (1922), 55ff.

———, *Genesis*, Goettingen, 1910.

Herodotus, *History* II, *LCL* London, Cambridge, Mass., 1921.

Hertz, J. H., *The Pentateuch and Haftorahs*, London, 1936.

Heschel, Abraham J., *God in Search of Man*, New York, 1955.

Himmelfarb, Milton, "The State of Jewish Belief," *Commentary* XLII (1966) 71-72.

Hirsch, Samson R., *Der Pentateuch Uebersetzt und erläutert* I, Frankfurt, 1867.

Hizkuni: Bible commentary of R. Hezekiah b. Manoah, c. 1260, France (*EBI*).

Honeyman, A. M., "The Occasion for Joseph's Temptation," *VT* II (1952), 85ff.

Hoonaker, A. Van, "Was Josef's beker (Genesis 44) een tooverbeker?" in *Isidor Teirlinck Album*, Louvain, 1931, 239-243.

Horovitz, Jacob, *Die Josephserzaehlung*, Frankfurt a.M., 1921.

Ibn Ezra, R. Abraham, Torah commentary, ed. Krinski, Vilna, 1927.

Jacob, Benno, *Quellenscheidung und Exegese*, Leipzig, 1916.

———, "Moses am Dornbusch" *MGWJ* LXVI, N.F. 30 (1922), 11-33; 116-138; 180-200.

———, *Auge um Auge*, Berlin, 1929.

———, *Das erste Buch der Torah/Genesis, uebersetzt und erklaert*, Berlin, 1934.

Janssen, J.M.A., "Egyptological Remarks on the Story of Joseph in Genesis," *JEOL* XIV (1955/56) 63-72.

Josephus, Flavius, *Antiquities, LCL,* London, Cambridge, Mass., 1926.

Joüon, P., *Grammaire de l'hébreu biblique*, (2nd ed.), Rome 1947.

Kaplan, Mordecai M., "The Supremacy of the Torah," reprinted from the *The Students' Annual* of the Jewish Theological Seminary, New York, in *The Reconstructionist*, vol. XXX (May 15, 1964), 7-17.

Katten, M., "Genesis Kapitel 41," in *Festschrift 75th Anniversary Breslau Seminary*, II, 151-171.

Kaufmann, Yehezkel, *The Religion of Israel, from its Beginning to the Babylonian Exile*, tr. and abridged by Moshe Greenberg, Chicago, 1960.

Kautzsch, E., and Cowley, A. E., *Gesenius' Hebrew Grammar*, 2nd ed., Oxford, 1910.

Keli Yaqar: Annotations on Torah by R. Shlomo Ephraim, Lublin 1602, Miqraoth Gedoloth, New York, 1965.

Kitchen, K. A., "Joseph," in J. D. Douglas, *The New Bible Dictionary*, London, 1962, 656 ff.

Knopf L., "Arabische Etymologien zum Bibelwoerterbuch," *VT* IX (1959), 247ff.

Koehler, L. and Baumgartner, W., *Lexicon in Veteris Testamenti Libros*, Leiden, 1948-1953.

Kornfeld, W., "L'Adultère dans l'Orient antique," *RB* LVII (1950), 92ff.

Leibowitz, Nehama, *Iyunim Besefer Bereshith*, Jerusalem, 1966.

Leqah Tob: R. Tobiah b. Eliezer ed. S. Buber, Vilna, 1880.

Maimonides (R. Moses b. Maimon), *Mishneh Torah* I, Leipzig, 1862.

MaLBYM: R. Meir Loeb b. Jehiel Michael Malbim, Bible Commentary, New York, 5710.

Mann, Thomas, *Joseph and His Brothers*, 4 vols., New York, 1945-6, *I Joseph and His Brothers, II Young Joseph, III Joseph in Egypt, IV Joseph the Provider.*

Meklenburg, R. Z. H., *Haketab Wehakabalah*, Leipzig, 1839.

Mendelsohn, I., *Slavery in the Ancient Near East*, New York, 1949.

————, "On the Preferential Status of the Eldest Son," *BASOR*, CLVI (1959), n. 38-40.

Meyuhas: Torah commentary by R. Meyuhas b. Elijah, London, 1909.

Midrash Tanhuma, 3 vols. (ed. Solomon Buber, Vilna, 1885).

Milgrom, Jacob, "Genesis translated with an introduction and commentary by E. A. Speiser . . .," *Conservative Judaism* XX (1966), 73-79.

Minhah Belulah: R. Menahem Abraham b. Jacob ha-Kohen Rapa, Cremona, 1582 (*EBI*).

Mowinkel, S., *Erwaegungen zur Pentateuch Quellenfrage*, Trondheim, 1946.

NaTsYB: R. Naftali Tsevi Yehudah Berlin, *Ha-'ameq Davar*, Jerusalem, 1938.

Oppenheim, A. L., *The Interpretation of Dreams in the Ancient Near East*, Philadelphia, 1956.

Or Hahayim: Bible commentary by R. Hayyim ibn Attar, Venice, 1742 (*Miqraoth Gedoloth*, New York, 1965).

Palache, J. L., *Semantic Notes on the Hebrew Lexicon*, Leiden, 1959.

Pashteh Deqra: Genesis commentary by R. Abraham Hayyim Kassel, Vilna, 1899.

Peck, J., "Note on Gen. 37:2 and Joseph's Character," *ET*, XLI 1971, 342/3.

Pesikta Rabbathi (EBI).

Pinto, B., de. *The Torah and the Psalms, JBL* LXXXVI Part II (June 1967), 154-174.

Pritchard, J. ed., *Ancient Near Eastern Texts Relating to the Old Testament,* Princeton, 1955.

Procksch, O., *Die Genesis uebersetzt und erklaert,* Leipzig, 1924.

Rad, Gerhard von, *Das erste Buch Moses,* Goettingen, 1952-1953.

———, *Genesis,* Philadelphia, 1961.

———, "Josephsgeschichte und ältere Chokma," *VT Suppl.* 1 (1953), 120ff.

———, *Die Josephsgeschichte,* Neukirchen, 1956.

———, "History and the Patriarchs," *ET* 72 (1960), 213 ff.

———, *Biblische Josephserzaehlung und Josephroman,* 3-28, Munich 1966.

RaDaQ: Torah commentary by R. David b. Qimchi, ed. A. Ginzburg, Pressburg, 1842.

RaLBaG: Torah commentary by R. Levi b. Gerson (Gersonides), Vienna, 1542.

RaMBaN: R. Moses b. Nahman (Nachmanides), Commentary on the Torah, *Genesis* [Hebrew], tr. and annotated by R.Ch.B. Chavel, New York, 1971.

RaShBaM: Torah commentary, R. Samuel b. Meir. (*Miqraoth Gedoloth,* New York 1965).

RaShI: Rabbenu Shmuel Itschaki Torah commentary, 1475, ed. A. Berliner, Berlin, 1866.

Redford, D. B., *A Study of the Biblical Story of Joseph,* Leiden, 1970.

Rosenzweig, Franz, See Buber, M.

———, See Simon, E.

———, "Der Ewige," *Kleinere Schriften,* Berlin, 1937, 182-198.

Rosin, D., "Beitrage zur Bibelexegese," in *Jubelschrift zum 90. Geburtstage von D. L. Zunz,* Berlin, 1884, 39ff.

Rubin, S., *Biblische Probleme, I. Die Josephsgeschichte in neuer Beleuchtung,* Wien, 1931.

Rudolph W., see Volz, P.

Ruppert, L., *Die Josephserzaehlung der Genesis,* Munich, 1965.

Ryle, H. E., *The Book of Genesis,* (Cambridge Bible), Cambridge, 1921.

Saadia b. Joseph, 882-942, Egypt and Babylonia, Torah commentary, Arabic, ed. Y. Qafih, (Hebrew), Jerusalem, 1963.

Samuel, Maurice, "Thomas Mann's 'Joseph and His Brothers,'"
Jewish Frontier Anthology, New York, 1945, 496ff.

———, *Certain People of the Book,* New York, 1955.

Sarna, N. M. *Understanding Genesis,* New York, 1966.

———, "Joseph," *E.J.* X, col. 202-209.

Sechel Tob: Menahem b. Shlomo (c. 1139, Italy) Torah commentary, ed. S. Buber, 1900.

Sefer Hayashar: One of the latest (11th? c.) works of Midrashic *aggadah,* tr. by M. M. Noah, New York, 1840.

Segal, M. H., "El, Elohim and Yhwh in the Bible," *JQR* ILVI (1955) 89ff.

Sforno, R. Obadia b. Jacob, Torah Commentary, *(Miqraoth Gedoloth,* New York, 1965).

ShaDaL: R. Shmuel David Luzzatto, Torah Commentary, Padua, 1871; Tel Aviv, 1965.

Sifthe Kohen: R. Mordecai ha-Kohen, *(EBI).*

Simon. Ernst. (ed.) *Franz Rosenzweig, Briefe,* Berlin, 1935.

Skinner, J., *A Critical and Exegetical Commentary on Genesis,* (International Critical Commentary), Edinburgh, 1930.

Speiser, Ephraim A.. *Genesis,* (The Anchor Bible), New York, 1964).

Strahan, J., *Hebrew Ideals,* Edinburgh, 1922.

Targum Onkelos, ed. A. Berliner, Berlin, 1884.

Targum (Pseudo) *Jonathan,* ed. M. Ginzburger, *Das Fragmententargum, Targum Jerushalmi zum Pentateuch,* 1899.

The Torah, The Five Books of Moses, NJPS Philadelphia, 1962.

Torath Kohanim, Midrash on Leviticus, called also *Sifra* (ed. Malbim, Bucharest, 1860).

T*seror Hamor:* R. Abraham Saba, Torah commentary *(EBI).*

Ungnad, A., "Joseph, der Tartan des Pharao," *ZAW* XLI (1923), 204 ff.

Vergote, J., *Joseph en Égypte: Génèse ch. 37-50 à la lumière des études égyptologiques recentes,* Louvain, 1959.

Volz, P. and Rudolph, W. *Der Elohist als Erzaehler. Ein Irrweg der Pentateuchkritik?, an der Genesis erklaert,* Giessen, 1933.

Ward, W. A., "The Egyptian Office of Joseph." *JSS* V (1960), 144-50.

Wellhausen, J., *Die Komposition des Hexateuch und der historischen Buecher des Alten Testaments,* Berlin, 1899.

Whybray, R. N., "The Joseph Story and Pentateuch Criticism," *VT* XVIII (1968), 522-528.

Yahuda, A. S., *Die Sprache des Pentateuch in ihren Beziehungen zum* Aegyptischen, I, 1929.

———, The Accuracy of the Bible, London, 1934.

Index of Biblical Citations

other than Narrative text

The book page number is followed either by the number of the verse-interpretation (v), of the note (n), or of the paragraph (x) in which the passage occurs